LEADING PEOPLE

TO BE

HIGHLY MOTIVATED

AND

COMMITTED

LEADERSHIP SKILLS

THE WHATs, WHYs AND HOW TOs

OF BECOMING AN EXCEPTIONAL

MANAGER OF PEOPLE

Bennet Simonton

Copyright 2005 Bennet S. Simonton

ISBN 0-9766748-0-7

Published by Simonton Associates
www.bensimonton.com

TABLE OF CONTENTS

ACKNOWLEDGEMENTS

To Admiral Hyman G. Rickover (deceased)
whose personal courage and demonstrable
respect for people were so inspiring.

To the many people who worked for me, whose
trials, tribulations and help played such
an important part in developing my skills.

YOUR FEEDBACK AND QUESTIONS ARE WELCOME

The author is interested in your comments and/or questions. He is also willing to provide advice on putting into use the methods of this book. Having successfully done so in four different organizations, he knows the pitfalls and obstacles that exist and how to effectively handle them. Please send any comments or questions to bensimo@juno.com or go to www.bensimonton.com to make contact.

INTRODUCTION

DO YOU KNOW HOW TO UNLEASH
THE POWER OF EACH SUBORDINATE ?

DO YOU HAVE A PLAN TO INCREASE PRODUCTIVITY
BY AT LEAST 30 AND PERHAPS 300%?

This is a book for bosses and aspiring bosses, from first line supervisor to Chief Executive, who desire to be able to answer "Yes" to the above two questions. Whether employed in a private business or government agency, if you want to produce a hard-working, highly motivated, creative, committed and "turned-on" group of subordinates who enjoy coming to work, this is the book for you.

As bosses, we constantly search for better ways to do every function, particularly ways that are easy to understand, easy to execute and compatible with other business functions. Our most vexing arena lies in achieving consistently outstanding performance from our people. In this arena, inconsistencies are more the rule than the exception and what works in one circumstance seems to fail in the next for unexplained reasons.

This book wipes away the confusion of conventional wisdom and presents a compelling, coherent and comprehensive set of whats, whys and hows for any boss to use in managing people. Its strength lies in its foundation in basic characteristics common to us all. Its clarity lies in the simplicity of the boss' actions that logically follow from these characteristics. Its appeal lies in its total coverage of all human conditions. Its true power is, for any boss as it was for me, only one choice away.

My Background

I have not been a management consultant, nor have I been a professor and I am certainly not a writer. I have been a boss for over 30 years. In those years, I made all the errors and experienced all the problems and frustrations that any boss encounters when dealing with juniors, peers and bosses.

I am a graduate of the United States Naval Academy and my management training began there. For the first year I was stressed mightily, both mentally and physically. We freshmen wondered why we were so stupid to return from Christmas vacation to such a hell. As a junior and senior midshipman, I learned how to dish it out by indoctrinating new freshmen using a very authoritarian approach. This hands-on, two year apprenticeship dictated my management style for the next 12 years.

I served in line positions on eight surface ships for periods totaling 20 years, 15 of which were in directing the operation and maintenance of naval nuclear propulsion plants. Five of those years were as a surface ship Commanding Officer, first of a destroyer escort and later of a nuclear powered cruiser. I had one year of training ashore in nuclear propulsion and also gained a masters degree in Computer Systems Management. My last 2 1/2 years were spent as a member of the Navy's Pentagon Staff helping to direct about $3.5B annually for research, development, acquisition and lifecycle support for all surface ship weapons systems.

I then went to work for a utility, Consolidated Edison Of New York, Inc. After over two years as the plant manager of a large electric generating station and seven years as an executive in charge of a 1000+ person powerhouse overhaul group, I left Con Ed in order to pursue other interests such as disseminating the management understandings and techniques of this book.

What Gives Me The Right To Write This Book?

Getting things done through people has been the focus of my entire working life, from the Naval Academy to present. I have read and studied, developed and tested techniques of managing people, over and over and over again. In an attempt to understand people, I studied history, religions, psychology, psychiatry and generally whatever man has wrought. For many years, I read every book I could find on management and leadership. In short, I did a great deal of searching for answers.

Through 14 different jobs working for 28 different bosses, the number of my subordinates varied from a low of 22 to a high of over 1300. While I have certainly made every error known to man and have seen them repeated many more times by seniors, juniors and peers, this is no different than what any boss experiences over time.

What is different is that I have experienced the sheer joy and personal satisfaction of knowing that the great majority of my subordinates could be trusted to perform in superstar fashion, that most were proud and happy to come to work each day. This blissful management state resulted from my focus on learning and on three rather unique conditions:

1- My father demonstrated a firm belief that our Creator was a good person who had made everything good, each good being synergistic with every other good. So if I had a solution to a problem that was not good for everything, he contended I should keep searching for the one that was good for all. And though he admitted I could be proficient at a technical endeavor at a young age, he said that I would not be able to find these truths about people without many years of experience. He was right on all counts.

2- A leader, Admiral Hyman G. Rickover, father of the nuclear Navy, demonstrated many times over that technical and operational excellence can be achieved through training people and having a consistent set of straight-forward, easy to understand rules and values for them to follow.

3- A concept, gained 12 years after starting my career, that the boss is not the sun around which subordinates (the earth) rotate, but is the earth that rotates around the life giving subordinates (the sun).

Because of my father and Admiral Rickover, I was confident a management system could be created that would be good for everyone and every thing. By the end of my first 12 years, I also knew the Navy's authoritarian management model, with its reliance on the "stick", was not very effective on mediocre and poor performers. I also knew that many bosses had turned these shortcomings into partial disasters. The authoritarian model's weaknesses had become more apparent as the 1960's created a growing distrust of bosses by their juniors. So by 1969, I had accumulated numerous unanswered questions and a myriad of incompatibilities between actions and human values. I was ready for a new idea.

I Got Lucky

#3 above was a bolt out of the blue. It came to me in 1970 from a very large behavioral science book while I was in the quiet academic environment of a master's program in computers. Thinking about the concept caused me to admit that the troops were producing the only useful output, while what I produced was solely to support and direct their efforts. And since I was not doing the production, they certainly knew more about it than I did. So why did I expect them to always listen to me? Perhaps I should listen to them! And perhaps if I listened, I could find ways to help the mediocre and poor performers to improve.

I decided to implement the concept by listening to my people rather than expecting them to listen to me. The timing of this change was fortuitous since my next assignment was as a surface ship Commanding Officer with considerable freedom from outside control.

As soon as I began using this new approach, the results surpassed my wildest dreams. This choice allowed me to eventually answer all unanswered questions, to resolve all apparent incompatibilities and inconsistencies, and to achieve true excellence through happy industrious turned-on people.

Making A Coherent, Comprehensive Set of Whats, Whys and Hows For Subordinate Bosses

However, I quickly learned that although I was able to find the most effective way to interact with juniors, my subordinate bosses could not go against conventional wisdom without considerably more knowledge than what I could articulate. This knowledge had to include easy to understand whys and simple to execute how tos without any need to be a rocket scientist. Therefore, I had to learn what was right, what was wrong and why, for each gradation of management action. I also had to learn how to adapt each to every personality and background. In fact, I needed a complete set of hows that could withstand critical scrutiny and everyday testing.

Although I had a partial set of tools in the early '70's, not until 1980 did I complete a totally comprehensive and coherent set of whats, whys and how tos that answered every possible question or concern. This set of tools turned out to be far simpler than I had expected. The final proof of its appeal to subordinate bosses and its effectiveness in changing an ingrained culture occurred during the ten years I spent at Consolidated Edison.

Success

Since my 1970 conversion, I have personally undertaken four serious management challenges. The words used by my bosses to describe their starting conditions ranged from "the crew is wrecking the ship" to "your customers hate your group and would get rid of it if they could". My set of whats, whys and hows allowed me to correct each one to a level not expected by anyone, particularly by the juniors themselves. Use of these tools assures a 30 percent productivity gain, but 300 percent is within reach if performance starts from a low point as in the four cases that I experienced.

The Book

I intend to expose you to my whats, whys and hows in the same way they were developed. They started with a necessity, a need which gave birth to a vision. From this vision, certain understandings emerged which were then used to create basic actions. And from these basic actions three superior techniques evolved.

This approach results in placing several of the most valuable pearls near the end of the book. Examples are: listening as the door to each subordinate's commitment and to the boss' achievement of excellence, and group meetings that are the only leadership mediums with sufficient credibility to effect changes in culture. However, I truly believe the reader will not be able to understand or appreciate these pearls without first understanding human characteristics common to all people, the basic features of <u>leadership/following</u> and the role of supplying high quality <u>leadership</u> through support and direction.

Two Apologies

I did not want to use the hackneyed and much misunderstood term "values". Between value engineering, family values and value-added, among others, the word has almost lost its meaning. But at the working level, there is no other adequate word. So with some trepidation I have used the term "values". I shall clearly define it so I doubt that the reader will have much trouble with the term once you are well into the book. I apologize for causing anyone heartburn.

The same identical situation pertains to the terms "turned-on" and "turned-off". The former has been used to describe reactions to drugs and other conditions. But once again, their meaning is very clear in the workplace. They are applied to one's use or non-use of the brain and to whether our morale is way up or way down. I do apologize for causing any heartburn, but we need to use terms that can be understood by working level people.

WARNING

This book addresses only one of the two major areas in which any boss must be highly proficient; that of managing people. The other area consists of the technical aspects associated with your chosen profession, whether it is building construction, making and selling products, providing financial services, or whatever. I'll refer to this second area as "things".

Achieving high proficiency in the technical area of "things" may require a significantly greater effort to master than does managing people (certainly my area of nuclear power was one of these). But the point is, both requirements must be satisfied. That is, a proper balance must be struck between the two and that balance will change for different conditions. I shall provide more insight on this issue of balance after you have had the chance to understand my whats, whys and hows for managing people.

My Goal In Writing This Book

I have watched America's fall from international commercial superiority. I have watched as we lost jobs in certain industries and created them in others. I have also watched our resurgence through the hard work and determined efforts of many bosses, at times in moving facilities overseas whose products were for U.S. consumers. These efforts were initiated in order to survive tough competition. Progress came by learning from our best competitors and quite often by copying their techniques.

Throughout this period of changing to meet newly emerged competition, great efforts have been made to achieve more output from our people. The new techniques focused mainly on methods to better motivate, empower and organize (Total Quality Management, Reengineering, small teams). The results of each have ranged from very effective to negative. What seems to work in one place fails in the next for unexplained or contested reasons. I believe the reason for the failures is that we have no universally accepted discipline for the management of people. What we have is a "have your own management style compatible with your own personality" guideline that is based on who the boss is rather than who the subordinate is or what he/she needs. We certainly have a defined discipline for quality that is independent of the boss' personality. But its implementation fails if the people do not cooperate fully; that is, if the people are not being managed properly.

Therefore, what U.S. business men and women need is a discrete, well defined discipline that meets all the requirements of this "machine" called "people" and can be learned and applied by bosses and administrators. Like every other discipline, this must include a comprehensive set of "whats" and "hows backed up by coherent, common sense "whys". This set of tools must be based on the characteristics of the people and must have sufficient clarity and appeal to be acceptable to the vast majority of managers and bosses. (Note: These general requirements have been met by all the major disciplines such as mechanical engineering, accounting and quality. Should they not also be considered minimum requirements for the discipline of managing people?)

The United States Of America has provided a great life for myself and my family. I owe to it a debt that is far more than I could ever repay. In traveling the world and seeing what happens in other countries, I have always been struck by how lucky I am to be an American and how good we really have it, in spite of its many detractors. This book is my attempt to make a small payment for the many, many good things I have received from America the Beautiful. I present in this book a proven formula for excellence in managing people in the fervent hope it will provide each boss with the necessary knowledge to make an informed choice, a choice to reap the great benefits that superstar people always bring. Good managing to us all.

CHAPTER 1

IS THERE A PROBLEM ?

Every boss needs a highly motivated, turned-on, industrious and creative group of employees. This would seem to be just a common sense statement, but is that what we have? Unfortunately, most management observers agree that very few bosses have highly motivated groups today and the vast majority of groups are much closer to being turned-off, poorly motivated and lacking in creativity. The most significant aspect of this condition is the difference in terms of productivity between the two. Best selling author and noted management consultant Stephen R. Covey in his book "Principle-Centered Leadership" indicates that this difference can be as high as 500 percent. My own personal experience, from four different cases of effecting a change from a low productivity state to a higher one, indicates the possible improvement is at least 300 percent.

So, is this a problem for American bosses? In our present day world of increasing competition, yes, yes a thousand times yes! And the most vexing part is that since the vast majority of bosses have never seen a highly motivated group, they believe that expecting a 300 percent gain is an absurd pipe dream, well beyond the realm of reality and not worthy of a moment's consideration. Please keep reading because the potential gain is real and the road to it is only one choice away for any boss at any level.

So most bosses have far too few motivated, turned-on, industrious, creative employees. Forty years ago when most competition consisted of American companies in the same boat, this situation was not important to the bottom line of profit. But now that we are competing against the extremely low wages of the Pacific rim or the technology of an entrepreneurial and creative company, turned-off and poorly motivated employees constitute a big, big problem. Before we launch into the whats, whys and hows of the solution to this problem, let's develop some understanding of its outward characteristics and probable causes.

The basic characteristic of the problem is a lack of respect and trust between a large majority of the members of the workplace. All too often, the people at the top distrust each other, the middle and the bottom, and this repeats at each level. In the early 1950's, this was not the case. By the late 1960's, however, the pendulum had dramatically swung toward distrust. Disrespect and distrust were hazards in the workplace since they significantly reduced motivation and created substantial disinterest, disharmony, insubordination and decreased cooperation toward any goal. The result was very poor productivity.

My own personal experiences certainly bore out this situation. By my upbringing, I respected my elders and particularly bosses. In the 1950's Navy, I found the great majority of my age group shared these feelings of trust and respect for seniors, making us very willing, compliant, eager workers. The twenty or so percent who were distrustful were considered to be troublemakers. However, by the late 1960's the percentages had reversed. After my own conversion in 1970 and by carefully listening to 18 year old recruits, I learned that their distrust was not just of military bosses, but of every person in authority. They believed we were only out for ourselves, were polluting the countryside and were generally a group of power-hungry people out to do no good. This belief created enough distrust and disrespect to de-motivate and turn-off these people, an effect that resulted in greatly lowered productivity and creativity.

CAUSES

I directly experienced many causes of this distrust and disrespect. We have no need to agree on the exact root causes, but I do want to discuss those that I have experienced since they pretty well explain why the present "well less than desirable" situation exists. In addition, it is important each boss understands that their own managerial abilities may have been severely degraded by these root causes. (Fortunately, relief from this burden is only one choice away.) There are three causes: the Second World War, the authoritarian society that resulted and the influence of new management theories on mid-to-large size companies, theories that were outgrowths of the distrust and disrespect created by the first two causes.

THE SECOND WORLD WAR

Quite simply, the U.S. was on the winning side and did not suffer any of the damage to plant and equipment inflicted on others, including allies. We emerged as the world's only industrial power. Since the industrial capability of

8

the rest of the world had been essentially destroyed, its rebuilding by foreign competitors required over thirty years of effort.

With the rest of the world rebuilding, we in the United States could pretty well do what we pleased. Demand out stripped supply to the extent that companies could pass most costs on to customers with little or no regard for the effect on total sales. Governments could raise taxes or regulatory costs at will since all of these could be passed to the customer. Labor costs could likewise be allowed to rise with unions pretty much getting what they wanted. The United States was a land of plenty with enough affluence to give everyone a piece of the pie. And there was no end in sight.

We all know the end came in the late '70's to mid '80's when the Japanese and the Germans caught up. And now we have the whole Pacific rim! Who will be next to grab a piece of the pie? The answer isn't worth knowing because we need to spend our time reducing costs. The days of affording increased costs from any source are over. That includes labor, raw materials, government taxes and regulation, staff, management levels or any other source. The competition is simply too stiff to allow us to pass unnecessary costs to valued customers. But I have gotten ahead of myself. Let's look at some results of winning the war that had an effect on the level of distrust in the workplace.

Affluence was one result and it gave bosses more money to hire more staff, people who could help the boss carry out a growing set of responsibilities. Also, numerous new levels in the chain of command were created as companies expanded to meet demand. Unfortunately, these actions served to distance bosses from their work force and from lower level management. As top bosses got further away and more isolated from the line by their staff, their decisions became less relevant and the top became the proverbial "they" in the eyes of subordinates. Product quality dropped while costs rose. The worker level was more aware of these problems than were bosses since they had to look at the poor product quality every day. This demoralizing situation caused worker complaints to grow, but resulted only in more frustration because bosses, distanced from the workplace, failed to adequately address them. The productivity effects were always negative. Coincidentally, higher costs and lower productivity caused bosses to increasingly distrust their workforce. Bosses gave this condition a seemingly descriptive name, "loss of the work ethic". Someone had to be blamed and it would not be the bosses who, like all of us, don't like to blame themselves. But these effects were not so bad because they could all be passed to customers, at least for 30 years.

Simultaneously, the anti-establishment movement of the '60's, Vietnam, Watergate and a host of other influences reinforced a growing belief that leaders in general were not to be trusted, a belief that is still actively circulated today. Labor-management conflicts became the norm as the distrust grew. There were many other negative forces, both in and out of the workplace, but the picture already painted is adequate for us to understand that winning the war indirectly created more than enough distrust and disrespect to account for a significant reduction in productivity. So let's move on to the second of the three major causes.

AUTHORITARIANISM

Defined as a blind obedience to authority, authoritarianism is what came to underlie all aspects of American life. Parents expect it of their children as do the children's teachers, church leaders, peers and last, but not least, their bosses. Even the media and the government get into the act as authoritarian powers who expect compliance. The torrent of desires, expectations and outright orders issuing forth from these all-too-numerous authoritarians has constituted a growing force in our lives. Although our country was founded in revolt against the oppression of authoritarians, memory of these hazards has faded. Authoritarians grew more numerous after World War I and World War II.

But the USA is also the land of the free and the home of the brave, a country rooted in a rugged individualism that rejects outside interference. Individualists have never rebelled against respectable authority, one that consistently demonstrates benevolence, a love and caring for those expected to accept the limits imposed by the authority. Our brand of rugged individualism has always allowed plenty of room for team playing and other group efforts. But it has never willingly accepted the clear arrogance reflected in authoritarianism, of "do it my way because you have no choice".

Our prospective bosses, like everyone else, grow up in this increasingly authoritarian society and are conditioned by it to act in an authoritarian manner once they put on their boss hat. While there is nothing wrong with authority and surely the buck must stop at someone's doorstep, authoritarianism is far too much of a good thing. It is a form of gross arrogance that is naturally offensive to every individual subjected to it. In any authoritarian environment, there are more than enough opportunities for each side to disrespect and distrust the other.

The upshot was and is that individuals do battle with their authoritarian bosses and these battles between team members result in a large reduction of teamwork, productivity and creativity. <u>The enemy is authoritarianism, not authority.</u>

NEW THEORIES OF MANAGEMENT

Our third cause is one that had a major effect on our larger companies since only they could fully afford to pay the purveyors of these theories. Although the larger companies have suffered the most, there have been some trickle down effects on their smaller counterparts.

Prior to the end of World War II, there wasn't much management theory available. What there was had only been designed to manage "things", not people. People had never been a significant problem to management because of a work ethic, or perhaps just because employees felt lucky to have a job and greatly respected or feared those who controlled the jobs. For whatever reason, the new theories retained this assumption and were mainly designed to address the management of functions and processes such as production, record keeping, accounting, procurement, planning, maintenance or quality. People were merely instruments to be used for these purposes and they were expected to adapt to the conditions and requirements of the workplace. When people caused recurrent work problems, the new theories assumed that something was wrong with the process and changed it in order to get the desired result.

So in spite of the fact people were the ones performing all these functions and processes, the new theories were based almost entirely on the processes themselves, not the people. This did not prove to be a major hazard until the people lost their respect and trust for the bosses. At that point, the theories served to augment the frailties of the people rather than their strengths and blew costs way out of proportion. To understand this outcome, let's look more closely at the new theories.

The Control Model
In simple terms, to manage is to control or conduct something and it implies a judicious use of the means to accomplish an end. The end would normally be to make profits in business or perhaps to provide a service in government. The "judicious use" feature would always be of our resources; computers, people, dollars, machines, blueprints, technical data and the like.

This sounds straight forward enough, but now we must define the meaning of control as it pertains to the boss.

The control model of the new theories was adopted from engineers who were familiar with machine control theory. First we sense a variable such as speed and compare that to a known set point. If the speed is too high, an error signal is generated to slow the device. As the machine slows, a speed sensor detects this decrease and a comparator generates an ever decreasing error signal. When the speed arrives at a desired set point, the resulting zero error signal causes no further changes. With a few added features to account for some complexities beyond our scope, this system can be adequately adapted to machines. However, using this model to control the output of people, the best of whom are self-controlled, has severe shortcomings. Nonetheless, this model was used because everyone knew that the engineers always made sense.

Managing Things

Therefore, as problems appeared in the workplace, bosses looked hard for solutions. During the '50's, '60's and '70's, bosses in the larger companies could afford to hire consultants who assumed a prominent role by developing a very impressive array of products. Some of these products were touted as be-all and end-all solutions upon which hinged the future success of every business entity. And since line management was too busy with production or was resistant to these new ideas, more staff was hired to put them into practice. These new methods arrived regularly over a long period of time and though they rarely gained the promised results, pursuit of them soaked up considerable management time and money.

These methods literally spanned the universe; time and motion study, sales projections, financial planning, work scheduling, organizational structures, artificial intelligence, visions, goals, RAM (reliability, availability, maintainability), organizational behavior, quality control, quality assurance, quality circles, financial planning, management by objectives, strategic planning, market research, benefits planning, operations analysis, industrial relations, demographics, participative management, excellence and on and on. Some went through evolutionary development and some went down roads later discredited. All of these products spawned many suppliers who continue to influence executives. But what was the result?

The overriding message for bosses was to use each and every one of these products, the more the better in order to gain excellence. As each grew in complexity and line management could not seem to appreciate their value, enthusiastic executives saw a need for more staff to control their implementation and long-term execution. In classic authoritarian style, many were literally forced down the throats of line managers and workers who resisted these new theories and their so-called experts. Of course, in order to gain excellence, the staff and their experts needed new inspectors, procedures, reports and policies.

Meanwhile, executives and consultants perceived a "loss of the work ethic" and began to realize that the work force and lower level management would continue to resist. So they took the obvious next step; to require sufficient reports to allow the good guys at the top and in the staff (supposedly the only ones who really cared) to catch the errors of the bad guys at the bottom who didn't care. This was what resulted from the control model, distrust and authoritarianism's clash with individuals.

Trend graphs of every sort came into being in order to prove to bosses the status of the above "things" and permit them to ensure that "things" would be done "right" as the new theories dictated. Doing "things right" also required more policies and procedures, rules and processes, all designed by the experts in strict conformance to the dictates of a particular viewpoint, their narrow base of knowledge. Doing "things right" was extended to the decision making process by requiring that each section of the staff be given an opportunity to agree or disagree on every anticipated action. The theory was that review by all disciplines would improve the quality of decisions over the old way of approval by only the line manager/executive. Didn't the bosses even trust each other? (No one seemed to worry about the greatly increased amount of time required to make decisions.) Of course, more staff was needed to carry out these increased responsibilities. <u>Centralized control and large staffs proliferated.</u>

In this environment our progress toward excellence was to be gained through perfection of structures, rules and processes, or so the new theories promised. We came to revere order, form and control. We had faith in process. With the large number of groups involved, we learned the importance of consensus management, compromise and bargaining. Corporate politics became central to gaining consensus and we became obsessed with team building, interpersonal relations and presentation skills. Best of all, we thought that by institutionalizing and depersonalizing the process, we had removed the perceived hazard of vesting authority in one person. In addition, the bad guys in the line could always be kept under control since the staff had the boss' ear and if he forgot, could always remind him/her about the line's lost work ethic.

This path was not without concerns. Politics and feelings seemed to take precedence over the technical quality of decisions. Line management complained of the bureaucratic delays in getting anything done since even small decisions took forever. Line became more alienated from staff. Also, so much energy was thrown into getting "things right" that few people had time for the customer. And in a political arena, didn't duplicity become a requirement for survival? Were we maintaining control at the expense of creativity and innovation? And the reports never seemed to include anything bad or contentious, but isn't that just the nature of the beast? But why should we be concerned when the customer was accepting the higher prices, lower quality and other consequences?

WHY BE CONCERNED?

You can purchase the best computers and they will never make a mistake. But computers need well thought out programs and programs need accurate data. Both the data and the programs will require a considerable amount of high quality, dedicated, caring, responsible effort on the part of many people in order to produce valuable output. We can make similar statements about sales, marketing, production, use of resources, manufacturing equipment, refineries, electric generating plants, automobile assembly lines and the like.

I recall that a brand new naval combatant surface ship was essentially ruined in a year by a fairly well turned-off crew. I know of a submarine that was removed from service mainly because the amount of money required to correct the effects of regular abuse by its crew was so great as to justify building a replacement submarine. I also know of more than one ship that was retained in service much longer than normal because its people had maintained the ship in a superior material condition.

Turned-on people are able to take unreliable, cranky equipment (computer or machine) and change it to being highly reliable and operating better than design. Turned-off people can reverse this process just as quickly. The secret is in the people. Turned-on people figure out how to beat the competition, while those who are turned-off only complain about being beaten by the competition.

In short, it's the people, stupid!

But what of the new theories? In placing into practice these theories and their assumption that people could be taken for granted, bosses focused on managing those "things" that the new theories addressed. Since many of these things were what their people were already doing, choosing to micromanage "things" from upper management levels committed the organization to considerable staff, extra time awaiting approvals, large amounts of reports and incorrect decisions made far from the scene of battle. This resulted in a considerable amount of bureaucracy (all of which held back people from producing, which was then used to justify more bureaucracy) and plenty of messages to the people that they could not be trusted to do the work. Giving responsibility to the process bred irresponsibility, duplicity and unaccountability in the people. This constituted a collapse of the moral foundation of management. Moreover, showing distrust of people, the sole source of ideas and energy, served to severely squelch innovation, creativity and self-respect.

OUR CURRENT STATE

By the late 1970's to the mid '80's, foreign competitors had managed to sufficiently rebuild their capacity to challenge American market dominance. Given a choice, customers naturally started to move away from the higher cost and lower quality American products. For the past 15 years, cost cutting and quality improvement coincident with new attempts to motivate and involve the work force have been frantically pursued by those threatened with competition. As concerns people, this was mostly accomplished by sticking to the new management theories and just trying to do certain "things" better. Personnel departments were upgraded, given more power and renamed Human Resources in order to treat people better and to sponsor involvement/empowerment of turned-off employees. A similar approach was used to embrace Total Quality Management.

While these efforts are certainly paying dividends, we have not yet begun to tap the true potential of our human resources. There is certainly nothing wrong with doing "things right". Every business has many "things" that must be done consistently to very high standards each day. The problem is that one of the most important "things" that must be done to high standards is managing people and the new theories did not provide for that.

In addition, technology has created a time when brainpower is fast becoming our most valuable resource, a time when ideas and their use dictate success or failure. No boss can afford to turn off even one subordinate's brain much less a majority of them. We must consider brainpower as a treasured resource that when unleashed will multiply our creativity, innovation, productivity and profit.

And don't lose sight of the fact that the potential gain lies somewhere between 30-300% in productivity, unless you choose to believe Stephen Covey's 500% number. The point is that the real effect is much larger than most of us realize, certainly far more than I initially thought possible, and a large productivity gain would be manna from heaven in meeting the competition.

So it is time to admit that the new theories have been unable to overcome the WWII legacies of distrust, disrespect and authoritarianism because they failed to provide an easy to understand and easy to execute set of whats, whys and hows for managing our most important resource, people. It is time to find a set of "whats, whys and hows" that by their nature will lower costs and raise the quality and quantity of output by making full use of everyone's brainpower to be creative, innovative, productive, motivated and committed.

No need to worry! A tried and tested set of tools are what this book is all about. These tools are securely founded on human characteristics common to everyone and include whats, whys and hows for every aspect of human interaction by bosses in the workplace. They are not dependent on the boss' personality, size, shape, race or sex. The power of these tools is that they are just the way each of us hoped they would be. I will not profess that the tools presented in this book are perfect, but they are far better than what we have and the promised 30-300 percent productivity gains are real enough to take to the bank.

STARTING WITH A VISION

Before we start, it would be nice to know where we are going. So the first element we need is a powerful vision, a goal that our tools will achieve. It must appeal to our sense of values and must give us unity of purpose. It must serve as a standard against which future actions may be judged.

Since we want to meet or beat the competition, let's choose as a vision that each employee becomes a well trained, industrious, strong and independent person who is successful and proud of it, a person who is happy to come to work every day. Let's examine this vision.

MANAGING PEOPLE TO BE WHAT? - 5Star

The reality is that down deep inside, every person wants to be a superstar. Although some want to expend all of their energy to be a Superstar, others will only put out a small amount for this purpose. For the boss, it not only makes sense to support such an individual goal, but to make this the boss' goal for each and every subordinate. This is a non-adversarial, teamwork and togetherness approach. Doing what is truly best for the worker turns out to be exactly what is best for the boss and the workplace.

In order to make this concept simple to understand, simple to discuss and somehow within the realm of possibility to achieve, I have created a vision of the superstar employee. I call it the <u>Five Star or 5Star</u> person. Each Star stands for a different key element as follows:

1. Well trained
2. Industrious
3. Strong and Independent
4. Successful
5. Proud

Stars 1 through 3 can be accomplished or controlled by the person herself while Star 4 is something provided by the boss. Star 5 results from establishing the first four Stars within the person concerned. A simple illustration may be helpful to explain this concept.

The Running Back

There once was a professional football player, a running back (RB) who had been piling up records for a number of years. This back did not have much of an offensive line in front of him, but whenever the opposition through error permitted the slightest hole, he could take advantage of it and get through the line. Once through, he could fake out most defensive backs. So even though the blockers could only infrequently help to get him through the line, his exploitation of opposition errors and his own superior open field running permitted him to rack up impressive "yards gained" records each year.

This running back was also considered an excellent blocker. Several professional peers refused to block saying that their bodies already absorbed too much damage when they carried the ball. No one should expect them to also get damaged by blocking when someone else had the ball. Not our man! He did whatever was needed and then a lot more. In fact, no one even had to ask him to do it. In spite of all this body damage, our running back held records for number of games played and had a reputation for playing hurt. You could certainly say that this person had the first three Stars of 5Star.

Unfortunately, the man was not proud (Star 5). When asked if he was proud of his records, he would put his head down and admit that they had little value since his team was losing most of its games! That is, Star 4, successful, did not exist for his team! One year, the old coach was replaced and the new one got the rest of the team doing better. The team suddenly won more games in that season than they lost. Our man's pride in performance increased to the point that his head was always up, a smile was on his face and he looked to be walking a couple of feet off the ground. The next season, the team won the Super Bowl. Our man was walking ten feet off the ground! Glory!

Was the running back setting higher records? No? Then why the change? Only because he now had all of the ingredients, Stars one through four and automatically received the fifth Star.

Let's take a closer look at these five Stars of a 5Star person.

WELL TRAINED

The more we know about our job, the better we feel. The less we know, the more anxiety. With good feeling, otherwise known as confidence, we can try to achieve. Without it, we can't get off the dime. Knowledge is power and more knowledge is more power. No one wants to shout out ignorance. Everyone wants to demonstrate superior knowledge and proudly show off their outstanding training. Knowledge supports and breeds confidence, strength, perseverance, forcefulness and the like. Lack of knowledge keeps us as timid as a church mouse.

Our best people know this. They search out and struggle daily to obtain whatever knowledge they need before they need it. They learn things for the joy of it on the chance it may be useful. They need no prodding. Our mediocre people need strong direction and plenty of help from bosses to achieve knowledge. But almost all of these will learn. Our worst people must be cajoled and almost forced to learn. Most we save while a very few will not make it.

Becoming "well trained" is greatly aided by being "industrious" and "strong and independent". Conversely, becoming "industrious" and "strong and independent" are greatly assisted by being "well trained". In fact, it's a two way street among all three Stars, truly a synergistic relationship where the whole is always well larger than the sum of the parts.

INDUSTRIOUS

Without this Star, no one can get anywhere. Even hardened criminals know this. People who fail to apply themselves are worthless to any goal, be it bank robbing or bridge building. But working hard, even while failing, gives us self-esteem. "Maybe I didn't make it this time, but it wasn't because I didn't try. Maybe next time." Hardly working is not something that makes anyone proud. Being industrious and diligent in our work turns us on and we do not have to make excuses for ourselves to anyone, no apologies needed. If we can apply ourselves diligently, we are better able to channel our effort into becoming well-trained. Likewise, working hard makes us recognize that better training will make it possible to achieve more goals in a given period of time. These two Stars feed on each other.

Being industrious or working hard builds our self-esteem, our morale, while hardly working gets us plenty of negative messages from our Gut.

STRONG AND INDEPENDENT

This is real glory for the individual person who gets this Star. It happens on the day the person decides they are their own boss and can control their own destiny, no matter what anyone else does. Think of the Running Back. Hopefully you can think about a few of your friends, yourself or others. These people think for themselves and as such are very innovative and creative.

Strong and independent people fly with the eagles instead of walking with the turkeys. They are aggressive self-starters who are dogged in their pursuit of getting "the job" done. They always try hard and never quit. They always do more than asked and rarely ask anything for themselves. These people solve their own problems through creativity and innovation and rarely need help. When they do need help, they actively search for it. They will never complain and using excuses for poor performance would never even be considered, much less done.

They generally have high standards for performance, but if shown a higher one may adjust to it. They never follow anyone who may lead them to a lower standard as they can quickly recognize the difference. They are too busy meeting their own obligations and personal standards to afford time to be critical of others. If in the minority, they often work extra to make up for poor performance of others. If in the majority, they may try to influence others.

These people come to the workplace with a willingness to work hard and offer to tell the boss how they can help. They believe it is their responsibility to accomplish whatever is needed, no matter what support or other things are missing. They believe they can accomplish anything by applying themselves diligently, mentally and physically, and do so always. They have very high morale, but may not smile often. They talk back to bosses to tell them when they are wrong, but never in an insubordinate way. They know that there is a need for a boss and willingly accept the boss' authority.

They know that they themselves are most important, "numero uno" so to speak. But at the same time, they are selfless in all things and have time to help others. They are strong believers in family and country.

Their creed is "when the going gets tough, the tough get going". Their strength and independence cause them to work harder and train themselves better. More synergism!

SUCCESSFUL

As indicated in the running back example, only the boss is responsible for creating success. Without success no one can feel proud even if they have met high standards in the first three Stars. Fortunately for bosses in the business world, there is no scoreboard everyone can watch as for a football game. So the boss can declare success any time desired, so long as reasonable justification is given. In this way the boss permits the fifth Star of pride to exist.

Success can be doing a little bit better today than yesterday. Improvement, as long as it is real, is always a great excuse for feeling good. Use whatever is available, but at least force enough progress so success can be declared credibly. Everyone knows inside that high morale is a must. The boss must provide success, our fourth Star, no matter the cost.

PROUD

We only get to be proud if we have a reasonable amount of the first four Stars. This is a truth that applies to every person everywhere. Ignore this fact at your own peril.

Pride within a person also includes the aspect of enjoyment in coming to work. If we are not able to look forward to most days with eager anticipation rather than halting trepidation, we will never feel real pride in our work. Loving to come to work can be the boss' goal for each person and is certainly within the boss' capability to create for most of us. This is a quality of life issue that is often expected by people today.

Our Natural State In Private Life

As defined, 5Star is the way we all want to be and know we must be in order to succeed in our private life. But somehow, when we come through the door of the workplace, most of us feel we must leave part of what we are at the door so that we can do what's expected by our bosses. By passing through that door, we suddenly turn from chief into indian and assume a role that is foreign to and incompatible with what's required in our private life. Wouldn't it be much better for us individually if no role change was necessary, if we didn't have to leave our values and whatever else we hold dear at the door and if we could remain in the natural human state of our everyday life?

As it turns out, my set of tools establishes this condition.

A MATTER OF EXTENT

5Star must be viewed as a spectrum with non-5Star at one end, fully 5Star at the other end and many points in between. The boss' goal is to move each person, boss or worker, from wherever they are to a state of being mostly 5Star.

Moving subordinates toward 5Star is moving toward <u>a culture that at some point takes over peer pressure and becomes a force of its own.</u> <u>A 5Star culture is, to a large extent, self-sustaining once established because no 5Star person will ever give up that state once they experience it.</u>

In general, closer to 5Star means; fewer safety problems, higher quality work, higher productivity, less performance errors, more teamwork, more cooperation, lower turnover, more creativity and innovation, higher tolerance, less discrimination, higher job satisfaction, less grievances and complaints, more motivation and commitment, more adaptability to change, lower cost, more often meeting schedules, more times beating the competition, better customer relations, less bureaucracy, greater profits and satisfaction for the boss, and last, a positive impact on family and community. The boss' road to a 5Star culture consists of easy to learn, easy to execute, simple and straight-forward steps.

FLASH!!

5Star people are at least four times more productive than average people. Converting average people to 5Star is what this book is all about

Are We Ready For These Steps?

Before we can understand the actual steps to achieve the goal, we must first take a close look at what a person is, at what we have before we start moving this person toward 5Star. Knowledge of human characteristics is prerequisite to effective management of people, just like knowledge of a car is essential to being a good auto mechanic. Our beliefs about people pretty much dictate how we treat them. We may be able to use a technique contrary to our beliefs, but most of us aren't good enough at acting to carry it off well.

Existing management books spend little or no time on this aspect of managing people and may lead us to believe this knowledge is unnecessary. A few psychologists have attempted to fill this gap, but what they gave us is not what's needed in the trenches. What I offer is understandable at the CEO or worker level and allows everyone to improve. For bosses, I make a clear connection in each part of the book between how people are and how bosses should manage them. These whys and their related hows are the road to creating 5Star highly motivated, committed, innovative and creative employees who are at least 300 % more productive than if poorly motivated.

So let's move on to the three characteristics of people in Chapter 2. I'm no psychologist, so what I have will be short and no more than you need to understand why you should manage one way versus another.

CHAPTER 2

THREE CHARACTERISTICS OF PEOPLE

Values, Choice, Following

During my first 12 years as a boss, I labored under several basic beliefs about people. These were: juniors like children are to be seen and not heard, a ship's Captain is a very important person and juniors should worship and listen to him, and all people are different except some are good and some are bad. Oh, how wrong I was!

I spent most of my management time preparing and giving orders and instructions, and finding and fixing things that the bad guys did incorrectly. In retrospect, for 12 years I was focused squarely on what to tell subordinates next, never on listening to what they had to say. Even though I had not intended it, I was often disrespectful and demeaning toward subordinates. On the plus side, I was considered to be one of the best bosses and had created a vision of the 5Star Superstar (well trained, industrious, strong and independent, successful, proud) and the desire to find a path to this goal.

My 1970 conversion, that the troops are the sun around which the boss as the earth rotates, turned me in a new direction. I became eager to support the troops and spent my time listening to them and their needs rather than expecting them to listen to me. This single choice greatly improved my personal effectiveness at my job and with subordinates. It opened the door to understanding how to help them to be 5Star. In listening, what I heard were the same sounds repeated over and over again. What I learned was people are not different from us. On the contrary, they are the same as us.

THEY ARE US

It's so simple that I missed it for years. They are "us"! They are just like us except that they have lived through a different set of experiences. Therefore, one key to dealing with other people is to first understand ourselves and then use that knowledge in determining how we should treat others. Conversely, understanding others is a great aid to understanding ourselves, if we believe that they are "us". The door to this knowledge is "listening". It was my door to the knowledge of this book.

I say they are "us" because <u>all of us believe in the same good and bad values</u>, most of us have been trained to conform to or <u>follow the wishes of</u>

society, and all of us <u>have an innate ability to choose</u>. These three characteristics actually dictate, repeat, dictate how any boss must interact with subordinates in order to be successful in business. These are the first of many "whys" from which the "hows" of this book were derived. Let's look at them.

VALUES – the first characteristic

We all have values and I have never found anyone who didn't agree with what I believed to be a good value or with what I believed to be a bad value. We all like love and dislike hate. We like honesty, humility, charity, positive attitudes, enthusiasm, trust, courage, independence, confidence, admission of error, industriousness, respect, success, high standards, neatness, loyalty, patriotism, fortitude, decisiveness, freedom, selflessness, compassion, smiles, knowledge, fairness, integrity, forthrightness, forgiveness and on and on. These are our good values.

And every one of us dislikes the opposite of each good value: dishonesty, indecision, lack of enthusiasm, disrespect, selfishness, arrogance, negative attitudes, etc., etc. These are what we know to be bad values.

But while everyone agrees perfectly on which are the good values and which are the bad, we differ as to the importance of each good or bad one. I will not agree exactly with the next person over how good a certain good one is, nor will they agree with me over how bad a bad one is. These extents are a matter for our accumulated experiences to decide, often our present circumstances and these are different for each of us.

For example, if I have experienced little love in my life, I will probably not think love is very important. On a scale of 1 to 10, 10 being the highest, perhaps I would give love a standard of 3. But perhaps you have experienced much love and grown to accord it a high level of importance in your life, so your standard for love might be a 9. Differing standards are a natural result of differing experiences.

If we accept the premise that mankind shares identical values, but differs on the standards, are there important tangible results? I can think of an infinite number. The person who has high standards for sacrifice, patriotism and forcefulness may turn out to be a soldier in wartime. A person with a lower standard for patriotism, just as high for sacrifice, but higher for compassion and love may be caring for the sick and homeless while demonstrating against the war.

Though this appears to be a remarkable difference, the point is we use our own unique set of value standards to control our life. Our set defines our idea of a better life, what jobs we seek, where we live and what we hold dear. In addition, we are our values and since they are good, we know we are good! Understanding of these conditions permits bosses to respect everyone's views as well as their natural goodness.

The Gut

Our Gut is conceptually the place where our values reside. It is not part of the conscious brain, but provides signals to it. The Gut uses our own good value standards to judge everything and sends these judgments to the conscious brain in the form of what we commonly refer to as emotions. Thus we "feel" good about good events and bad about bad events. The Gut is our good-bad compass and as such it is perfectly accurate.

While it is easy to understand the Gut's use of good and bad values, how do differing standards affect its signals to the conscious brain? If I witness an event that shows a 6 standard for love, since my personal standard is 3, I will respect the event and the associated people. I will get a warm and fuzzy feeling from my Gut. Meanwhile, another witness with a standard of 9 will have the opposite response. Each person's Gut and the value standards that reside therein are what they use to judge every external act. Their response is totally predictable if one can figure out three things: which values are reflected in the event, the reflected standards for each of those values (good or bad), and lastly, the standards held for those values by the person doing the judging. A reflected standard lower than yours results in disrespect, equal to means "fine, but so what", and higher than results in respect. The greater the difference, the greater the signal or emotion. If the event meets a very high standard for good, it will always be warmly received because we respect the effort required to meet a very high standard, even if we have a very high standard for that value.

Since the Gut is independent from our conscious brain, the Gut and the conscious brain make a very effective team. The conscious brain does the reasoning by determining and carrying out actions while the Gut provides signals as to whether the action is a good or bad thing to do. The Gut, our good-bad compass, tells us the correct answer.

Gut level emotions, the ones we were born with, are necessary to our proper functioning as a human being. They are great joy over great good and great anger over great bad. They get us going and are the fire in our boiler. They are the fear that keeps us from going too close to the edge of the cliff or driving too fast. They are the fervor that infects others and inspires the team. If we ignore the messages of the Gut, the rational brain on its own is capable of justifying the Crusades, the Inquisition, the Holocaust and many other very serious good value standard violations that form a history of man's inhumanity to man.

If our Gut is such an accurate compass, why do people perform so many obviously bad acts? There are three basic reasons that are relevant to managing people. First, we created most of our behavior while growing up, before we had a conscious understanding of values or our Gut level signals. Second, some of us are educated away from our Gut. And third, when we become aware that another person has committed a bad act, we may use that event to excuse a bad act of our own. "Everyone else is doing it, why can't I?" This happens in mob actions such as looting. Excuses are of such importance to the workplace that they are explained in detail later in this section. Let's now look at the first two, growing up and education.

GROWING UP -- Behavior Without Value Standards

Each of us started life without behavior or understanding of value standards. We developed our behavior by copying it from the people around us, our parents and others. The law is that we almost always become like those with whom we associate. And as we grew up, we also learned about values and standards from those around us. Hopefully, all of this is quite obvious. But are the implications obvious to you as a boss?

I am convinced that non-human living species may have been equipped at birth with a significant amount of knowledge as to exactly what to do in life. The process butterflies go through is impressive, but so is that of a female turtle. She can traverse thousands of miles of open sea to return to her beach of birth in time to lay a clutch of eggs in a hole of her own making. These are actions that she never witnessed, but somehow "knew" how to do.

Humans, on the other hand, do not appear to be born with any pre-programming as to what to do. Through genes we receive guidance on the way to carry out actions; how aggressively or meekly, how emotionally or unemotionally and the like. But the "whats" must be learned by watching what goes on around us and then attempting to copy those examples. This is a monkey see monkey do routine wherein we can only copy actions repeatedly seen or heard.

We practice a little, watch the example some more, practice some more and repeat and repeat, most done sub-consciously. Eventually we develop behavior and we reapply this process until we have copied most everything our parents presented as examples; walking, smiles or frowns, getting happy over this or frustrated over that and generally all that we saw them do to interact with others. And since we copy from others besides parents, each behavior becomes a mixture of what we witnessed from all sources. Unfortunately, we do not gain a conscious knowledge of values and standards until after much of our behavior has been developed. The value standards reflected in our behavior, therefore, are those reflected in the behavior we copied and <u>may or may not have been placed there on purpose</u>. More likely, they were passed from the behavior of their parents or peers and so on back in time.

Beyond how we got our behavior, bosses must realize that <u>all of us do what we do for what we believe are good reasons</u>. There are two "whys" for this. First, we know we are our good values, not our behavior, so we are good. Second, we developed our behavior with good intent and got it from those we respect and/or love. So when bosses disrespect us by assuming from our bad behavior that we don't care or are just bad people, they are attacking us and all those we respect and love. This is a serious error. Its message will be quickly evaluated and the response will always be negative.

So thinking about each of us, what chance is there that our behavior reflects our own value standards? And what chance is there that our behaviors meet high standards for all good values? Slim chance? After puberty, if we understand values and the signals of the Gut, we could take charge and start improving our behavior. How many of us recognize this need? Will our boss help?

Education Versus Gut Values

If growing up has its pitfalls, so does advanced education. It focuses on use of the conscious brain and attempts to convince us that by itself the brain is able to solve just about anything. We are not taught the teamwork process between the brain and the Gut, and are even led to believe emotions generated from within are basically bad. Since the signals that come from the Gut are what we call emotions, they fall into this "bad" category.

The more educated we are and the less we use our hands, the more we rely on our brain. In addition, success leads educated people toward more reliance on the brain for all reasoning and decisions. But <u>without a Gut as a good-bad compass, the rational brain can only try to do "things right" rather than do the "right thing"</u>. Does this sound familiar?

The result is that most people who do not go on to higher levels of education still have use of their Gut as a good-bad compass. And being creatures of habit, the more they use their Gut, the more useful it becomes. Conversely, for those who use it less, the harder it is for them to hear its message.

This outcome could be the cause of a serious disconnect between well-educated, senior bosses and their Gut level workers. The boss could decide with his/her brain to do something that only an accurate Gut could recognize as being good or bad. And how about being reserved and calculating when the troops need fire in the boiler (passion) to charge up the next hill? Workers tend to read any lack of passion by a reserved boss as a lack of sincerity.

This disconnect is easily resolved if one follows the tenets of this book. While it doesn't require regaining one's own compass, it does require teamwork. Bosses need only ensure that those who can clearly hear their Gut level responses are on the team with "protected rights" to participate. Bosses who believe they can hear their own Gut level responses must still use this approach for two reasons; first, we can all be fooled by our conscious brain and second, no boss can actually get into the shoes of the people affected by his/her decisions (more on this later).

VALUES GIVE US TRAITS

Knowing that everyone has identical good and bad values with differing standards, we can now discuss those human traits that result from our values and are relevant to managing people. These traits, like the values from which they emanate, can be viewed as laws. <u>A boss' success or failure in managing people will be dictated by the extent to which he or she chooses to follow or not follow these laws.</u> These traits are associated with two human arenas; first, our hopes and fears, and second, our responses to the actions of other people.

Understand that because people are "value-centered", they react in very predictable ways. We each have certain value standards and they decide our actions and reactions.

Hopes and Fears, Superstars

In our hopes and fears, people agree totally on having good outcomes. Since we share the same values, we all hope for the same basic things and fear the same things. We all want to be reasonably well-to-do, happy and secure, living in a world that is itself safe and secure. We want the same for our children. Each of us wants to be a superstar at something. Our poets have probably expressed most clearly and succinctly what soars to the heights of human dreams and plunges to the depths of human despair. We respond identically to these. We cry over the same things, in happiness and in sorrow.

For bosses, the most important of these outcomes is our desire to be superstars (5Star). This trait is not difficult to understand, so in spite of its great importance, we'll move on to another outcome from values.

Hopes and Fears of Consequence (Carrots and Sticks)

As small children, we quickly learn that consequence follows action or inaction. We can be silent and continue to suffer from hunger, or we can make noises and be rewarded with food. We don't actually connect these events at first, but with sufficient repetition, the cause and effect relationship is understood. In some families, crying out evokes a negative reward in the form of angry shouts and even physical abuse. Some of us will tough it out and continue to cry. For others, any price is too high. We'd rather live with the problem (hunger) than suffer the consequence of communicating it.

In order to understand a little better how the brain functions in using consequence, the costs or benefits resulting from an action, consider a simple example such as pricing of TV sets. A friend runs over to you and announces that all TV's are on sale for $1.00. Since most of us enjoy TV, $1 is a very, very small price to pay for such a large benefit. Because of this very favorable cost-benefit relationship, I am certain that you will be catapulted into action. How many rooms are in the house and do you want a TV in a bathroom? Perhaps you should put one in the garage to be able to watch it while working on the car. You wonder if any friends and relatives are aware of the $1. Should you spread the word or just keep it to yourself? So at a price of $1 there will be a great deal of thinking.

What happens when we raise the price to $100 and the benefit remains the same? How about $200? How about $500, $1000 or $5,000? As the cost increases, we spend less and less time thinking about alternative actions. At $5,000, do we bother to think about how many rooms are in the house? The point of this exercise is that the first characteristic of any possible action to be evaluated, by every human being, is its cost-benefit relationship. And if we think the cost is too high or the benefit too low as compared to those of other actions, we may not bother to think any further. This is a program or algorithm that the brain uses over and over again in order to evaluate alternative courses of action. Are value standards the first step? No! <u>The first step is cost-benefit or consequence!</u>

For a second example, examine the case of a 90 mph driver on a 55 mph speed limit road. A policeman pulls the car over and chews out the driver, but doesn't issue a ticket. The outcome in most of these cases is no behavior change.

The driver easily shrugs off the chewing and goes back to 90 mph, no cost, only a slight delay. However, a $200 fine probably stops 60 percent or more from ever trying 90 mph again and another 30 percent from doing it as often. Ten percent never get the word. The principle is, "Sticks and stones will break my bones, but words will never harm me".

So cost-benefit is always the first thing analyzed and it is a necessary element in our lives. How would we decide where to live and in what, what schools to attend, what clothes to wear, where to work, where to play and all of the other myriad decisions we must make without cost-benefit criteria? How can we decide what to do with our time without knowing the consequences of alternative actions as concerns rewards or costs?

Another aspect to consequence is "no news is good news". Assume that a worker is doing something wrong and a management person walks by within seeing distance. The worker usually knows the action is wrong. If the management person passes without saying anything about it, the worker immediately gets the idea it must be acceptable because nothing was said. In fact, the worker will most likely object strenuously when, after repeated cases of no news, someone finally does chew him/her out for it. The worker was previously led to believe it was OK and how come someone is now objecting? The wisdom is we must never passively walk by and thereby sanction unacceptable actions. At least wag your finger or stop to point out the error.

A corollary to consequence is we all expect to be charged for our errors, our mistakes. No one expects to escape some reasonable retribution based on the severity of the error.

So what is the bottom line of consequence for the boss?

First, do not, I repeat, do not think of rewards and disciplinary action as being motivators. Motivation is a much bigger issue and <u>turning on people is the subject of this entire book</u>. Carrots and sticks only serve the narrow function of being consequences that are used in everyone's decision-making process.

Second, bosses must only reward acts that meet everyone's value standards. This is everyone's workplace, no more so the boss' than anyone else's. <u>What we do must be satisfactory to all.</u> The same is true for disciplinary action. If both are not predictable outcomes in consonance with everyone's concept of fairness, then they are incorrect and will produce far more Excuses for poor performance than motivations for excellence. Recognition, the least expensive form of reward, is a very powerful consequence, but it too must meet fairness standards. Too often we encourage the wrong behavior and gain a result never intended. <u>The secret to success is to spend plenty of time listening</u>

to the <u>Gut level responses</u> of people who are both low in the organization and very much attuned to fairness issues. The "hows" of doing this are presented in detail later in the book.

This completes discussion of superstars and consequence, traits that emanate from the hopes and fears created by our value standards. Now let's look at two value-based responses.

VALUES DICTATE OUR RESPONSES TO OTHER PEOPLE'S ACTIONS

Actions of other people have direct and indirect effects on us; good, bad and indifferent. The good and bad cases contain some valuable laws for bosses.

Good actions cause Indebtedness

This is an influence through which people become grateful. <u>The more gratitude they feel, the more industrious they are.</u>

Isn't that powerful! Think about immigrants to the USA who came from countries where oppression and lack of opportunity prevailed. If they had it really rough where they came from, the chances are very high that just getting to this glory hole called the USA is enough to commit them to very diligent, hard work without complaint, no matter the difficulty, for the rest of their lives.

As a second example, a dentist, whose office was located in Manhattan, once told me the story of a young female employee with the diction and accent of one of the other boroughs of the New York City. She wanted to date Manhattan men, but was unsuccessful due to her accent. After finding out how much this meant to her and seeing her unhappiness, the dentist paid the cost of speech/diction schooling. Not long after completing school, she achieved her dating goal and her work performance dramatically changed from average to outstanding. She became the office morale booster and as a receptionist, had customers convinced that this was the best run outfit anywhere. This was indebtedness because the event was so significant to her. How to strike it rich with people! Can we produce indebtedness in the people we manage? Yes, if we can:

1. Make the company so good that people will be thankful for the opportunities presented and for all the good feelings they get from coming to work each day.

2. Invest in people through training to be 5Star, helping, meeting their needs and sharing our hopes, fears and woes through three different people (perhaps two bosses and one support person). These three people must act out high value standards. Helping would include when people have their day in the barrel. Everyone has one of these and if help is provided we pay it back ten times over just to make sure we've worked off the debt.

The principle involved is, <u>bosses who make things good for their people are paid back in kind through industriousness several times over the original cost</u>. This may be part of the reason why the old axiom, "it is better to give than to receive", is true. If going to work is a real turn-on, gratitude and indebtedness will always follow. Any boss choosing this road makes out in spades.

But this "indebtedness" principle has its flip side. If you hurt them badly enough, people will go to any length to retaliate. The cases that are in between the extremes aren't so great either. This opposite effect to indebtedness, the other side of the coin, is what I will name the excuse principle.

Bad actions cause Excuses

Everyone has the same good values and naturally wants to take good actions. If so, why do people take incorrect or wrong actions in the workplace? There are three basic reasons:

1. They don't understand it is wrong because they lack the correct facts or necessary judgment criteria.
2. They copied it from others and never thought to evaluate it against their own value standards.
3. "Well, since the boss got away with that, I think it's only fair that I not be charged for doing this."

My experience indicates a large majority of problems in the workplace originate from #3 above and this is what I call the excuse principle.

People and events often violate our value standards. <u>While those of us who are 5Star ignore these violations and don't allow them to affect our</u>

performance, what do the rest of us do? We can forgive and forget because of indebtedness or force of reason, or we can get mad about it and save it. The ones we save I call Excuses because we will use them to excuse our own bad performance, past or future. For instance, if we have a bad attitude today, that can be excused because of the bad national economy, the disrespectful and degrading actions by our boss, the denial of a promotion, the receipt of a pay raise that is not as good as that given another employee, change, rain yesterday, stress we perceived or the moon was blue last night.

Excuses are filed in a Box and are readily available to justify not working while being paid for it, unsafe acts, not meeting the boss' deadlines, incorrectly performing work, theft, destruction of property, alcoholism, dishonesty, drug abuse and violence. Any person with an operable "excuse box" in which to file excuses is a hazard to themself and others. The entrepreneur who bribes government officials, drug dealers from the ghetto, welfare cheats, incompetent bosses and executives, and workers who slough off on the job all suffer a common affliction. They all are operating in violation of their own value standards for what they believe are good reasons. Their conscious brain managed to rationalize away one or more of their own value standards in favor of one or more other values such as fairness or security. "Everyone else is getting some, including the President and the Congress, why shouldn't I?" These are all excuses!

In the workplace, excuses are referred to as "what goes around comes around" and are controlled by the bosses. If bosses remove all excuses, each person will be left to their own value standards when deciding on action. Some of these actions would be meeting relatively low standards of good, some would meet much higher ones. But all actions would be good because we all agree that bad things should not be done..

This is a powerful statement. It tells us that all human beings are inherently capable of producing great good if only the boss will support us. It tells us that we are all capable of reaching our dreams and shows us that our hopes for comfort, security and happiness can be realized. For managing people, it says the sky's the limit because everyone can be led to be a superstar.

Admittedly, the removal of all boss-supplied excuses may seem like a large undertaking. The only other course is to develop people who are strong and independent (5Star) who aren't equipped with an "excuse box" and thus have no possibility of saving an excuse. Perhaps we should work on 5Star as well as removing excuses in order to assure success in our business.

Wouldn't it be nice if there was a way to work on both of them at the same time, "kill two birds with one stone"? Later we will find out there is!

This completes discussion of values and the traits that result from those values.. Now for the second characteristic.

FOLLOWING OR CONFORMING – the second characteristic

A follower is a person who decides how to act only after knowing how their peers and bosses are acting. The art of following has two parts to it. The first is to copy the actions of peers and bosses. The second is to record for future use the value standards implied so we will know how to act in the workplace. For example, if the boss is unfair to us at a standard of 6, a follower will act unfairly toward other people at about the same standard. The same is true if the boss treats a follower fairly to a standard of 6. And the following process holds true for arrogance or humility, hardly working or working hard, lacking in technical knowledge or having lots of it and all the other good and bad value standards that our boss and our peers care to display with reasonable repetition.

A non-follower is a person who decides to act only after determining what he/she personally wants to do. If a non-follower works next to Sally all day long, a question of "What was Sally doing today?" would elicit a response of "How would I know? I really wasn't watching her because I was busy with my own work." Conversely, a follower would be able to recount quite a bit of what Sally had done because that is what followers do, watch everyone else to see what they are doing. Needless to say, following takes a lot of time, effort and brainpower, all of which are lost from the work. In contrast, a 5Star person is a non-follower and thus has more time and brainpower to apply to work. The 5Star trait of being independent means using one's own value standards to determine what to do, independently of what other people expect or what existing conditions might imply.

As with 5S, an entire spectrum exists between totally following at one extreme and totally not following at the other extreme. But the distribution between the two is greatly skewed. The fact is, over ninety percent of us are much closer to being followers and this includes bosses as well as their juniors. But why are so many of us followers? Are we naturally this way?

All of us start life as non-followers and this is our natural state. This state supports taking charge of our own life and being responsible and accountable for our actions. Everyone knows the good life is not possible if we let other people dictate to us. Non-following also permits us to listen to the signals of our good-bad compass (Gut) more closely and to follow its dictates rather than the value standards implied by the actions of others.

But the United States is very much an authoritarian society. Our parents tell us what to do. And so do our teachers, churches, peers, government, media and eventually, our bosses at work. Pressure to conform to the expectations and the implied value standards of these authorities is enormous. We often conform just to escape censure and reduce the amount of flack that comes our way. As a result we become less and less non-followers and more and more followers. Some of us traverse the entire spectrum and have trouble knowing who we are since what we do bears no resemblance to what we want to do.

The bottom line is, <u>90% of us are closer to being followers than non-followers</u>. As such, we end up with two sets of value standards. One set has been developed from interpreting the actions and wishes of authorities who demand conformance. This set is used to produce actions, to the extent we have become followers. The second set resides in our Gut and is used by the Gut to judge everything and send the resulting evaluations to our conscious brain.

Now for our third and last major characteristic.

CHOICE – the third characteristic

Each of us has an innate ability to choose. We may choose how we act in every circumstance. That is, we may choose what we think, what we say and what we do every minute of every day. We may choose to act by reacting or not reacting to what people do or say and to events that happen near to us or far from us. Our range of choice extends to what we think and what we communicate by way of body language and tone of voice.

This great power of choice, each human being's most important asset, was given to us by our Creator for our use and <u>it cannot be controlled by any other person or thing</u>. Like every other piece of human equipment, it improves with use and does not, like a machine, wear out from use. If it falls into disuse, its value is lost. However, it can be restored to full use at any time and will regain its value as it is used more and more from that time onward.

This ability to choose is so obvious a human characteristic to non-followers that it is as natural as breathing. They know that without it they might just as well be dead. Followers, on the other hand, have been convinced to partially or fully lay aside this God-given right and subjugate themselves to the wishes and desires of authoritarians. The full fledged follower rarely acts, but mostly reacts to other people and conditions. If it is raining, they most often feel depressed. Traffic jams are a good reason to feel frustrated, as are many forms of actions by people around them. "I'm only human" is a common response to why they feel bad. Their feelings come from their reactions and they believe choosing to be happy isn't possible for human beings.

As stated before, following is not our natural state. It prevents us from using our ability to choose and using our own good value standards when working. Therefore, following subverts our natural control system and tries to replace it with a system based on the value standards reflected in the actions of others. Of course, those we follow are mostly followers themselves who followed the standards reflected in the actions of other followers who had followed ----- (who knows how far back this goes). Since these actions rarely reflect high standards for the good values, followers will often be prevented from achieving high performance standards.

Failing to use our ability to choose takes on new meaning as we learn more about what makes humans tick. Many studies have closely linked our health to our attitude. The body's repair abilities have proven to be greatly enhanced by an uplifting and positive attitude, while a negative one has proven to have the opposite effect. Success in any endeavor has likewise been linked to a positive outlook and attitude. In fact, it has become obvious that beyond our God-given abilities, choosing an uplifting and positive attitude gives us our most important asset.

That completes our discussion of the three characteristics of people that have significant implications for bosses. In fact, we shall see in succeeding chapters how these characteristics dictate the proper techniques for managing people. Before proceeding, let's review some important conclusions that should have been picked up from this chapter.

CONCLUSIONS from the three characteristics

From a managerial standpoint, all people are alike! They are us! If bosses accept the three characteristics (identical good and bad values and the traits that derive from them, 90% followers, and our innate ability to choose), there are several actions that bosses should take:

- Remove excuses that can be used by people to rationalize actions that do not meet their own value standards.

- Respect subordinates for believing they were doing the right thing when they developed their behavior. Trust that their behavior is not them and that they are good because their values are good.

- Cause/encourage subordinates to use their own value standards, their Gut to judge everything, self and boss included, and to use them to decide on their own actions.

- Help subordinates to better understand values and to learn how to improve their behavior to a level that can make them proud of meeting their own value standards.

- Accept that all behavior, including following, was learned and therefore can be unlearned and reprogrammed.

- Openly acknowledge that each person wants to be a superstar and take concerted actions to help each to achieve that status (5Star). Remember! We were all non-followers when we started and we can be again.

Flash!!

Followers waste most of their brainpower attempting to conform, trying their best to discern what expected of them. Non-followers spend 100% of their brainpower on their work because they don't waste time attempting to follow. Since brainpower is the source of a person's innovation, creativity, productivity, motivation and commitment, followers have very little while non-followers operate at their full potential. *Think about it!! This is the reason for the huge performance difference between the two.*

The actions above are woven into the "how tos" of Chapters 4 through 9. But don't forget that:

VALUES ARE OF PRIMARY CONCERN TO ALL PEOPLE AND ARE CENTRAL TO EVERY MINUTE OF EVERY DAY OF THEIR LIVES. AS BOSSES, WE IGNORE THIS FACT AT OUR OWN PERIL.

With that said, let's proceed to Chapter 3 for the basic management approach that the three characteristics dictate.

CHAPTER 3

HOW SHOULD WE MANAGE PEOPLE ?

IS THERE A CHOICE ?

Managing people would seem to be just another discipline, just another area in which a body of knowledge, including theory, has been accumulated. This knowledge should form the basis for a set of discrete, definable procedures that if followed should yield the desired results. But "should" never occurs on any day of the week. If it had, there would be no need to write this book.

If you want to become a mechanical engineer and are willing to invest 4 years and $100,000, a host of universities and colleges will eagerly commit themselves to the task. I would say your chances of emerging with useful knowledge, assuming you graduate, are as high as 80 percent. After graduation, if I line up ten of you and direct you to analyze a machine with a problem, at least 6 or 7 will agree on the problem. If I make you all agree on the problem and ask for a fix, I may get six of you to agree on the same fix.

The above can be done in many disciplines like accounting and nuclear physics. Don't try it in management of people. From what I have seen, <u>the chance of getting even two of ten bosses to agree on the problem or on the fix is low</u>.

The reason for this inability to agree is that management styles vary considerably and we are encouraged to pick one that suits ourself, our personality or whatever. But who would recommend that a boss' personality or style be taken down to a machine, instead of intimate knowledge of that machine, and used to determine what to do with that machine. "Hey stupid, don't pull that stunt. Study the machine and then get yourself down there and try like hell to determine the problem using specific tests and determine the solutions based on a specific set of defined knowledge. It has nothing to do with you personally." But somehow when it comes to dealing with people, knowledge of the machine is not required. Instead, we are encouraged to superimpose our style and our personality, our likes and dislikes on the process. You dislike Phillips head screwdrivers, but you like flat head screwdrivers. I am certain that those feelings will not help you when you try to turn a Phillips head screw with a flat head screwdriver. The same is true for managing people.

The people management arena is strewn with hundreds of these excuses, such as "I don't like to ---" or "I can't bear to ---". We have all heard them. The actions evaded range from not being able to get up in front of a group to not wanting to counsel an employee, from not wanting to terminate to not being able to provide succor in a time of need. The excuses to justify these evasions range from personality to "I don't want to hurt someone" to "the moon was blue last night". There are also many people who would like to blame the sociologists, psychologists, psychiatrists, religious, consultants and others for their own management errors. Excuses will always be available to anyone who is looking for them, especially to those who enjoy the permissiveness of the "doing your own thing" vogue. But recognize that all of these excuses are invalid and their use signals that the user (boss) is not 5Star.

As with machines, excuses will always limit your success with people, if not cause outright failure. Listen to yourself using them (we all do) and get as far away in the other direction as possible.

You must not decide what a person should be given based on what you have to give, only on what that person needs. Throw away your excuse box and your management style. Use your common sense and the same logical, methodical approach required to solve technical issues. That approach will be developed in this book.

THE NATURAL LAW

Although a large number of additional whys will be presented in the following pages of this book, it is appropriate at this juncture to disclose that the science of managing people is the science of leadership, pure and simple, no more, no less. Whether or not the CEO or boss wants to admit it, "the ship is its captain". This is what actually happens and the boss (CEO or lower) has no control over this. He/she can't stop it, modify it, wish or order it away. It is a natural law that operates inexorably and without regard for the human beings involved. The process that results waits for no one. It just happens day in and day out.

Therefore, no matter what the actions, words, facial expressions, body language, verbal or written orders or policies, habits, personality traits, inactions through silence, or other boss behavior are, these are followed by most juniors simply because a great majority of them are followers. The subordinates become what the boss projects. If the boss works hard, they tend to work hard. If the boss has little knowledge of certain things, they have little knowledge of them. If the boss encourages, they will be encouraged. If the boss cannot bring him/herself to do certain things, they will not either. Followers clearly discern the implied value standards and set out to use them in their everyday routine.

This sequence is a natural law, one that makes the boss either the subordinates' biggest ally or their greatest enemy or something somewhere in between.

The boss by virtue of appointment becomes the leader whether great and fearless or tyrannical and unsupportive or whatever. It is the boss who decides how subordinates will act by choosing his/her own actions. The boss can, of course, decide not to decide, the "what they see is what they get" or the "I was the one promoted so I must be OK the way I am" approach. The first quote represents a "to hell with the subordinates" tack, while the second is the height of arrogance. I don't mean to seem judgmental about this, but my true desire is to make crystal clear that each boss chooses, consciously or unconsciously, what their subordinates will be led to be,. <u>That they will follow the boss' lead has been preordained</u>!!!

So! Do we really have a choice on how we manage people? Do we get to choose a management style of our own? The answer is, the "natural law" dictates that we have no choice. We can only choose how we make use of the law and this is a choice of the value standards toward which we lead.

LEADERSHIP ???

If we walk into a race track and the horses are in the middle of the race, I am certain we will all be able to agree on which horse is in the lead. It will always be the horse "in front" of the other horses, the "leader". The other horses are "following" the "leader". So leading implies being in a position followers will try to attain. Two questions emerge.

1. In what does the boss (CEO or supervisor) lead?

2. What do subordinates look to follow in a workplace?

Fortunately for us, these two questions are merely different sides of the same coin. The name of the coin is "values". From the boss' view it is his/her leadership, while from the subordinates view it is what they follow. It makes no difference that we analyze.

FOLLOWING OR LEADING

To start the discussion, recall that ninety percent or more of all subordinates are followers, people looking to produce their behavior through copying that of others. This copying process is applied to values as well as to actions. In the workplace, people want to find out as quickly as possible what is expected of them so they can meet those standards and thus keep down the hassle, avert possible censure and keep the paychecks coming to feed themselves and their families. Conforming to peer pressure is also a part of this process. None of these are surprising revelations.

Remaining with the subordinates, how do they find out what's expected of them, what the standards are for the different values? The process is the same one used during childhood, the one that absorbs everything around them. After soaking up everything that is available, the brain's computer is used to sort out the "do as I say not as I do" events, consequences presented by management or peers, and other nuances.

Through this process, new employees can very quickly get to act like all the other employees. They check what is happening to others and what is happening on-the-job in terms of normal values: attitude, cleanliness, industriousness, honesty, integrity, admission of error, knowledge, perseverance, fairness and all of the other ones. Their brain automatically performs computations and suddenly they know what the standards are for each. They have, in effect, <u>translated actual conditions into value standards</u>.

So equipped, they begin to use these standards to perform their work, standards for precisely the same values all of us have. This is the "natural law". Recall that the <u>followers do not use their own value standards</u> to produce behavior in the workplace. <u>Only 5Star people do that</u>!!!!

So, employees detect the workplace value standards and use them to decide how to carry out their work. If these standards are high, we fly with the eagles, beat the competition most of the time and love our workplace. If these standards are low or toward bad values, we walk with the turkeys, lose to the competition and generally dislike coming to work. Can the boss afford to leave this situation to the whims of chance? Can the boss take a chance on which good or bad values and their standards are utilized in the conduct of work?

The leader's only recourse is to commit to frequently and clearly <u>communicating only very high value standards</u> through the normal management <u>actions</u> of supporting, directing and developing. <u>Actions speak far louder than words and the real truth is no one listens to words</u>!! As children, we didn't understand the language of words and could only learn through the language of action, through what people do and their tone of voice and body language. This develops into a habit and is carried into adult life. <u>Communicating values is thus an action oriented process</u> in which each boss must be proficient.

The boss' actions range from one-on-one discussions to group meetings, from providing tools to training and benefits, from discipline to promotions and rewards, and from action or inaction when it's their day in the barrel to termination for cause. Both actions and inactions transmit value standards, the latter often being the loudest. On a scale of 1 to 10, 10 being best, these actions and inactions must repeatedly reflect 8-10 standards for all good values if we expect to have real excellence in the workplace.

Carefully note the wide range of actions from which followers extract value standards to use in performing their work. For high level bosses, what they personally say and do may constitute a very small part of a subordinate's sources. The leadership value messages received by a person consists not only of the personal actions of their immediate boss, but also of what other people do to this person. "Others" includes staff, other bosses, peers and the rumor mill. Over the past week, a person may have received 200 messages on fairness, 100 on quality, 50 on industriousness and only 2 on humility, very few of which came directly from the immediate boss. The person computes a new standard for fairness using past data combined with the latest 200 messages and repeats this for each value. If these standards are low or reflect bad values, the bosses are in real trouble.

The Boss' Only Choices

So the boss is the leader and leads in value standards, whether he/she wants to or not. Once appointed boss, he/she is the leader who will be followed and that is the law. The boss' choices are extremely limited. He/she can choose the direction in which to lead, whether toward the good or the bad value, for example whether toward humility or arrogance. The boss can also choose the standard for that good or bad value from 1 to 10. Making the wrong choice or choosing not to make a conscious choice is to choose mediocrity or even anarchy with all of its attendant problems.

Leadership is simple. Unfortunately, it has been revered and placed on a high pedestal, out of reach to most of us common folk. If it was ever knowable, it has become less so over the years. There is some belief that it belongs to a previous heroic age and is incompatible with participative management. Some people also question whether concepts such as democracy and equality are compatible with leadership. Although I did for years share these concerns, they all disappeared as I developed and practiced the whats, whys and hows of this book. I am certain leadership will become just as clear for you once you've placed into practice the knowledge of this book.

Changing Workplace Performance

Unfortunately, bosses tend to believe their job is mainly one of giving orders. This consists of choosing the goals and the visions, directing actions by their employees to get there and then checking for the results. Bad results simply call for some form of re-direction.

But from the boss' "leadership", their employees have already computed a set of value standards that they are using every day in the execution of their tasks. Let's call these the "how tos" of doing the job and admit that they will determine the success or failure of the employee's endeavors and that they emanate from the boss, not from the subordinate. "How tos" are how industriously, compliantly to rules, cooperatively, neatly, cleanly, creatively, safely, independently, resourcefully, confidently, qualitatively, compassionately, enthusiastically and the like.

So if the boss is unhappy with the results subordinates are achieving, he/she must change the support and direct management functions so as to communicate higher good value standards. Only after these changes lead subordinates to use higher standards can the boss expect performance improvement. In effect, subordinates are always waiting for the boss to change before they themselves can change. An example may shed some light.

Transmitting Values

Bill joins the work force and soon is told by a foreman that the work cannot proceed because he must wait for a part. So Bill puts his hands in his pockets or sits down to wait. The foreman says nothing more. The next day it's waiting for a welder and so on. Soon, Bill gets the message that doing nothing is OK as long as there is a good excuse. No matter that he could do something else or could figure out what's missing before starting a job and thus go to one that requires no waiting.

Bill probably didn't believe he would be paid to stand around doing nothing. Likewise, Bill would not pay a plumber to fix his own sink if that plumber chose to stand around doing nothing in Bill's house. But Bill as a follower easily falls into becoming unproductive. What if Bill was 5Star and used his own value standards to decide his actions? I assume it is becoming obvious why 5Star people are so valuable.

There may be a multitude of similar bad influences or low value standards being transmitted in the workplace. Bosses must be able to detect these problems and provide workable solutions to use in changing each and thereby improve the standard being transmitted for each value.

Before getting down to the specifics of leadership, let's now discuss four other issues important to understanding effective leadership. They are: repetition, conflicts, respect for bosses and leadership toward 5Star.

REPETITION

From Chinese lore comes the tale of telling a person one thousand times that he/she is a pig. The first few times cause major negative reactions, possibly even shouting. These die down and by the one thousandth time the person responds with an "Oink". This is the essence of the natural law of leadership. Good or bad, it happens almost every time. The exception is that 5Star people do not surrender easily and never do so inside the brain. Their examples have been recorded within the concentration camps of past wars and the dungeons of past inquisitions.

These outcomes from "oink" followers and "non-oink" 5Star were preordained. They are not something to complain about since they can be used to great advantage. The U.S. Marine Corps is well-known for producing dedicated privates from followers by using their response to repetition.

The implication for leaders is that without a large number of repetitions, the communication will not be accepted. Therefore, the only question for the leader is how many times has it been repeated and how long will it take to complete the desired number. Given this requirement for repeating the same message a great number of times before it takes effect, <u>leaders would be well advised to spend more time making certain each of their intended actions will meet an 8-10 standard and only then get on with the repetition.</u>

For example, the leader's standard for fairness will be communicated through the management actions of job assignments, promotions, commendations, discipline, selection for special training, access to the boss, suggestion awards and others. Each category may achieve tens of repetitions in a given time period (each person will have a slightly different data base and thus a different standard).

So the leader must get many different management functions all going in the same direction (fair versus unfair) and at a high 8-10 standard. The consequence of conveying unfairness or a low standard for fairness is a considerable loss of productivity and innovation/creativity, higher personnel turnover and poorer product quality to mention a few. "Not really being fair" is a great de-motivator and creates many uses of the excuse box. "Really being fair", on the other hand, creates considerable indebtedness and unused excuse boxes. Bosses have a great exposure over fairness and the solutions are explained in this book.

What can be done if there isn't sufficient natural repetition to drive home a particular value standard? For example, even if the actions reflecting humility do meet high standards, each junior may directly experience only a few cases. With so little repetition, a standard for humility cannot be established and people will continue to use whatever standard they acquired outside the workplace. The same exists for compassion, forthrightness, charity, admission of error and courage. The boss will have to create opportunities to clearly demonstrate these in order to meet the need for repetition.

The leader's solution is to talk with subordinates one-on-one and in group meetings. In group meetings, forthrightness, admission of error and humility come across very quickly and only in this way can the leader infuse them into the workplace. <u>Group meetings can attain a level of credibility not possible through other mechanisms</u> and as such they are indispensable to communicating values through demonstration, never but never through preaching. The solution, of one-on-one and group meetings, is covered in detail in Chapters 8 and 9.

CONFLICTS

Unfortunately, life in the United States teaches us we cannot have our cake and eat it too, that acting out high value standards may be a great dream but it is not a possibility in the real world, and in order to get a full cup I will probably have to take part of it away from someone else. The methods of this indoctrination include all facets of life; politics, community, work, schools, religion and all others.

The result for the boss is that subordinates, in their belief that all good values cannot be satisfied, will "accept" conditions in which two or more high value standards appear to be in conflict. Accepting means they will not take actions to resolve these apparent conflicts in spite of the fact they experience considerable unhappiness and lowered morale over them! So the unsatisfactory condition will remain a thorn unless the boss acts.

Therefore, the leader/boss must ferret out these conflicts and take whatever corrective action is necessary to resolve each. Through this process, subordinates learn to no longer accept conditions that do not meet all high value standards.

A small sample of these conflicts might be:

1. You can't have great safety without losing productivity.
2. You can't be forthright and still observe privacy.
3. You can't be forthright with employees because their goals conflict with the corporation's.
4. You can't be loyal to your subordinates and also be loyal to your boss.
5. You can't be forceful and not interfere with humility.
6. You can't have effective discipline and still be loved by subordinates.
7. You can't be compassionate and terminate employees.
8. You can't chew out someone for error and still be considered loving.
9. You can't be authoritative and still be participative.
10. You can't back your subordinate bosses and still be fair to workers.
11. You can't be fair without being consistent.
12. You can't act like a boss and still promote creativity.
13. You can't be warm and loving and still be the boss.
14. You can't be promoted and not be a yes man.
15. You can't be honest and still succeed in business.

Fortunately for the boss, none of these beliefs are correct. The present status is merely a self-fulfilled prophesy dictated to us by the purveyors of these negative beliefs. The truth is, our Creator was a good guy who made everything fit together perfectly. If we choose to act out this truth, the overriding counsel of this book, life can truly be a bowl full of cherries!!! Belief in this by our leader turns out to be fantastic for us followers and we love it.

More opportunities exist than those above. They are each invitations for the boss to excel, to teach that "you can have your cake and eat it too". The goal is to have the individuals involved start to resolve these conflicts on their own and help others to do likewise. This is a big move toward 5Star or taking charge of your own life, rather than doing and feeling as others want or expect. Although I will not give explicit solutions to any of the above opportunities (even though I have resolved each in the past), this book provides sufficient answers for you, the reader, to do so on your own.

RESPECT FOR THE BOSS

This issue proceeds from the fact that <u>the leader's actions are always evaluated against each individual's own personal value standards</u>. If I as a junior think a particular value standard is important to me:

> When you violate it by action or inaction, I may hate you.
>
> When you meet it, I may appreciate your action.
>
> When your actions meet a higher standard than mine, I am deeply impressed and may even change my standard.

This effect is very powerful! It means if you as boss make your actions, on a scale of 1 to 10, meet an 8-10 standard for each of the values, you will be very respected by everyone. Being very respected provides you with one more key element. The guidance and orders you issue will be received by more receptive and responsive juniors who will try harder to carry them out. While I have heard many bosses object that their orders were not being followed, when I had time to investigate I always found the boss was to blame.

Increased receptivity by followers reduces the requirement for repetition by a significant percentage. So receptivity through respect really makes the leader's job far, far easier. All subordinate leaders will bask in this sunlight and will thank the day the big boss arrived.

Bad leadership can go just as far in the disastrous direction. It is seen in messages and actions that violate the values of subordinates. Instead of humility, there is arrogance. Instead of showing confidence and trust in people, it demonstrates a belief that they are bad and not capable of much on their own. Instead of praise, there is fault finding. Instead of a positive, uplifting attitude, it is glum and downcast. Instead of cooperation, there are adversarial actions. Instead of heroes, there are martyrs.

Do the juniors follow bad leadership? Unfortunately for the juniors, yes! They do it by loading up their excuse box. Most of their attitudes go negative and many do damage to themselves and their families. When they went to work to be managed, they didn't realize they would be treated to such harsh fare.

Only the strong and independent survive almost unscathed. Truly 5Star people can withstand this onslaught. Their performance alone keeps the workplace functioning at a low vice zero level.

While good leadership results in juniors who want to take orders from above and carry out the wishes of the appointed bosses, the exact reverse is true for bad leadership. No one respects bad leadership, even if they cannot define it. They know it in their Gut and no one needs to tell them. Their bosses may not want to sabotage the workplace, but the troops think they do.

So the troops cease taking the orders of the bad guys and look around for new leaders. This is called anarchy and exists in many places. Links in the chain of command become disconnected. Loyalty disappears. <u>Any team concept fades and each person is an individual ship in a sea of trouble.</u> Dissident groups start to form. Peer loyalties develop to replace the lost loyalty to the top. Pay becomes something every person deserves just for coming to work at such a bad place.

The above situation exists in more places than most of us would like to admit. Most of us are employed in companies that are in between the two extremes I have described. This is the area of mediocrity or walking with the turkeys instead of flying with the eagles. Mediocrity is bad in and of itself.

LEADERSHIP TOWARD 5Star

So far in this chapter we have only discussed leadership toward high good value standards. Unfortunately, this effort alone will only achieve about 40% of the available gain. While leadership toward high standards is a prerequisite to going higher, the remaining 60% will come from turning your followers into non-followers. Following is equivalent to bondage and as such we are always waiting for the next message rather than proactively taking charge and doing what's needed. However, non-followers are always proactive and this comes from their being strong and independent (living by their own value standards), the third trait of the 5Star person.

Because they think independently, 5Star employees are able to achieve their full potential of innovation, creativity, productivity, motivation and commitment. So leading everyone to be 5Star, or as close as they can be, is terribly important.

In addition, the gains from this achievement can be more easily maintained because new 5Star people will refuse to give up their new-found control over their destiny, refuse to return to being followers. For this reason, a 5Star culture is far more stable and self-sustaining than one of well-led followers.

Thus, causing people to become strong and independent is the ingredient that must be added in order to achieve the entire potential gain, the 40% and the 60%. Leadership that causes people to practice taking charge of their destiny is the road to this achievement.. For this we will need a very powerful leadership forum, one that will be far more credible than any one-on-one session can ever be. That forum is a group meeting.

At this juncture, that is all we need to know about leading people to become 5Star non-followers. The path will become clearer as you proceed through the book. Group Meetings are not covered until Chapter 9 because of their dependency on the first eight chapters.

CONCLUSIONS

Leadership is simply leading in values because they are the only things followers are looking to follow. They know exactly what the values are and are fully capable of computing a set of standards from what goes on around them in the workplace. And this is the set they will utilize when performing their work. Values and their standards constitute the boss's leadership, whether or not he/she likes it. This is a "natural law" that is always in effect.

The point I am making in this chapter is that direction (orders) and re-direction (more orders) are at best only a small fraction of what we need from the boss/leader. What we need is for the boss to improve the quality of his/her leadership. Employees, including subordinate bosses, will thus see a set of higher standards that they will then use to improve the quality of their work. The faster the boss gets to very high standards in leadership, the faster subordinates arrive at excellence.

Bosses waste time feeling frustration over subordinates who don't do what they <u>should</u> do. For the great majority of juniors, <u>what they do is what they are led to do</u> and the exceptions only serve to prove the rule. This is the natural law and it gives bosses no choice over how to manage people. The boss can choose whether to lead toward a good or a bad value and can choose the standard for that value. These are the only choices open to the boss and this is the law. But there is still much to be learned about how to use this law to our advantage.

Before leaving this chapter, let's review the path we will take from here.

HOW WE SHALL PROCEED

We now have a vision, the three human characteristics (values, following and choice) and a basic management approach dictated by those characteristics. Armed with these, we can now build a set of tools, a set of whats, whys and hows by which to carry out the leadership approach. Our path to do so is:

1. Define and discuss those specific values that the leader boss will attempt to communicate to subordinates through leadership (Chapter 4).

2. Show how to transmit high standards for these values by leading through the normal management support functions of providing tools, parts, material, training, procedures, peace of mind, direction and the like (Chapters 5 and 6).

3. Provide a thorough understanding of the boss' most important management tool, listening. It is the door to success for both bosses and their subordinates (Chapter 7).

4. Provide a thorough understanding of the two mechanisms that bosses use to discover existing leadership deficiencies, take corrective action and <u>convert followers into 5Star non-followers</u> (GOTYP and group meetings, Chapters 8 and 9).

In addition to the above, there are certain workplace conditions and personal behaviors that so often cause problems that knowledge of their whys and hows, how to manage and change them, is a necessity.

Appendix A. Workplace Conditions: bosses, peers, change, bureaucracy, unions, customers, priorities, competition, relief of the boss, communication, committees, discrimination and life's problems.

Appendix B. Personal Behaviors: personality, likes and dislikes, ego and prestige, assumptions, bad morale, bad attitudes, stress and emotionalism

CHAPTER 4

VALUES FOR LEADING OR FOLLOWING

Those values that are especially relevant to the workplace are listed below. Some of the values have been placed in Groups to support better understanding of leading.

honesty *	wisdom	patience	high standards
confidence *	selflessness	firmness	rule compliance
industriousness *	decisiveness	knowledge	risk taking
Integrity	freedom autonomy	- trustworthy	passion
Charity	respect	eye contact	neatness
inner strength	creativity	commitment	patriotism
courage	cooperation	competence	loyalty
independence	quality	sacrifice	dedication
responsibility	forcefulness	cleanliness	fortitude

GROUP I	GROUP II	GROUP III
positive attitude	compassion	grit
Smiles	humility	heroism
Cheers and praise	admission of error	
perseverance	fairness	
success	forthrightness	
winners	forgiveness	
	trust	
	courtesy	

VALUES AND THE BOSS

For my first 12 years, I believed each person had different values and their behavior reflected their values. I treated them as their behavior led me to believe they were and if they took offense, it only proved they were worse than I had thought. For example, when their work was incomplete, I concluded they didn't care and I told them so. When their work lacked high quality, I concluded they were sloppy and I told them so. In retrospect, I used my value standards to judge them and many fell short of the mark. These actions bordered on being moral judgments. I now realize all these actions and thoughts were completely wrong.

After my 1970 conversion, I learned through listening that everyone's life revolves around values and I did not hold the moral high ground. I also learned that calling people sloppy was a totally unproductive action on my part, while taking the time to help a person to improve their work quality was a big positive.

As a boss, I began to appreciate that a sound understanding of values and an ability to explain their application to the workplace were prerequisite to sustained success through people. How else to ensure that subordinate bosses would project high standards? How else could I aid all subordinates in becoming superstars in their own right? In short, I now realize that <u>high good value standards are essential to outstanding performance and success in business,</u> and <u>causing their use is every boss' main function</u>.

In this chapter my aim is to relate relevant workplace values to the roles of bosses and juniors. I am certain all will be familiar to you and your own experiences will confirm what I write. My purpose is to present each value in such a way that you can understand how to project it at high standards and explain it to others, so they can use it on their journey to 5Star.

The Table Of Values

There are more values than those given above. I had no intent to list every possible word describing a value that humans use. I do have most of the ones important to the workplace. The values in Groups I, II and III have need of detailed understanding as they relate to managing people, and some of the others are worthy of special mention. Using these values at a high standard in our lives is the way to satisfy our individual hopes and fears. The less consistently our actions meet high standards for these values, the more problems we will have in dealing with everyday life, whether it be private or job related. Meeting the requirements of some are less necessary for certain vocations, more necessary for others. Round pegs in round or square holes, or what actions reflecting specific value standards are appropriate to which vocation could be discussed forever. I only intend to cover the vocation of managing people.

I will first address the asterisked values in the left column. These three values are not special for just bosses, but for all of us equally. Actions that meet high standards for these three have a significant positive effect on our lives. Meeting low or negative standards means "we don't make it", we don't make the grade.

HONESTY

When anyone finds out that one of your acts was dishonest, the game is over. They don't ever want to see your face, much less follow you, and all the excuses in the world will not help you. I might justify my own dishonesty to save my job, to get my fair share, because others do it, or for a myriad of other excuses. But don't anyone else try to be dishonest to me!! This is just as true between peers or friends as between juniors and bosses.

INDUSTRIOUSNESS

Without it you can't get anywhere. People who lack it are worthless to any goal. We all need to meet a high standard in this value; for the boss to prove his/her worth to the junior, for the junior to prove his/her worth to the boss and, most importantly, for each person to prove their own worth to themselves. Not being hard working means not trying hard and strips us of our self-respect.

Every person knows down deep inside that very little can be accomplished at home or at work if they do not apply themselves diligently to the task. And every boss has sufficient control to cause subordinates to be reasonably industrious at work. If the boss fails to do so, this is failing to help a person who is in great need.

In addition, industriousness makes up for a lot of other faults such as lack of expertise or efficiency, being new on the job and the like. Although it is impossible to instantly change your efficiency, it is possible to work twice as long until you are able to fix your efficiency. Others, including juniors and bosses, become very forgiving when they see you burning the midnight oil. Being industrious gains you considerable respect while a lack of it gets you mountains of disrespect.

CONFIDENCE (or SELF-ESTEEM)

Some say a loss of national confidence destroyed a civilization that had reached a human height of accomplishment not since achieved -- the Greeks of 600 to 400 BC! Powerful?

A total lack of confidence is a disaster of the first order, whereas full confidence tempered with humility is one of the keys to success, to being 5Star. Confidence is faith in oneself rather than despair. Confidence is doing in the present rather than fearing for the future. It is a sense of self-worth. It is the ability to learn from our errors and failures rather than constantly re-living them in the "I can never do it right" mode.

Each one of us has a great need for confidence and the boss/manager wields a lot of power over this characteristic. Can a bad boss make us sick? If he/she takes away our confidence, the answer is yes! Confidence gives us the will to be industrious, to gain knowledge without fear of being labeled as stupid, to be forceful when needed, to strive for high standards, to have courage and fortitude in the face of considerable odds and in general, to be able to afford compassion, trust and fairness for others. Once again, without it we are reduced to acting out the role of a weak, very dependent person.

HONESTY, INDUSTRIOUSNESS and CONFIDENCE are thus traits we simply cannot do without. Lacking any or all, we flunk life.

GROUP I   positive attitudes, smiles, cheering, perseverance, winners, success

Let us now discuss some aspects of values that have particular meaning for leaders. I have grouped under roman numeral I those values that are most important to all of us being managed. Therefore, these values must be demonstrated at the highest possible standard by all bosses. Look at them carefully. Poor attitudes and lack of enthusiasm must be replaced with positive attitudes and tons of real, genuine enthusiasm. Without a fire in the boiler, without plenty of get up and go, we simply cannot concentrate on or perform the job at a high standard of excellence.

POSITIVE ATTITUDES

Productivity and creativity are almost directly controlled by attitudes. Negative ones reduce productivity to a level 80 to 90 percent below true potential and make little difficulties into big problems. The more positive our attitude, the more we turn problems into challenges, lack of knowledge into the fun of learning, old practices into applications of new technology and new ideas, and failure into success. <u>There are few solutions a positive attitude cannot find.</u>

The principle is, the ten most important things to bring to the workplace are attitude, attitude, attitude -------- ten times. In my experience, I have rarely been able to determine an eleventh most important trait. I did learn for welders, before the advent of robotics, it was eye-hand coordination since without it the person could never become a top grade welder no matter how good the attitude.

The point is that a positive attitude, or approaching everything from the right direction, is essential to achieving a high quality outcome. With the power of a positive attitude, an individual person can solve most of the problems that constantly plague management. These people do it on their own with little aid, whether it concerns quality, cleanliness, training, rule compliance, productivity, cooperation, safety, reliability, cost or whatever. Therefore, attitude should be the most important personal characteristic considered in any hiring decision.

Conversely, a positive attitude soon fades when subjected to a steady diet of unfair practices, poor quality or quantity of tools, lack of spare parts, poor procedures or planning, poor training and the like. These conditions prove to everyone that the bosses do not care about subordinates since with their power bosses could easily fix these problems. In addition, bosses who frown over problems support negative attitudes, while bosses who smile, eagerly accept the challenge and embrace the opportunity to fix a problem send a positive message. "Preaching to the choir" is negative. Having fun fixing is positive. Bosses should shout and cheer at the disclosure of problems in order to lead subordinates toward better attitudes.

So the boss must support positive attitudes through actions to remove Excuses, not preaching. It is through the corrective action process subordinates learn that the boss would want us to have the right tools or the proper spare parts. But the boss cannot do everything and with our positive attitude we realize this fact. With a positive attitude, we do not reach for the excuse box as often, if ever. We get moving and get the problem fixed before it causes the job to fail or a bad attitude to start.

The person with a bad attitude waits for the boss to remove the Excuses. Correction comes through leadership in responding to these challenges and persevering to real solutions. Or the boss can validate a bad attitude by sitting around and bitching about the problem or the people who are causing it and thus create more excuses.

Although these understandings and the actions they require are crucial to job outcome for the person in the trench, a positive attitude is also crucial to his or her personal success in life. <u>Since we spend our most productive hours at work, what we develop on the job pervades our entire life.</u> No boss would want to wreck the children or spouse of his/her work force, but that is exactly what happens when bad attitudes are created on the job. For most of us followers, our attitudes are the same at home as they are at work. The very positive attitudes embodied in a 5Star person are of great value to the person's family. Needless to say, friends, community and fellow workers are not far behind the family in experiencing the effect, good or bad.

I know of no greater gift that a boss can provide to the work force than outstanding attitude. And I know of no gift that has a greater payback to the boss. This borders on 5Star status. Who needs perfect control and power over subordinates who already want to do everything needed. And yet I hear bosses mumbling about if they only had better control, if people only did what was asked. Hogwash! It's just disrespect for people and leading in the wrong direction. People don't want to be bad, but are led to doing so through excuses provided by the boss.

So the big boss must require all bosses to act out a <u>value standard of 10 for attitude and enthusiasm</u>. And the troops will follow. It's the law and they know in their Gut that they need it dearly.

SMILES

Smiles indicate plenty of confidence as well as enthusiasm and a positive attitude. They send a message of confidence that we are going to succeed at whatever we are trying to do. Who needs to have smiles? Bosses! The troops receive most of their communications non-verbally. Grimaces mean things are bad (the troops know not what) and smiles mean the opposite. Tom Peters tells the story of the Ohio titanium plant with its signs all over the place - "If you find a man without a smile, give him one of yours." This is a powerful message, one we can easily learn to project.

Anyone you manage needs their confidence badly and having it enhances our industriousness. Lacking it, in even small amounts, starts to depress industriousness. As that goes, so goes morale. If you do not understand the value of a smile, you have never listened to your own Gut level response when others smile at you. If you cannot smile in order to demonstrate enthusiasm, <u>you cannot be an effective manager of people</u>.

CHEERS OR CHEERLEADING AND PRAISES

To sustain the fire, we all need someone to cheerlead us once in a while. Who must be the most performing cheerleader? It is, of course, the highest boss. If the big boss does not set the highest example, the under-bosses will do less and they need cheers just as much as do the people in the trenches. As with attitude, praising and cheerleading must be made a requirement for all bosses so the troops get enough. After all, they are the ones actually in the heat of battle. Remember, a cheerleader leads other people in cheering by <u>bringing up their accomplishments and leading them in clapping for themselves</u>.

The troops dearly need to understand and take pride in their successes. Praise them about these. This is very powerful and leads them to repeat their successes. And then we praise and cheerlead again and so on. Look at what we did! Hooray!! How else to sustain the fire in the boiler, the confidence, the industriousness and the positive attitudes that we so dearly need in order to overcome the difficulties presented to us every day of our lives. This is the greatest gift anyone can be given by another person and the payback to the giver is likewise great.

Praise should not just be for excellence, but for improvement, for moving in the right direction, for making progress toward a high standard. This permits more opportunities to praise sub-par employees and encourages them to move toward being 5Star. Many will successfully make the journey with praise. Without it, only a very few will even try. With lots of negatives, they go in the opposite direction. As usual, it is the boss' choice.

PERSEVERANCE

Without perseverance no one can get anything difficult accomplished, boss or worker. Mountain climbing simply is not possible without it, and everyone wants the joy and satisfaction of climbing their own mountain. Perseverance requires lots of faith, lots of grit, a great attitude, plenty of confidence and perhaps sacrifice, courage, fortitude and even heroism.

Perseverance commands great respect from others. Without it (giving up, quickly or not) the boss loses respect, but with it gains deep respect. With a middle grade standard, the boss and his/her people will not accomplish many difficult tasks. If the boss has a high standard, real personal glory and satisfaction from a job well done suddenly become possible for the juniors.

This one trait does a lot to differentiate winners from losers. A thorough study of perseverance and much introspective examination pays big dividends. The key is to never forget the interdependence of perseverance with the many other values listed above, each of which the boss influences strongly.

SUCCESS and WINNERS

As said by some quite intelligent but visceral people, "Show me a good loser and I'll show you a psychopath". I have already told you about the Running Back and tried to convince you of the great need for success and winning.

Recall that this value is one of the stars of the 5Star person and it must specifically be provided to the employee by the boss. Fortunately for most businesses and other organizations that manage people, there is no scoreboard and often no beginning or ending to the game. In sports, when the game ends, any person can check the board to see who won. But as a family, as a business, as a governmental agency or as a union, success can almost be declared by the boss whenever he/she chooses. The boss can choose the goals and even if we don't make them, can then declare we have done a great job because we did better than the last time or just better than expected.

There are literally hundreds of ways to declare success and keep everyone moving ahead. Remember, it's only winners who have enough energy left to make the next attack or take the next hill. If convinced we are losers, we lose our confidence and our attitudes, the very tools needed to succeed in the next assault. Admittedly, like bankruptcy, there are some losses that cannot be hidden, but these are less than 10 percent of all cases.

Bosses must take control of all aspects of success/winning, the public relations aspects as well as the substantive issues, like those embodied in the Running Back case. And who should be best at knowing which game is more important to win? And who knows more about what it takes to win? The boss, the boss, the boss!!! So the boss alone shoulders the responsibility for winning! He/she alone decides when and where to step in and make us winners in spite of ourselves - to snatch winning from the jaws of defeat.

FIRE in the BOILER

The above completes the traits listed under Roman numeral I, the most important ones for the boss to infuse in others. These must be displayed by the boss in every action and inaction that can be seen, heard, touched, read about or tasted by any juniors. Bosses should <u>make a 10 level standard in these values a firm requirement for the entire management team</u>. If they are willing to take a management position, they must accept this as a condition of employment. <u>Leading the work force in the wrong direction is the biggest single error a management person can make</u>, especially for these basic values (as well as for honesty, industriousness and confidence).

I recommend a routine, at least monthly, review of all your actions in the past month to check your compliance with these standards. And you must also check each subordinate boss when you are in his/her presence, and again in a serious, thoughtful review at least semi-annually. <u>If these values are demonstrated correctly, you will be on your way to 5Star on the job, and your people will have far less tendencies to use the excuse box. They will carry these values home to their family and community, and they may actually want to work for their bosses and enjoy coming to work.</u>

GROUP II — compassion, humility, admission of error, trust, fairness, forthrightness, forgiveness and courtesy

The values grouped under roman numeral II can be summed up by the word caring. The question is whether or not the boss really <u>c</u>ares about subordinates. Only if the boss demonstrates caring for hem will subordinates <u>c</u>are about the work, each other and the customer. Each junior decides on their own whether or not the boss <u>c</u>ares by adding up a large number of events and actions for which they hold the boss responsible. <u>The boss' choice is whether to provide subordinates with excuses for poor performance or a positive lead toward excellence.</u>

In addition, each person is affected by the outside world. Too often this world is dog eat dog, buyer beware, I am more important than you and the hell with you. It is a place where there are many men and women, of all ages and races, rubbing up against each other with plenty of opportunity for discrimination and disharmony. They bring these, along with the ill feelings and the bad habits formed from them, into the workplace. A boss has no choice but to deal with this situation.

All of these people want to be treated caringly. The boss chooses how to treat them, and through that leadership, how they treat each other. Cooperation and teamwork are at stake and the outcome has a large impact on productivity and the bottom line.

But there is much more to caring. people cannot be committed unless they feel a sense of ownership, cannot feel ownership unless they can influence all aspects. But influence depends on being able to put in our two cents and this depends on a listening boss who shares what he/she knows, redresses our complaints, welcomes our suggestions and provides succor in our time of need. So a boss must listen carefully to subordinates in order to even begin to be considered caring. If the boss "cares" about us in this way, we care about everything else and gain commitment. This path to commitment is such a powerful tool that it will be fully developed in Chapter 7. Let me make clear, however, that <u>listening is intimately tied in with the caring values</u>.

Once again, as it was for attitudes, what we develop at the job we take home. Or for the parent, what we present in the family environment (at least partially derived at work) is what our children take with them to school, to play and the like. Those managed need someone to help them with being caring or humane toward others, someone to set the example and coach us to meet the standard. Who else but the boss! Let's look at these values.

COMPASSION

When I have my day in the barrel, what will you do? If you help me without regard for our differences, to the best of your ability, I am forever thankful. I may become deeply indebted to you depending on the extent of your help. Just a few kind words, however, go a long way. This example set by the boss is greatly appreciated by everyone else as well. They think about their own upcoming day in the barrel and realize that you might help them.

However, if you beat on the sides of the barrel, a few others will beat with you, many more will be confused as to what is the correct action and still many more, with common sense, will never expect help from you. If it was over a death in the family, everyone will be openly against you. If over a drug problem, you will only lose a few.

Bosses must demonstrate a high standard in compassion. People need the example to use in the workplace and to take back to their family and community. Besides, the recipient pays back ten fold for any compassion received. The on-lookers follow the lead and also are thankful that they may get compassionate treatment when their turn comes. Recall the indebtedness principle and realize that all involved will like to come to work at your place, to say nothing of their high level of productivity while there.

Unfortunately, the need for compassion is sometimes confused with the need for discipline or negative consequence. Giving people another chance and thus stopping some subordinate boss' corrective disciplinary action is not compassion. Progressive discipline is a necessity and outside interference that interrupts or reverses the process sends very negative messages, most importantly to the person needing the discipline. The result could be called cruel and inhumane, but never compassionate since the offender and the on-lookers often choose to interpret the action as proof that no wrong was done and therefore no change in future behavior is necessary. This kind of negative compassion is hazardous to all.

HUMILITY

Here is a message every boss should give.

"As a boss, I am no better and no worse than you, my junior. I only have a different job. If you are in the trench you are more important than I since you are doing the work, not I. We can't sell what I do, only what you do. The organization will never be better than the quality and quantity of what you produce. This workplace is just as much yours as it is mine. We each come here to do a job, to earn $$$ to keep ourself and our family in decent condition. We each need to enjoy coming to work and to be proud of what we have done today so that there is increased joy to take back to our family. We each want to go home in the same condition in which we came, undamaged. I may have more education, drive a better car and have a higher salary, but that doesn't mean I am a better person. It only means my problems may be different and it's how we handle our problems that is our measure. If judgment of us occurs, it should not occur through other human beings."

The troops will really appreciate hearing the above message. Acting it out is not easy, but the boss must view him/herself as a supplier to subordinates, not as their master. They are the boss' customers and should be treated as such. If we have humility, we treat others as though they are superior to us.

Tell your subordinates you do not judge them good or bad. That's not your job. It is your job to decide whether or not their actions support the goals of the company and it is your job to decide what to do about that, from support and coaching to reward and promotion or demotion and termination. Good or bad is not your job, but there may be someone up above who makes that judgment. Tell them everyone makes mistakes, including yourself, but the important point is that we help each other to learn from them and fix them. So you will always help and support because that is your job.

ADMISSION of ERROR

This is an extremely respectable trait and possibly the single most important creed needed by every chain of command. The top bosses never can fix anything they don't know is a problem. So all errors must be reported up the chain in order to have even half a chance of being fixed. Lacking this knowledge, the organization is doomed to repeat its errors forever. Knowing doesn't mean it will be fixed, but does allow us a chance to try.

Bosses must go out of their way to publicly admit to their own errors since only transmission of a very high standard has any chance of success. The boss' errors are those made by him/herself and every subordinate and include errors made by any predecessors and the people who worked for them. Apologizing for your predecessor's errors as if they are yours is a powerful technique that clears away the old grudges and permits others to stop rehashing the past. While the boss can only apologize for the old bad effects, if any of those errors are still having bad effects it is as if the present boss caused them. So admit to all, ask for their forgiveness and get on with correction.

Admission of error by the boss also projects humility. Go out of your way to admit and tell how you corrected. This example is sorely needed so others can accept the natural process of problem creation through human error followed by correction. This "fact of life" process is one that everyone needs to understand.

However, setting the example in only this way is never enough because actions speak far louder than words. The opportunity for action arrives when the rule is broken. I recommend harsh treatment for anyone caught trying to hide an error. Action reinforces the boss's example and provides positive leadership, while inaction would counteract the example thus negating it.

Although I have not before mentioned this negative reward system as an aid to the setting of standards, where compliance to a minimum standard cannot be gained through instruction/training, negative rewards must follow. Only in this way can the boss demonstrate respect for the standard and show appreciation to those who took the trouble to meet it. If the boss will not back up a standard through providing consequence, people's compliance with that standard will cease and compliance with others will be brought into question. Failing to back up is a case of "Do as I say, not as I do", a very clear signpost that every subordinate will quickly read.

FAIRNESS

Although we might want more, all we ever expect is a fair share. If we don't get it, we will not go out of our way for those who are unfair. Fairness is not always getting our fair share, but it is always being given a chance to ask for it. This is the value that reflects to each of us whether or not we are allowed to put in our two cents and thus, to a great extent, our level of commitment.

If we cannot get reasonable fairness for ourselves, we can be very callous about worrying whether fairness is obtained by others. In fact, some people are happy to see others get treated unfairly. "I went through it, why can't you?" Unfairness can have numberless bad effects on human productivity throughout any organization. Unfairness gives us lots of material for our excuse box and thus results in many negative job related actions.

Fairness, on the other hand, has a tremendously positive effect. Everyone is actually surprised to find a consistent reasonable standard and their considerable appreciation is reflected directly in the effort they put out on the job. I will not spend much time defining fairness examples because actions or inactions that indicate unfairness are easy to detect, just because everyone wants to talk about them. Therefore, all the boss needs is to listen to the Gut level judgments of his/her troops and to have the will to reverse the unfair action or explain the unperceived fairness. Most can be fixed in a few months or less. Those that remain become insignificant as the people respond to this new fairness. But bosses who will not get out with their people are doomed to being unfair by definition. The only true test is in what others believe. Think of excuses!

FORTHRIGHTNESS

In my experience, most bosses play their cards close to the vest. They are guarded and circumspect. They share few if any of their thoughts. The more enlightened give some rationales for what they are doing, but may not brook any deviation from what they believe is right. Often, dissenting opinions can be given only at the junior's peril. "You'd better be right!" These actions are quite incorrect and reflect low standards in a negative direction.

For subordinates, without full knowledge of a particular aspect of the business, any conclusions reached about it have little chance of being correct. Though they will be supported by those with the same lack of knowledge, they will suffer derision from those in the know. This seems to happen in union-management relations today. The truth is, the people who work for any boss must be considered to be on his/her team.

The less team members know about what might affect the outcome of the team's endeavor, the less identification they will have with the team. This is a road to less commitment and achieves far lower levels of excellence than is possible or acceptable. In addition, if the boss plays his/her cards close to the vest, juniors Follow this example and will not report what the boss needs to know of their ideas, errors, etc. Poor performance is pre-ordained because when people know they aren't on the team, their industriousness, commitment and confidence are severely degraded. There are a myriad of excuses that bosses use for not being forthright; lawyers, it is too complex, the people don't care, they always take advantage, there's not enough time, etc. And as usual, these are all wrong.

Conversely, sharing information with people sends the powerful message that they are on the team. Being forthright gives all your team members a full deck of cards. I have found that the number of things that I could not discuss down to the lowest level occurring in a 5 year period could be counted on one finger. This kind of openness is stunningly positive. Suddenly, it is our team and even low achievers start participating and becoming involved.

Sharing your thoughts, your dreams, your cares and your woes is also powerful. Everyone can relate to them because we all have them. Sharing the whys is also very important. Anyone who is able to understand "why" can usually come up with "what" on their own. And through this process the boss changes from being one of "they" into a real breathing human being, one of "us".

I refer to this entire effort as the 52 Card principle. No one wants to play when they only have half a deck and the boss has a full one. Knowledge is power and more knowledge is more power. Full decks gain commitment to the team, as long as they can put in their two cents and be given a reasonable response.

But what are the limits? The boss can openly discuss just about everything concerning people's performance, corporate goals, corporate or group performance, every problem, every solution, every union-management situation, every support deficiency, every aspect of financial health and, in fact, everything that is or should be considered public knowledge. The rules are quite simple. If it is of concern to the person, it will probably affect how well they do their job and so the boss should provide the answer. The limits are:

1. .PERSONAL ISSUES

If the person has made an issue public, you as boss must treat it openly, publicly. If the person has kept it quiet, kept it private, the boss should respect that with confidentiality.

As an example, assume Doe has a bad attitude. May the boss discuss Doe's bad attitude publicly? Yes! Bad attitudes hurt everyone in contact and therefore are by definition public. The boss should apologize to the person's peers and juniors at the first opportunity and perhaps again in the future if the situation continues. The best example is set by telling everyone the boss knows of the problem, is working on it and asks for subordinate forbearance until it can be corrected. Would the boss not do the same for a lack of tools or a lack of proper lighting?

Now let's examine a case wherein Doe has cancer and tells no one. The boss should keep that private. What if Doe has a lack of knowledge and is a supervisor? The boss must handle this exactly as was done for the bad attitude since all juniors will know, even though they might not go out of their way to bring it up. If the subject surfaces about foremen with low knowledge levels, the boss can use Doe's case and Doe's name to demonstrate to the troops that the boss understands these kinds of problems and is willing to work on solutions. If this embarrasses Doe, the time to worry was before it became an issue for other people. <u>Bosses cannot be seen as sweeping reality under the table.</u> Go out of your way to prove the reverse.

What if Doe was turned down for promotion. Assume the boss never promulgates such things. Another employee objects that Doe was treated unfairly. The boss now knows Doe must have made it public and has probably made a good case for unfairness. Assuming the boss believes it was done fairly, the boss must relate to the inquirer and anyone else who has been listening exactly what Doe's performance has been, not in adjectives, but in objective fact. Then the promotional rules must be reviewed and the inquirer asked if Doe should be promoted in spite of the rules. More discussion may be desirable.

The point is, you cannot allow Doe to turn off your people. Meeting high standards in forthrightness will prevent this problem and serve to lead everyone toward using this standard. If you do not seize this opportunity, your people will be feeling badly for no reason and will have one more unneeded excuse. Meanwhile, you have lost a chance to reinforce values. In the workplace <u>what goes on is everyone's concern since we are all on the same team.</u> The boss' job is to protect every person's right to knowledge by acting out high standards for good values, of forthrightness in this case, to say nothing of trust, humility, respect, fairness and a bunch more.

The above is what I call the Public/Private principle of forthrightness.

2. BUSINESS ISSUES.

If the person is interested enough to ask or complain about a policy, a rule, a condition, or whatever, you certainly do not show humility or respect for that person by dodging or refusing to answer. You can always put off giving an answer until you research it since this prevents hipshooting and shows respect. But you must come back with an answer. Do not even try to dodge! You take the chance of teaching others to be street-wise and slippery. I know of few business considerations that cannot be discussed, at least at the common sense level. Many military considerations had high security levels and could not specifically be shared. There are likewise some important bits of proprietary information in businesses. I am sure all can be declassified enough by removal of key facts to permit discussion with your employees. I am not talking herein about discussions with outsiders, only with those to whom you owe loyalty, bosses and juniors.

The main point is, people will never believe it is their workplace or their company if they are denied knowledge of it. Without knowledge, there cannot be commitment. This is one more choice for the boss.

Another aspect is worthy of our attention. Some bosses "insulate" their people by not telling them about bad things, supposedly to prevent negative effects. This is not forthrightness and will damage efforts to achieve 5Star. If your own boss is the source of the problem, insulating may be appropriate. However, for others such as support staff or the competition, insulating prevents team members from understanding considerations important to decision-making. Sharing the good and the bad causes everyone to be more realistic and improves the quality of their decisions.

And lastly, without forthrightness the boss is unable to discuss values and is soon forced to "preach to the choir". <u>Forthrightness renders preaching unnecessary</u> because it gives more than enough opportunities to communicate values as solutions to real problems and workplace issues. People do not need to be told of values that they already hold dear. What they need is an understanding of how to apply their values to their work, an understanding that they can only gain from the forthrightness of the boss.

I have spent considerable time on forthrightness because I have found it to be a very powerful, but little used tool. Go out of your way to use it at every opportunity because it so clearly demonstrates respect, humility, compassion, fairness and courage. It also provides opportunities to teach many values since it generates open discussion of all aspects of the environment and the values that apply. It also is the only mechanism you can use to get the team to function, to believe themselves to be voting members as you openly discuss with them their hopes and dreams, their fears and woes, the real problems of the workplace. If they cannot tell you the problem, you will not be able to help with the solution. Bringing up problems is encouraged by forthrightness and discouraged by lack of it.

FORGIVENESS

"To err is human, to forgive divine". Though this is one of the last caring values to be discussed, it is by no means the least important and may be the most. I do not know how to choose its relative ranking. The quote says it all.

Lack of forgiveness destroys creativity, independence, entrepreneurship, industriousness, risk taking and, in general, 5Star. If we are to be beaten about the head and shoulders over human failings or over our inability to surmount the large obstacles that often account for our failures, we will develop a fear of trying, a loss of confidence and the like. People who manage people must learn that a line must be drawn between acceptable failures/errors and unacceptable ones, and then communicated. If the line appeals to our people, they will be able to retain the positive human values just enumerated.

Where to draw the line? If the error or failure does not reflect a lack of morality, repetition of work performance errors or repetition of actions demonstrating very low or bad value standards, forgive it. This is a line in the sand that will be embraced by everyone. Here are the details:

1. Lack of morality could be stealing, falsifying the books, embezzlement, obtaining kickbacks and the like. These are NOT human errors. They are done on purpose to achieve an end and demonstrate a lack of morality. (Note: this definition does not include the failure to develop a new product after several million dollars are invested. This is not a human error or a failing that the boss must censure. Just forgive it and chalk it up to learning.)

2. Repetition of work performance errors, or making the same error repeatedly, must eventually be squashed. After the first, a discussion takes place in which the errant person demonstrates whether they knew it to be errant and if so why they did it. If they honestly did not know, they are taught. If they should have known, they are told so and we move forward. As the second and more occurrences of the same error appear, the discussion

gets more and more one-sided, boss talks more, louder and starts to make it hurt. Loss of pay, etc. otherwise known as progressive discipline. But strictly forgiveness the first two times, maybe more. In cases involving the safety of themselves and others, they had better be charged a consequence the first time since personal safety, or not going home in as good a condition as we came to work, can have serious implications for ourselves and our families. Progressiveness continues to re-assignment or termination to get this round peg out of a square hole. Besides, every person wants to be helped out of a job where they are repeatedly unsuccessful.

3.　　Repetition of actions demonstrating a low value standard is our third and last definition. Negative attitudes and a lack of industriousness, admission of error, knowledge, honesty, cleanliness, rule compliance or the like are examples. These are treated almost identically to repetition of work performance errors, with two exceptions. First, those who hide their errors are enemies of the group, pure and simple. Treat them that way by being harsh. Second, do likewise for dishonesty since without honesty we cannot function. For bosses, dishonesty could be a cause for outright dismissal. By contrast, admission of error can be taught and developed in any group with few exceptions.

Who must draw this line? First line foremen are the most numerous management level. If they serve as judges there will be just as many different standards or different lines drawn as there are foremen. What we need is a high level of consistency because of the bad consequences of error and the need for fairness toward everyone who is expected to toe the line. Probably the boss just below officer level is the best person to consistently apply the same standards. This person may not be the one who actually conducts the discipline, but must review each case before disciplinary action is taken in order to protect both forgiveness and fairness.

The Boss' Forgiveness Error = Treat A Good Guy As Bad or A Bad Guy As Good?

A last consideration of forgiveness. Should we draw the line as tight as possible or as loose as possible. We could draw it such that the error is in the direction of treating a person who actually did the right thing as if they had done the wrong thing (good guy as bad). Or we could err in the direction of treating a person who actually did the wrong thing as if they had done the right thing (bad guy as good).

Good guy as bad? You may think you are doing the company a favor by playing tough cop. The result is that you reprimand or discipline someone who has done no wrong and this person holds a grudge against you for at least 6-9 months. And that's if you do everything perfectly for the next 6-9 months, no repeats. All the other good guys out there see the action and know but for some luck, they too could have been struck down as being bad when what they did was actually good.

In your attempt to be tough, you've created a serious morale problem for anyone with knowledge of the event. Lost productivity and quite a bit of hate and discontent will result.

Bad guy as good? So you failed to discipline when it was appropriate. As long as you have shown in the past that you do discipline people when the case is clear, all the good guys watching just think the person got lucky. But assume the boss makes this error several more times. As the person continues to escape punishment, some good guys get interested and begin to believe the boss may be a bit stupid. They watch while symbolically the bad guy erects a platform in the town square, erects the overhead scaffold, installs and tests the trap door, and finally stands on it, noose around neck. Suddenly you, the boss, arrive on scene and trip the trap door. All the good guys leave satisfied, shaking their heads because you almost had them fooled. Note, it only took a few seconds to correct your error and did not meanwhile result in significant bad effects. So making damn sure before reprimanding or disciplining is very important!!

The bottom line is, forgiveness gets you indebtedness as well as a fire in the boiler. Without forgiveness, bosses reap negative benefits from providing many excuses to subordinates.

TRUST, By Bosses Of Juniors

This is a very misunderstood value.

> "I cannot blindly trust you will do a particular thing correctly. What I will do is trust that you are a human being who is trying to do well, not one trying to make mistakes. In addition, I trust you will make mistakes and when you do, it is my job, as boss, to ensure there will be few if any bad consequences from your error. I will ensure you are

provided sufficient backup protection such that in the event you do err over something of consequence, you will not have to suffer the pangs of defeat, only the benefit of learning from an error."

Let me explain. In the normal course of business, certain things are undertaken. If one human error will have no significant negative consequence, I as boss need only think about how well trained and practiced you are. If less trained, I would check on you sufficiently to ensure that you will succeed. You may need occasional help or knowledge. I cannot afford to let you fail because I do not want you to be demoralized. I want you to have one more thing of which to be proud. If you are very well trained and experienced, I may not bother to look at the job except at the very end and then only to keep you thinking that I care.

As the consequence of failure starts to rise and eventually becomes quite high, my frequency of checks and use of other tools starts to rise and eventually peaks, for both the experienced and in-experienced. When consequences get quite high, I may have a person assigned to check execution as well as have a written procedure with worker signatures on each step as well as specially calibrated tools as well as compliance reviews, as well as cautious testing, as well as ------------.

The point is, we should only trust people to be human. Extremely competent people make far fewer mistakes, but they still make them. Making errors is human, no big deal, just the normal thing. <u>Bosses must concentrate on not setting their people up for bad conscience trips when they make their human errors.</u> Likewise, bosses must not be caught <u>not trusting</u> the less experienced or less responsible of their people. Trust that their behavior will repeat on a probability basis, but that errors can always crop up unexpectedly. If you plan for them, errors and mistakes will not bother anyone and you will have many, many less.

Now that we understand how to "trust", is there anything wrong with not trusting? Don't even think of it because the consequences are all bad. Distrust is a clear sign of disrespect and a non-caring boss. No matter who the boss openly distrusts, every person knowing about it thinks they could be next and thus starts distrust and disrespect for the boss.

So don't commit suicide over such a simple issue. If you are unable to trust a person in their job, it is time for re-assignment to a job more suited to the person's capabilities or for severing the relationship through transfer or termination. Not taking action often causes bosses to make a bad situation worse, through distrust or by formulating restrictive rules that apply to all subordinates and serve to squelch innovation and creativity.

TRUST, By Juniors Of Bosses

Juniors cannot trust what they do not know, especially when society in general teaches them to distrust and disrespect bosses. Juniors are fearful that they are only numbers, pawns for the boss to manipulate to further his/her ends. These ends are believed to be at odds with what is best for the subordinates.

The boss gains their trust through two mechanisms. First, bosses must act out 8-10 level standards in all values, but especially in forthrightness. Second, <u>the boss creates trust by turning the workplace over to subordinates such that everything they do is of their own making</u> (more on this later). After these steps, there is literally nothing for people to distrust since there are no unknowns and most everything is of their making. Since this fits nicely with making 5Star people, it works like a charm. Some people call this empowerment, but I personally have disliked the term since it has been so mauled in recent years.

This brief treatment requires more detail (given later), but it is the essence of how bosses can gain their people's trust.

COURTESY/COOPERATION

"Do unto others as you would have them do unto you!" "Love your neighbor!" These are the Golden Rules and they could not be more important to the smooth functioning of the workplace. Only the boss can put them there firmly so as to achieve the necessary harmony, cooperation and courtesy.

Courtesy and cooperation are not wishes. They should be made into <u>requirements, conditions of employment</u>. When people are allowed to excuse their bad performance with "I just can't work with John", the boss is in real trouble. They cannot be asked to like the other person, only to treat that person in such a way as to make him/her believe that the other person Cares. <u>Courtesy and cooperation are prerequisites for teamwork. Liking is not part of the deal.</u>

CARING

So the above seven caring values and their standards exist. They are very important for the boss to <u>demonstrate</u> through action and inaction so juniors may feel indebtedness to the company, are willing to put up with the difficulty of working with others and want to work hard for the good of all. Once again, this brings them much closer to 5Star commitment and ownership while removing many of their tendencies to use the excuse box. And once again, in this way the boss strongly contributes to the employee's family and community.

Caring is not a feeling. Caring is action and it is tangible. If not, subordinates know the boss doesn't really care!

WHAT IS GROUP III

Grit and heroism! Certainly values that we all revere. John Wayne portrayed it in a movie titled "True Grit". The establishment in the U.S. seems to have lost these concepts. Vietnam took away our heroes as did corruption at the top. Believe me when I tell you that your employees know grit and heroism when they see them and they love them. While both are needed, every day of our lives, many bosses can't figure out where grit and heroism fit in the workplace.

GRIT

Stands up and is counted! When the going gets tough, the people with grit hunker down and pull or push harder. They keep pushing until the objective is achieved. They don't give in to the elements and Mother Nature can't defeat them, only temporarily set them back. They are willing to fight for what is right and accept sacrifice if necessary. Perseverance, rule compliance and high standards all require grit to achieve. It takes grit to have humility. If you care enough to act out high standards for all values, you have grit and everyone knows it!

HEROISM

Superman and John Wayne set the example. First, a hero must fight the enemy. Second, the hero cannot win the first battle and must go away from it bloodied. This bleeding may continue for several battles. Third, the hero wins in the end. The hero never reflects on winning, says "Aw, shucks" to show humility and then rides away into the sunset to the next challenge.

Who are the enemy? The juniors? Hell no! They are on our team. You have never seen Superman hurt Superwoman or John Wayne shoot the town folk, have you? As a boss in a business environment, your enemies, as viewed by your subordinates, are those who control things that the subordinates need. Outside organizations, such as purchasing and engineering, and your own boss are members of this group.

Your own boss is an enemy? Subordinates know you are "sticking your neck out" if you try to get your boss to provide what the troops need, simply because "making waves" can be dangerous to your pay raises, your promotions and other possible benefits. So when our boss goes after his/her boss to get things our group needs and it requires effort (some bleeding by our boss), subordinates will view these actions as heroism. This is "talking back to the boss", not being insubordinate. It may be showing your boss that a new policy put in place will create conditions or events that are not in the best interests of your people or "things" and requesting a change. This is "sticking your neck out" or "making waves" in comparison to the relative safety of being quiet and saying nothing.

How about outside organizations? Does Dad stand up to the garage mechanic who repairs our car incorrectly? Or does he avoid any confrontation and pay the bill? A peer organization within our Company fails to do their job for us. Does our boss "go to bat" for us and talk to a counterpart or have his/her boss or boss' boss talk to a counterpart and get us what we need? Or do we just suffer the consequences quietly because our boss fears for his/her next promotion and uses "don't make a wave" as the action criteria. Heroes are not necessarily wavemakers, but they never ask their own people to suffer so that they can stay away from battles. This is called cowardice and is greatly disrespectable.

So Group III sets an example of inner strength, intestinal fortitude and sacrifice that turns on the people you manage. Those being managed will encounter many occasions in their lives when these qualities will be needed, both at home and at work. These can be routine events or emergencies wherein significant risks must be taken. If you are afraid to take a chance, you might just as well hang it up. Without grit, you will not be dependable when the going gets tough. Without heroism, you will demoralize your people.

COMMENTS ON OTHER VALUES OF CONCERN TO MANAGING PEOPLE

There are five more values important enough to discuss how they relate to the workplace.

KNOWLEDGE

If you want to manage people who manufacture cars, I suggest you learn a lot about manufacturing cars. Likewise for oil drilling or home building or making electricity. With knowledge, you may be able to develop and maintain proper training programs for your people. Without it, you cannot understand whether training has any value and you will thus promote a lack of professionalism, otherwise known as generalism or jack of all trades, master of none. And without sound technical knowledge of your product and how it is constructed, you will not be able to have a positive impact on quality, material, tooling, production lines, documentation, changing technology, or even hiring managers who can. Without considerable technical knowledge, you may only be able to assist in the demise of your organization as compared to the competition, otherwise known as mediocrity or plant closings. With technical knowledge and <u>without knowledge of managing people</u>, you likewise can achieve mediocrity as a boss.

This knowledge requirement grows as you are promoted from first line to CEO since the numbers of subordinates and different skills that they require increase with each management level. Having watched this done correctly and incorrectly, I am aware of the considerable satisfaction and confidence gained when done correctly, and the Excuses, dissatisfaction, stress and fear of failure when done incorrectly. The former are turned-on while the latter are unhappy. Don't let yourself be fooled by the management gurus who say that a good manager can manage anything. There are exceptions that prove any rule, but most of us will not like the results, particularly the results for all those people below you who rely so heavily on your knowledge and skills. It is not so bad hurting yourself, but when you do it to tens, perhaps even hundreds of others, everyone has a reason to feel bad.

The above is true for any level of boss or first line worker.

INTEGRITY

It took me many years to define integrity and then many more to get some. Understanding integrity as compared to honesty is very useful to bosses and to being 5Star.

Honesty - a person has honesty if they never say anything they don't <u>think</u> is true.

Integrity - a person has integrity if they never say anything they don't <u>know</u> is true.

So the key is <u>knowing versus thinking</u>. In order to know, we must study, evaluate and test. We must examine what we believe to be true from every possible approach, aspect and direction. We must also test our beliefs in the market place, again and again until we are quite certain we are correct. Then and only then could we truly have integrity when declaring "that" to be true or I know "this"! In most disciplines, this means years of effort and numberless practical attempts in the workplace, or wherever the action is, to gain high quality results. It means bosses must approach their best and most professional machinists with great respect and defer to their judgment over machining issues <u>unless they can be proven wrong</u>. It also means, people without years of effort and experience can speak with integrity over very little.

It should be intuitively obvious that lack of knowledge stops us from speaking credibly, but not from being honest. But honesty is far too low a standard for business decisions. If, however, we are willing to expend energy, we can achieve integrity in some areas of endeavor, but never very many. As people begin to understand this concept, <u>they learn how to test the "integrity" of contentions made by others and learn to recognize who is blowing smoke</u>. When they cease to follow those without integrity, their respect increases for those who have made the effort to gain integrity in their area of expertise.

Bear in mind, the troops dearly need to have trust in their bosses. So bosses must be good to their word. Bosses who are suppliers to their people have little difficulty with integrity since they give less orders and play a supporting role much of the time. On the other hand, authoritarian bosses have little or no chance of being good to their word because they attempt to pronounce what is right over almost everything.

Teaching this concept, this value, to your juniors has a sizable payback for both teacher and student. It helps bosses to maintain their humility by realizing how little they really do know. It helps subordinates to be strong and independent through recognizing two truths. First, they can be a true expert in their own field. And second, others who profess to know what is right for a certain issue may not have done the things necessary to gain integrity and therefore should not be followed. All juniors need to appreciate that "professors" often profess knowledge that <u>has not been subjected to the rigorous testing of the workplace</u>, and that people in the workplace can truly become "professional" through the experience of testing the usefulness of associated knowledge. "Professors" hypothesize, but each hypothesis <u>can only be proven</u> <u>"down where the rubber meets the road" in the workplace</u>.

5Star people have integrity. This must be explained to everyone while applauding those who have it. Only in this way can non-5Star people understand how to move toward integrity. The same is true for all values.

LOYALTY

Loyalty is being true to any person to whom one owes fidelity. This is an up and down value, up to the boss and down to the junior. The relationship founders as soon as the boss is not good to his/her word to the junior or vice versa. Like integrity, this value is very difficult to define and just as difficult to convert into action. But if we expect our boss to keep paying us or our juniors to keep turning and burning, our loyalty to each must be tangible.

Loyalty to the boss is: making the boss look good, doing more for the boss than asked, carefully explaining to the boss any bad effects of decisions or policies and persevering until the boss changes them, never judging the boss, never Following the boss' bad leads only good ones, telling the boss all problems and solutions so that the boss may interfere if desired but never be blind-sided, never usurping the boss' authority, always being courteous and respectful of the boss whether the boss is present or not, never bypassing the boss without approval, never misleading the boss, meeting all deadlines or explaining ahead of time why you cannot, building up the boss to your juniors and admitting that the boss is human. <u>Do unto the boss as you would have juniors do unto you.</u>

Loyalty to the junior is fulfilling the responsibilities of being the junior's manager by always leading in the GOOD direction while supporting and directing the junior, <u>as needed by the junior</u>. (We have not yet addressed these two management responsibilities, but you should understand the concept pretty well having completed a fair share of the "leading" function.)

Loyalty is carrying out an obligation well enough to have no regrets. If done to that standard, the recipient will have no complaints and plenty of praise. Loyalty requires a concerted effort, but the positive payback to yourself is large.

Loyalty is not mutinous behavior. I have listened to peers discussing their boss on numerous occasions, never without witnessing criticism of the boss, often with outright disrespect. I have learned to steer clear of these since it makes me less able to be loyal and starts me on the road to self-destruction and poor performance. There is nothing positive to gain from disrespecting your boss. So what if he or she does something incorrectly! Does that give you the right to err? Two wrongs do not make a right. So avoid any thought of disliking or disrespecting your boss. The other possibility is that juniors become aware of this and guess what? Since they are Followers, they learn to criticize you and whoever else they deem deserving. Throughout any organization, disloyalty causes large negative effects.

QUALITY

Everyone loves 8-10 level quality. High quality products sell well in spite of higher initial cost because everyone knows they are cheaper in the long run. We all want to be associated with high quality at work and its presence is a turn-on, a source of pride. Valid quality programs are therefore relatively easy to sell in the workplace. Even though quality takes time, effort and great attention to detail, most people will join a quality parade.

Bosses are watched intently by subordinates. Actions as well as inactions are automatically judged. Bosses who fail to take the time and effort to pay attention to the little details of their own leadership will by default act in ways that demonstrate well below 8-10 level quality standards. And these same bosses wonder why subordinates are using low quality standards when working.

When a problem occurs, how does the boss react? Does the boss give an opinion (partially unprepared) or wait and take the time to develop a high quality response? When trying to correct a certain "thing", does the boss jump quickly or act deliberately after time for careful review, analysis, commitment building and the like? Does the boss have quick answers and seem to know everything?

Quality before quantity is the key, the answer for everything. Take whatever time is required to establish; all relevant facts, the judgment criteria, various alternatives and which is the best through challenging every aspect. Then execute the best alternative with careful recording of parameters, pausing at every opportunity to review results before proceeding further. For repetitive processes, it is very important to achieve 8-10 standards, at whatever pace that requires, before increasing speed for quantity. This applies to all workplace processes, leadership included, because people are involved and, to my knowledge, there is no other way to beat the competition of today.

High quality responses and actions by the boss not only lead in the right direction, but demonstrate respect for the troops. On the other hand, loose cannons and hipshooters are perceived as being disrespectful and hazardous. Bosses who flit around hitting many things a little bit are just as bad. This entire book is an attempt to define and cause understanding of what must be done to achieve 8-10 quality leadership, the boss' primary function. Don't expect your people's efforts to reflect great quality or attention to detail unless yours clearly do so.

SELFLESSNESS

If you carry out the requirements of those values which I have explained, you will be selfless rather than selfish. Selflessness is concentrating on your obligations to others before worrying about yourself. My own search for high standards is far from complete and selflessness is one of the toughest. But trying to make the journey is very rewarding, both personally and to subordinates.

I am not recommending that you fail to give proper attention to your own health, to your own body, mind and soul. On the contrary, if you do not spend time and effort learning how to and then doing these very important tasks, you will not have the wherewithal to meet your obligations to others. You must decide what your obligations are, then determine how to meet them, and then repeat those tasks until you get it right.

We all have obligations to most of these; self, spouse, children, parents, community, country and perhaps to clubs, social and political groups, bosses and juniors. I put self first because of the body/mind/soul problem and then prioritized the remaining ones. Each of these people or entities have different needs, all of which we are obligated to meet because of our own decisions and our needs. After all, we decide to have the spouse, the children, the boss, the juniors, etc. Much time and effort is required in order to determine how to meet these obligations and then do so. I submit that all of this will keep you busy for a lifetime and will be terribly satisfying if done well.

If, however, you get taken in by self pride, by prestige, by the glory of a high level position or the promise of promotion, by the lure of money and material wealth, by sex, by pleasure, or the like, you will have become selfish instead of selfless. You will spend so much time on these pursuits that your obligations to others, particularly family, cannot be met. Likewise, your juniors will lack for many things and be in bad shape, turned-off and uncared for by you. And you will have failed by not leading in a good direction!!!

COMMENTS ON OTHER ASPECTS OF LEADING
THE HAZARDS OF ACTIONS AND WORDS BY LEADERS

The leader is the appointed boss, first line foreman or CEO. All of the leader's words, acts, body language and acts by others in the boss' name must line up in the same direction in order to gain needed credibility. If in different directions, the "do as I say not as I do" syndrome, the leader gains disrespect and little in the way of positive effects. When the actions and words do not line up, there is no integrity and it is an ugly sight to those with a higher standard in such an important value.

In this regard, I witnessed a military boss who consistently accentuated the negative. Nothing ever done correctly was noted, except to suspect that the facts or data indicating success were invalid. All emphasis was on the negative; "Why can't you get control of them?", "Watch out for this because I'm certain they will screw it up again!", or "We did it better ten years ago and why can't you do better?" There were some constructive results from his discussions on doing better, in spite of the negative approach, but no one got to share in the glory, only he. On occasion, he would "wax philosophical" and instruct us that praising people should be done much more often. He would immediately lapse into negativism on the next agenda item.

We have all heard many other examples of not walking your talk. "Why don't you approach John on that subject? I don't really like to do that." "I don't really like to chew her out, why don't you do it?" "I don't really like to get up in front of a group to speak. You do it." "Make sure you get rid of that person", but when it is the boss' job to do so, the answer is to give the person another chance. These are all variations on the "do as I say, not as I do" theme. Bosses who do this are not listening to themselves or to subordinates who would tell them if asked. These bosses should change as quickly as possible. Sending the troops in the wrong direction only loads up excuse boxes and results in higher costs and lower productivity.

LEVELS OF MANAGEMENT AND BEING 8-10

All levels of management must be 8-10 (10 being the best) in the Group I "fire in the boiler" values (positive attitudes, smiles, etc.). Everyone needs them all to succeed and management personnel must clearly demonstrate them at all times. The big boss must do the most demonstrating to keep everyone else on track.

As concerns the Group II values (humility, compassion, etc.) first line foremen may not be able to explain them perfectly, but they can play their part in procedures that implement these caring values. The higher the boss' level, the more effective he/she must be at explaining values and at ensuring their use. The CEO certainly must be the most proficient player in Group II since only the CEO can inculcate them in new upper management personnel. These value standards are so generally misunderstood and violated that it would be safe to assume bosses do not understand their importance to managing.

As concerns Group III, grit and heroism, these values must likewise be fostered by the top, but they can be easily assimilated at all levels. Humans naturally tend toward these in organizations where 5Star is encouraged.

So, how do we become 8-10 in each value? First, please recall the earlier discussion about creating behavior as children and values. Your own personal behavior will not reflect your own value standards unless you did a lot of work on yourself after gaining adulthood. This is a journey worth taking. It is not your fault you are what you are, but it will be if you fail to correct it. Fixing is a real turn-on and the payback is enormous.

Second, find out from your troops what they don't like, what gives them heartburn and go after correction of these. They always know what turns them on or off and for the most part will share this with anyone who has the power and a reasonable willingness to correct ills. They infrequently understand what the real problem is, but that their Gut says something is wrong is valid to a very high degree. Your Gut level people are the best judges of your leadership and there is no substitute for their input.

Third, I recommend making a page for each value and writing down workplace actions that would reflect high, medium and low standards. Also choose the negative value, the bad one, and describe actions that would reflect it. Then try to recall your own actions and compare them to the standard. Do not waste your time on being surprised or hurt if you find your knowledge or your execution of a particular value to be lacking. Be concerned if you can't find numerous cases for improvement. After all, you're human! Use patience that is also a value. Start on Group I.

When you get your own performance over 7 for a certain value in Group I, you can start judging your juniors and get into the habit of counseling them on how to improve. Make sure you share your own errors with them, as well as how you went about changing. Open discussions of values are mandatory and cause everyone to play as a team to make things better. We know that everyone shares the same values in the conscious brain, but we also know that the subconscious may be acting out a script that is contrary to the value in question. Test a little, fix a little and test again. As we do better, we want to do more. This is a time for praising and cheerleading to maintain very positive attitudes while we change. <u>Good humor from the boss makes it all possible</u> and this, of course, is the reason Group I values must be reasonably mastered by the boss before starting to work on juniors.

DON'T DISREGARD THE INFLUENCE OF "SOCIETY"

Values were taken for granted 50 years ago. Since that time our society has become uncertain about values. The 1960's and its flower children best depict what happened to values. In many parts of society, values and character have been supplanted by "do your own thing", "there are no absolutes" and "it's society's fault, not yours". Many of our leaders have accepted these new standards while others argue against them.

The result for bosses is that everyone is less informed about and more suspicious of the viability of values than before. All of this has had a negative effect on people's ability to produce. To be effective at anything <u>people need judgment criteria, standards for conduct</u> by which to decide the "right thing" to do on a daily basis. <u>Without them, self-control and achieving excellence are almost impossible.</u>

For the above reasons, bosses must now be far more effective than 50 years ago in transmitting good values and in helping subordinates to use them and build their own character. Overcoming these bad influences, as well as distrust and authoritarianism, requires better, clearer leadership by each boss. The payback to the bottom line more than justifies the effort.

TONE OF VOICE AND BODY LANGUAGE

Transmitting values and communicating them to followers are greatly affected by your tone of voice and body language. There have been many studies of human communication. My own experience supports one which concluded that 7% is verbal, 38% is tone of voice and 55% is body language. So <u>93% of most communication is non-verbal</u>. This is a very large number and probably results from learning how to effectively receive messages from our parents and others when as a child we didn't understand their words. If this 93% number is anywhere near to being true, bosses must especially take note since so much of their job is communicating high standards for all good values

OBSERVATIONS

1.   Leading starts with subordinates (followers) who need value standards in order to perform their work. In accordance with the natural law (following), they get these standards from the supplier (boss). When their good-bad compass (Gut) judges these standards, if they don't like them they will tell a supplier who cares enough to listen. The supplier can correct the standard and then ask subordinates (customers) if they are satisfied. This is an iterative process. Belief in the viability of this process and in the boss' role as a supplier of standards are keys to success as a boss.

2.   Leading is done through the leader's actions and inactions to support the work force through tools, training, planning, direction and the like. While these functions appear to be oriented toward getting specific work tasks completed, the value standards which they establish are far more important in the long run.

3.   The "natural law" tells us that followers, all people except 5Star, absorb implied standards and use these to determine how they do their work. Bosses choose the standards transmitted, consciously or not.

4.   If the leader's people are executing poorly, they do so because that is what they were led to do by the leader.

5.   The real quality of the boss' leadership can only be judged by the <u>response of the best performers</u>. If they give a thumbs up about a certain issue, it is not far wrong, if at all. Thumbs down means the leader is way off the mark and may have even gone in the wrong direction. Thumbs horizontal means you should try a different way. These Gut level responses or votes are unerringly accurate signposts that the boss must constantly collect and evaluate. Only through their use can we keep well meaning office designs from defeating our chances for excellence.

6.   Change must first come from the boss, must flow through clear, repetitive actions that will demonstrate the new desired standard, and slowly but surely gain acceptance by the people. The faster the demonstration rate and the more

frequent the repetitions or reinforcements, the sooner the change will be effected.

7.   Leading is by far the most important function of any boss and is a logical outgrowth of the natural law. The higher the boss, the more impact his/her positive, neutral or negative leads have on subordinates.

8.   Opportunities for leadership occur with great frequency and must be seized as they occur. Unless effort over a period of time has been applied, low standards will be evident in many ways. Bosses must take the time, when face to face with the people involved, to articulate each case and gain their concurrence on the need for 8-10 standards. While doing so on paper is generally a waste of time, face to face recognition of sub-standard conditions or acts is a powerful positive leadership event. Seizing opportunities will be expanded many times in the next five chapters, because to let them escape is to lead everyone to believe the low standard is acceptable. And they will follow these bad leads no matter what you think they <u>should</u> do. That is the law.

PRINCIPLES

By this time in the book, we have covered many whys and hows, specific actions that have been designed to meet high standards for all values. The whys may be more important than the hows since no one wants to adopt a new way unless it has compelling reasons behind it. There have been about three dozen , such as 52 Card, the Gut, 5Star and the natural law. I shall hereafter refer to these and others in later chapters as "principles", in the sense of rules or guides of conduct. We shall see in later chapters that these principles and the values from which they stem will be in constant use by the boss in the everyday routine.

Now that we have covered leadership and the most important values for the boss to demonstrate in that leadership, let us see how these values are used in routine management functions.

CHAPTER 5

SUPPORTING

WHAT CAN I DO FOR YOU?

For my first 12 years, I thought that my subordinates had been hired to do my bidding and to get my work done as I decided. I also knew that besides people, I needed to get together tools, parts, planning and other elements in order to get the job done. I considered these, including the people, to be individual "things" that bore no particular connection to each other. Using the new management theories, I tried to do each of these "things right". I never paid much attention to what the troops thought about the elements of support, mostly to what I thought. After all, weren't the troops supporting me and weren't they supposed to listen to me? <u>OH, HOW WRONG I WAS!!</u>

In 1970, after I gained an inkling that the troops were not just one among many elements necessary to getting the job done, I began to listen carefully to them. I quickly learned they had many objections about the other elements, most of which made a lot of sense. As I made efforts to resolve these, their objections changed to being suggestions and increased in number. While I became very busy improving "things" requested by the troops, they became more 5Star and as such their performance rose far above their previous norm.

I soon realized two truths: that all of these "things", including discipline and direction, were the boss' support for the troops since only he/she had the authority to make them right, and that these "things" would be adequate <u>only if they met the real needs of the troops</u>. The more I listened, the more I recognized that the best judgments of adequacy came not from bosses or staff, but from the Gut level criticisms of the users, the troops.

My next step was realizing that their great improvement in performance had been caused by my change from an authoritarian to a respectful, listening approach born of the hypothesis that they were the sun and I was the earth. This "you are more important than I" approach had made it easy for them to object about support deficiencies, while the fact that I responded in a timely fashion served to urge them to do more. By comparison, my previous authoritarian, "you were hired to listen to me", approach had been a real loser (even though my performance had excelled that of most contemporaries). As a result, I concluded that <u>the boss-junior relationship is one of a supplier to a customer</u> and should be conducted with this standard as a guide.

Listening also led me to understand that their values did not differ from mine, but that they used theirs only to critique my performance. For their own work, subordinates were mainly using the value standards implied in the support that I provided and it didn't matter whether the standard was high or low, or in the direction of a bad value. This discovery about leadership was a significant breakthrough. My concept of excuses followed soon thereafter. All of these revelations made me realize <u>support that is not tailored to meet the exact needs of each subordinate degrades their performance</u>. By this time I was also beginning to realize that juniors are capable of performance far superior to what I had believed possible. Much later, performance that I learned to recognize as being degraded was still good enough to be considered outstanding by most bosses.

The point is, making the choice to be a supplier to juniors for all needed support, no matter what it is, is a choice for an excellence that is far superior to normally accepted standards. It is also a choice that sheds light on what makes people tick.

SUPPORTING

Supporting is the act of leading subordinates to become turned-on 5Star superstars. It is accomplished through providing, at 8-10 level standards, those elements that <u>they agree</u> they need in order to be superstars. The principal elements of support are: training, discipline, rewards, tools, parts and material, technical advice, planning, information, documentation, procedures, rules, peace of mind and direction. The quality of this support communicates value standards for use by non-5Star subordinates, followers, in their work. These standards are their "how tos", such as how clean, safe, neat, industrious, honest, quality conscious, knowledgeable, cooperative and the like, to be when working.

As defined, support must be available at an excellent standard <u>before</u> production can be expected to achieve consistent excellence. There are two obvious reasons why this is true. <u>First</u>, if the tools reflect low standards by being hard to use, the work will proceed at a slower pace than could be achieved with easy to use tools and thus valuable time is lost. In this way, low standards in support functions permanently limit elements such as quantity or quality in production even if workers do their part at the highest standard. <u>Second</u>, the natural law causes production to be conducted by non-5Star followers at the same standard used in, or reflected in, the support functions. So a low standard in tools achieves an effect that is at least twice as bad as that of the inadequate tool itself.

From the above, it is clear bosses are suppliers of both support and standards through that support, making subordinates the boss' customers. In addition, planners, trainers and policy makers may report to the boss, but in the boss' name they supply the boss' customers. These are, therefore, support roles and the wisdom lies in making them act out that role.

Bosses who regularly go into the workplace to find out how to serve their customers and improve their leadership through better tools, planning or whatever, are seen as caring, humble, hard-working and worthy of respect. Those bosses who go to the workplace to exhort and push the work force are viewed as enemies worthy of disrespect. In truth, pusher bosses are getting the cart before the horse since great support must precede great production. The boss should get his/her own act in gear first.

Let's look more closely at low standards of support in order to understand more about their negative effects.

Raising The Degree Of Difficulty

Picture the case of a garage mechanic repairing a car. The degree of difficulty of a particular repair has already been determined by the car designer, the manufacturer and by Mother Nature. These forces have combined to rust up the nuts and bolts as well as make them accessible only to a contortionist. This, therefore, fixes the difficulty of the job for the mechanic. It cannot get any easier than the result of these three forces.

But wait! Doesn't the boss have a say in all of this? Absolutely! The boss can make this job far more difficult (but rarely easier) by ensuring that the mechanic has not been trained for this repair, thus making it at least twice as difficult. The boss can also ensure the instruction book is not available or spare parts are not available or are the wrong size, or only half of the correct tools are on hand or that union-management strife exists or a host of other obstacles get in the way. By the time the boss finishes, the job could be three or four times as difficult or almost impossible. Are variations on this theme deliberate attempts to cause mechanics to fail, or just attempts to frustrate, de-motivate and turn them off? We all know bosses don't deliberately create these frustrations, but they are devastating nonetheless.

Subordinates down in the trench are amazed that such simple problems are allowed to exist. From their standpoint, the issue is "Why don't the bosses just get out of our way?" because they believe they could develop better support on their own. The solution is to let them do what they want unless the boss can logically convince them of a better way.

I wish that reducing productivity through raising the job's degree of difficulty was the only damage caused by these deficiencies of the boss' making. At the working level, it becomes clear that the boss doesn't care. "Why should we care if the boss doesn't? Why should we bust our humps?" Poor support is thus a negative lead that will get you carelessness, sloppiness, errors of inattention and plenty of just plain non-effort, to say nothing of outright disrespect. In such circumstances, even the people who do work hard out of a sense of self-pride (5Star) take long rest breaks or knock off an hour early just because their sense of justice demands it. With everyone feeling disgusted and unhappy, the whole flavor of life at work turns sour.

Filling Up Excuse Boxes

Although we have already expressed several problems above, lack of support also fills up to overflowing each and every excuse box. There are so many excuses not to do well that the person managed has almost no chance of having a positive attitude or working hard. I describe this extreme because even being close to it is bad for everyone.

On the other hand, high quality support produces feelings of indebtedness among juniors, whether they are bosses or workers. Seeing what the boss has done for them, they have many positive reasons to perfect their own behavior, their own on-the-job efforts. This is the state wherein external influences not only do not hold us back, but propel us toward high quality performance.

What choice will you make as boss? What standards will you provide to subordinates so they will know "how to" do the work? With support at the 8-10 level, you can be sure they will know you care and they will have no excuses for sub-standard performance. And with that knowledge, they will show plenty of tender love and care for the work, each other and the customers. If the boss doesn't demonstrate the highest standards in the treatment of his/her customers, how can subordinates be expected to learn how to provide outstanding service to their customers, the external ones. This supplier role cannot be overly emphasized as it is essential to your success as a boss of people.

I will now provide guidance on each of the individual elements of the boss' support.

TRAINING

Training was included in the 5Star (Five Star Person) definition because of its potential for significant impact on work behavior. Knowledge is power and more knowledge is more power. Knowledge in an individual brings with it many positive results; confidence, personal pride, self-esteem, peer respect, safety, productivity, quality, autonomy, entrepreneurship, independence, creativity and others. Training can be a very significant competitive edge, especially for the future. And also, there isn't another single investment that the boss can make in employees that has such a significant payback and through which a faster advancement toward 5Star is possible. Yes, 5Star! <u>Do not forget for a moment that 5Star is the real goal.</u>

Training in any quantity creates a bond of indebtedness. The trainee sees it as a broadening and an opening of new horizons. Often, it is a way to advancement and promotion, most likely to a higher standard of living for the family. Thus, the trainee attaches great personal value to effective training. Also, because of the fact the boss had to expend corporate assets in order to provide the training, not to mention time off the job, the trainee is extremely thankful to the boss as if in receipt of a personal gift. Trainees have no way to repay this debt except through hard work and dedication, being 5Star.

One often hears the view that we don't need training programs if we just hire well trained people. Unfortunately, there are too few well trained people to meet every company's needs, and four other considerations also exist. <u>First</u>, people forget a sizable percentage of what they have learned as each year passes. <u>Second</u>, new knowledge appears regularly. If the loss is not replaced and new information not regularly absorbed, there will be a loss of professionalism that will soon hurt your business. <u>Third</u>, this loss of professionalism has a profound negative effect on all 5Star qualities. 5Star cannot be enhanced or even maintained without regular training. And <u>fourth</u>, hiring of well trained people has no indebtedness aspect. Thus, reliance on the hiring solution doesn't have as much of a payback as some would have you believe.

Who Must Be The Champion Of Training?

Who needs to believe in training the most or to push it the most -- first, second, third line or CEO? The closer you are to the work being done, the more involved in meeting schedules and cutting costs you are. Both of these appear to be in direct conflict with training since it takes time away from the work. Thus, training must be a very visible and high priority goal of higher level bosses in order to overcome these natural workplace influences.

In addition, while the bottom of the chain is capable of understanding the benefits of training, they cannot risk being at odds with a boss over something that removes people from direct work. These cause questions like "where are all your people and why aren't they on the job? Can't you get control of them?" Fear of these alone stops training. This fear disappears only if replaced by fear of a different question - "Why aren't your people at training and don't you understand the long term effects of untrained people?" Which way will you, as boss, lead?

So the CEO must be the champion of training. CEO approves investment and uses of resources and should have better knowledge of cost-benefit ratios. If CEO doesn't strongly embrace training and take a very personal interest in it, only a few subordinates will take the political risk of directing such an apparently expensive approach.

Another key to training is, bosses should assume a goodly share of the training load for their own people. If bosses personally train juniors and prove to be a valuable source of knowledge, juniors' respect for seniors is greatly enhanced. Recalling the dictates of the "indebtedness" principle, it should be obvious that bosses who go out of their way to personally train their juniors are building up corporate credits which the junior can only pay back through hard work and dedication. For first line supervisors, this is called on-the-job training. The principle is true for all levels of bosses.

The quality of training programs must be of real concern since they constitute such large doses of the boss' leadership. Programs must be relevant to the work and never general. Only your best workers and their bosses, those truly professional in the subject material, can design and critique these programs. Their efforts must be supported by the authority of a higher level boss who can override any education specialists as to content and testing. The teacher must be a person with real expertise in the course material who was respected as a performer and has a true desire to help others to learn.

The boss must also utilize other knowledgeable people to initially attend the training in order to critique it. As a final step, listen to the comments of the graduates and their bosses. If the person with the training and his/her boss are not both impressed with the overall gain in knowledge, you are not getting your money's worth.

The last pearl of wisdom is, training should be scheduled in advance, preferably a few months ahead and executed regardless of the work in progress. Bosses should tell juniors <u>training is the #1 priority because it, more than anything, dictates the future</u>. In other words, once you decide how much and to whom, that commitment must be considered to be more important than any other operational requirement and must be carried out without fail. The trainees will feel great about this commitment, but eventually, all of your people will support this policy enthusiastically, even the first line who are trying to get the job done. And since everyone knows why there are less workers available today and knows they themselves also benefit directly or indirectly, <u>almost everyone will pick up the slack</u>.

The principle involved with training is "you only get what you give", but in this case the return is far greater than the investment. The expenditure of resources on training, with an announced plan ahead of time and then executed fully as promised, pays you back many times over through the 5Star characteristics and indebtedness instilled in your subordinates. Great synergism exists to the hard working and strong and independent 5Star qualities. In fact, training is so important that no boss can afford to leave it to the whims of others.

Although only the CEO can lead everyone, lower level bosses must try their best to do this in their own organizations since the payback is so great. There may be some pain, but the cause is good. It is one way to be a hero to your troops.

DISCIPLINE

While not as important as training and far less difficult, fair and timely discipline is an absolute essential to success in any organization. Because it is generally misunderstood and is often viewed as being in opposition to "loving your neighbor", only bosses can credibly cause willing acceptance of its great value. To this end, I shall attempt to convince you that fair discipline is "loving your neighbors", lack of it is disregard for them and a clear set of reasons exist that explain this.

While 5Star employees or those with significant "indebtedness" do not bother to produce incorrect behavior, the remainder of us often look into our excuse box in order to justify it. If the proposed behavior has a probability of resulting in negative consequences, a decision must be made as to whether this risk is acceptable. But what if there are no consequences?

For those who manage people, this is the great question of force versus help. Let us presume, for the purpose of understanding, the boss was allowed to use only one of the two methods on employees, force or help. Which to choose?

Help

The manager could train, support, lead and coach the person being managed, but could not charge negative consequences. This means if the employee did something incorrectly and did not meet a standard, the employee would only be coached in an attempt to change the behavior. The standard, the reason for it and the way to meet it would be discussed. Re-training, re-evaluation, re-discussion and re-coaching as necessary to achieve the standard would also be used.

In this case of help only, no harm comes to the employee, no matter the act. In very small groups where there are few if any membership changes, help alone might not cause many problems. But my experience with medium to large sized groups shows help alone creates serious problems. In these, when there are rules to be broken, there will always be a small percentage of the work force who will break them as they see fit and be relatively steady repeaters. Some people believe they can hide in a large group and thus produce cases of lateness, being off the job and poor workmanship. There will be some "hard cases", people who for one reason or another will not change. With no disciplinary measures, the people involved rarely change and choose to defend their actions with excuses, as if they were right in making errors. Knowing the rules, they laugh at their bosses. "They can't touch me!"

Meanwhile, those not erring watch carefully. They think the acts are wrong, but seeing no management response except help, they slowly but surely begin to disrespect management. Most would not let their own children get away with such events. Supervisors, ineffective at handling the hard cases, begin to fail to report infractions by "better people". "Why should I when those really bad people get away with it?"

And thus, all levels begin to disrespect upper management. After a while, everyone gives in, accepts the situation to the extent they even stop complaining about it and performs work to standards far below their potential. Even the best people (5Star) are eventually dragged down - "Why the hell do I bother to do my job when the person over there hardly works and gets paid the same as I do? Why don't the bosses do something about this?" So help alone in a sizable group results in severe problems, slowly but surely over time as people turn off.

Force

Let's now examine force alone, no help. In this case there are a set of negative consequences whose severity varies with the value of the act, the number of repetitions and the person's record. These consequences include suspensions, reduced pay raises, reduced pay, failure to promote, demotion and termination. If the employee needs coaching in order to effect changed behavior, this is not provided.

Force alone results in a bit more fear of the boss and a few people who believe they have been too harshly treated. A very few have a tendency to try to get back at bosses, but no one can be heard saying "They can't touch me!" A more important result, however, is that the hard workers who never get in trouble are very pleased the slackers can't get away with anything and people without adequate skills or knowledge are not being promoted or paid as much. Rather than slacking off themselves, the hard workers do more work while the slackers do not dare to slack off as much. Your best people feel vindicated for making the effort to comply with the rules while the mediocre ones do better in order to keep away from having force applied to themselves.

The overall result is that under force alone, productivity is much higher, perhaps double that of the help only case. In addition, your best people, the ones who get most of the work done and make the fewest infractions of rules, feel great! Let's hear it for the Best Guys and Dolls!! This is respect for your best people. This is fairness.

The important conclusions from this exercise are:

1. Coaching (help) and progressive discipline (force) must both be provided, <u>fairly and consistently</u> to all members of a company, including bosses. Force and help are both necessary to achieve 5Star. Coaching gets rid of the fear from force alone and none of the bad results of help alone come to pass. The help aspect inserts a level of humanity that is <u>greatly appreciated</u>, a powerful way for management to say they care about each person. This is the same answer given under the consequences section, with the important addition of respect for humanity.

2. Temper force with the humanity of forgiveness in order to encourage more risk taking and <u>be ever mindful of the error of treating a good person as if they were bad</u>. The grudges and the negative effects on bystanders, as explained under forgiveness, are too terrible a price to pay.

3. <u>Never confuse force with help or vice versa. They are totally independent of each other!!</u> Discipline to be effective must be progressive. Depending on the violation, it can start at the verbal warning or suspension level. But it must be progressive or at least not be less than the last time, otherwise the signals to the offender get confused and may lead to a belief that a price will not be charged. Discipline is only an effective deterrent to the extent it is perceived as a consequence that <u>WILL HAPPEN</u>. If the big boss decides to "have compassion", as if he/she is the only one who cares about people, by forgiving a disciplinary action meted out by a subordinate, the message to the offender is that immediate superiors are not in sync and the action was not really a violation. This course of action could be termed hate or disrespect, but never compassion. Compassion can only be displayed by help, spending time to assist the offender to improve, change, or solve problems. Listening just once to these people telling their peers about how

they got away with something is really convincing for anyone who supports remission by reason of compassion.

4.   Force is the only way to make good people realize their compliance is appreciated.

5.   The way to protect all disciplinary criteria is to have the authority high in each group, as high as possible and still be able to execute discipline in a timely fashion. The more people executing this function, the larger the number of different standards being enforced and thus the greater the level of unfairness.

6.   Recall the leadership values in Group II, those concerning the word caring. Your disciplinary actions, from reporting through application of actual discipline, will be a major part of an employee's historical data base and will be used to judge the boss' leadership. Your actions must pass the <u>Gut level judgments</u> of your work force, not the book theory of sociologists. If they pass with high marks, tick off another giant step toward 5Star and a terrific reduction of excuses. When someone is "screwed" by the bosses, the "There but for the grace of God go I" syndrome demoralizes everyone. The opposite (fairness) really turns us on!!

REWARDS

Recognition is something everyone wants. It has no hazards if done publicly by recognizing a specific action. Reasonable use sends a warm message to everyone, particularly to the person being recognized. This person need not be one of your best, but the act itself must be noteworthy, at least as compared to the person's normal performance.

I have had little experience with financial rewards beyond base pay. Merit based rather than seniority based pay makes common sense when judged against value standards, but beyond that I cannot be of aid. I can unequivocally state, <u>no financial reward can replace our human need for personal satisfaction from work, our joy at having a caring boss, or our desire to enjoy just coming to work.</u> I can also state, 30 to 300% productivity gains can be achieved without special financial rewards for merit.

TOOLS, PARTS, MATERIAL, TECHNICAL DOCUMENTATION, PROCEDURES, PLANNING

These essential support elements determine for subordinates whether "today" is frustrating or magnificent, a turn-off or a turn-on. Workers always know whether the planning was foresighted or not. The difference between available, superior tools and unavailable or poor quality tools is immediately apparent in the workplace. The communicated standard may not be discernible in an office, but to the people in the trenches, it is instantaneous and clear. While even small changes are obvious, large ones are like foghorns blaring in their ears.

Tools, parts, planning, etc. are generally not issues that can be adequately controlled by workers or their immediate superiors. Often, only bosses very high in the chain have authority over every aspect that can affect the final result, the frustration level. The worker and his/her boss may be reduced to being beggars who can only hope the bureaucracy in a purchasing or planning department will play its part in a timely fashion. Support groups will perform well <u>only if</u> held accountable to the worker by their common boss and required to be suppliers to the worker. Only if they must respond to the worker's (customer's) needs or be censured will the worker's frustrations be minimized and organizational success be assured. <u>Done correctly, workers become valued team players rather than frustrated beggars.</u>

Let's look at these roles more closely. Bosses often believe workers like to stand around doing nothing. This is so far from the truth as to be laughable!! No worker believes they will be paid to stand around, at least not until they are told to do so by their foreman because the parts are not here, the welder is on the way, the equipment has not yet been shut down for maintenance, or whatever. After a few of these, workers learn that standing around doing nothing is expected. They would never let a plumber working in their own house do so, but here at company Z it must be OK. Workers learn to accept the frustrations of looking for tools that are not readily available, for material that must be here somewhere and for plans that must have been clear to the originator but are not clear to the workers. <u>It is not their choice and it turns them off, but followers follow the boss' lead as the law requires.</u>

And who believes in quality more, the boss or subordinates? Workers must face their product day in and day out. They know the product is a direct reflection of what they have done. I have not found the case where management believes more in quality, but that is really not the issue. Bosses must rid themselves of any "holier-than-thou" feelings or Excuses and get on with <u>providing subordinates with what they need in way of support and leadership in values</u> so as to augment rather than limit excellence in production.

Besides a proper attitude, one of serving their customers the workers, the only other secret to achieving success in tools and others is that <u>failures and most opportunities for improvement can be readily determined by talking with those in the trenches, the customers.</u> Expressing your excellence goals, your understanding that you might be obstructing the work and then asking detailed questions about where improvements are needed, will quickly surface problems.

Not only can the boss get a good list of things to fix, the chance to communicate standards through the quality of the boss' fix pays big dividends. More about this in Chapter 8.

RULES

The KISS Principle, "Keep It Simple Stupid", really applies here. If they aren't easy to understand and execute, they aren't worthy of being rules. If you do not pay people for being late, do not allow foremen to decide how late is too late. If you do, you will have as many different standards as there are foremen and this damns you to unfairness in the eyes of the work force. One second is late, so if foremen report on this rule, it's easy to execute, easy to be consistent, easy to be fair and most of all, easy for subordinates to understand. rules concerning poor work performance or loafing on the job will always be more subjective, but everyone expects that.

Beyond KISS, reasons behind rules must be easy to understand and known by all. Everyone will comply with a rule that they know has good reasons because we all believe in the same good values. Very few will accept and comply with a rule when they don't understand the reasons for it.

The last issue concerning rules is whether or not management makes a concerted effort to enforce the standards required by rules and use discipline appropriate to the case. This is an issue of accountability, one that today requires considerable attention by senior management as compared to thirty years ago. <u>Accountability is expected by all Gut level people and they become surprised and angry when it doesn't occur.</u> No one really minds being held accountable so long as others are held to the same standard, particularly bosses. Unfortunately, society has clouded our straight thinking of past years such that many bosses did not learn accountability while maturing and cannot be expected to enforce rules on their own.

Thus, the fair disciplinary systems described earlier cannot exist unless reporting of infractions is enforced by upper management. This leads us to the most basic and important management rule of all.

Most Important Management Rule

This is the only managerial rule that must be enforced at all costs because through it all things are possible. The rule is, <u>all problems must be reported up the chain</u>. A problem is any condition that the reporter believes to be incorrect in any way. Our goal is to reduce filtering as much as possible. And this rule fits perfectly with the boss' supplier role.

Management cannot fix a problem it does not know and may not even with knowledge of it. But because knowledge is a necessary first step to any fix, a person having knowledge of a problem who fails to make a report must be considered an enemy of the group. Any problem that has no resolution must be reported up the chain until a resolution is found. If the problem has been adequately resolved at a lower level, the report is still needed since knowledge of the problem's occurrence in one group may enable a higher level boss to reduce costs by alerting another group or addressing a root cause not recognized by juniors. Therefore, any resolved problem must be reported high enough to arrive at a boss common to other similar groups.

Reports of problems must be short and sweet with only enough detail to allow the boss to appreciate its significance. "Short and sweet" is a necessity in order to reduce the time demands on both the boss and the junior.

The intent of the rule is to ensure the boss is aware of the existence and frequency of occurrence of problems. This awareness permits him/her to decide to ask for more details, recognize a trend, search for a root cause or take no action. The idea is to give the boss a chance to interfere, if and when he/she decides.

In the nuclear Navy, I personally witnessed the extremely positive effects that use of this rule had on professionalism, technical expertise and achievement of excellence. This rule permits bosses to <u>maintain their focus on problems of the workplace</u> and those are the ones most important to the success of any organization. In my experience, bosses not using this rule became disconnected from reality and frequently turned into masters to be served. The result was that the boss' programs, initiatives and orders, as a whole, dissuaded juniors from reporting problems. For these reasons, <u>this reporting rule is prerequisite to excellence</u>.

For reports of unresolved problems, bosses gain the obligation to respond with a fix to the reporter in a timely manner. This is an obligation that must be met or the rule will lapse into the abuse of disrespect, no matter what enforcement is attempted. The response may only be that the boss doesn't know a fix, but will provide help in trying to find one.

Rank - Does It Have Privilege?

The last major guideline is that the degree of rule compliance must be directly proportional to rank of the person in question. How can the lowly troops be expected to comply if bosses do not set a high standard. As a generality, show me a boss with a standard of 4 in a specific arena and I will show you people with a standard below 4. If the boss raises the communicated standard to 8, the people will slowly raise theirs until they are slightly below the boss on average. So if rule compliance is important, bosses must meet the highest standard.

Any "Do as I say, not as I do" requests by a boss are never followed. The followers know inside themselves the boss got promoted doing what he/she is doing, not saying. They know if they copy the actions, the boss will be pleased most of the time and they might also get promoted. "Do as I say, not as I do" is leadership that has significant negative effects because followers can see through it easily, even if the boss cannot.

The answer to this question of whether rank should have privilege over subordinates is a resounding NO!! Privilege negates the boss-as-supplier role and demonstrates no good values, only bad ones. I recommend staying as far away as possible from privilege <u>since it degrades the vaunted position of the first line soldier on who's back the success of the entire undertaking relies</u>. The only thing that rank does have is more obligations and these should be compensated through pay, personal satisfaction and respect from customers, if warranted.

Peace of Mind

Without it, we cannot properly concentrate on the job and always suffer a performance degradation that causes our work to drop off in quality, quantity, safety, et al. High productivity is not possible without it. Lack of peace of mind can stem from two sources; our inability to deal effectively with personal or work related problems and a lack of trust in our bosses.

Bosses can effectively supply peace of mind to subordinates through two avenues. The first is to educate employees about the problems they face, personal or job related, and how to resolve them. The second is to care about them by listening when they have a need or specifically have a bad day in the barrel, accepting the obligation to give juniors reasonable succor and help, and welcoming criticism of our management systems/support so that these cease causing problems for subordinates. These paths mitigate, to a great extent, feelings of insecurity, helplessness, powerlessness, or lack of control. They place management squarely on the employee's team and give them a real sense of security through trust.

Five Problems Related To Peace Of Mind

<u>First</u>, many managers do not listen carefully to anyone and most juniors know it. Juniors are quick to recognize that if they cannot be heard, few of their problems will be addressed and this realization causes their insecurities to grow. The most important action a boss can take is to make the same choice I made in 1970; to be a supplier to the troops through the only road available, listening. Since it is so important to getting on the 5Star road, I cover this easy to learn art of listening in detail in Chapter 7.

Second, most managers have not realized that <u>the way they treat subordinates is the way subordinates become</u>. If they encourage them, the juniors become encouraged. If praised, they become more praiseworthy. If the boss is forthright and shares information, they in turn become more open and share more with the boss. And if bosses focus on errors, their people become more error prone. All of the positives cause juniors to think bosses care and cause juniors to feel important, wanted and needed. The negatives cause the reverse. If the employees are ignored, they begin to look like uncared for children, shabby, insecure and crying. In this way, the boss chooses whether juniors have peace of mind or anxiety.

Third, while most managers realize all workplace problems can be worked out, they feel almost no sense of responsibility to help with personal problems. This is an error. Whether your company provides expert help or not, a boss who doesn't listen to problems, such as alcohol/drug abuse or mental anguish and provide a minimum level of compassion, is not a caring boss. Reporting these problems up the chain often finds someone who can give advice on who to see or how to go about arriving at a solution. Often, encouragement is all that's needed. Knowing senior bosses cared enough to learn about the problem is greatly appreciated by the employee, reduces anxiety and provides the security blanket of a sort of family. People need these peace of mind actions and the payback in the workplace is many times the effort.

I'm Unhappy With --- !

Fourth, all small peace of mind issues, the ones that sound like "I'm unhappy with", must be addressed. Bosses must work toward 5Star and expect their fellow employees to feel secure and well-adjusted. Unhappiness breeds the reverse. Each unhappiness reflects a problem that has a solution, one that will require action by one or more employees. It is the boss' responsibility to set a very high standard of perseverance in order that these problems are illuminated and their solutions achieved. Juniors will interpret this as caring. Less perseverance in addressing unhappiness will be interpreted to mean the boss cares less or expects us to be unhappy. Two examples follow.

Labor-management issues may appear to be sensitive and overriding, but sharing knowledge and openly discussing issues directly with the troops who have strong feelings always makes things better. If these are left to someone else, they fester and worsen. Everyone wonders why the bosses are hiding and will not talk, especially since bosses are very outspoken when they have concerns about something. How come when the troops have concerns no one wants to discuss them? <u>Go out to your people and discuss their concerns!</u> If you have good reasons for what you do, they will know it. If you don't, you find out from Gut level responses. Both events are valuable. Both are necessary steps toward peace of mind.

For the second example, lack of peace of mind or unhappiness over your disciplinary treatment of Doe could be an issue. Assume you know that Doe has been out garnering support. Make certain you discuss totally the aspects of the case and all the reasons why what was done was done. If caught in an error, correct it and always give the benefit of the doubt to Doe. If the action passed reasonable Gut level value standards, everyone listening will accept it down deep inside, although they may not do so publicly because of loyalties to Doe or for a myriad of other reasons.

No matter to the boss. It only matters that a free and open discussion with those unhappy voices was held in which the boss set a high standard of forthrightness (the 52 Card Principle). Perseverance along this path will convince everyone of the fairness of your discipline, or you of the need for change. Trust and good will are the outcome. To do otherwise is to allow Doe to cause a lack of trust in the boss, which in turn creates a loss of productivity.

Thousands of other "I am unhappy with" exist. The time spent openly discussing those which come to the boss creates a positive result, whether it is by subordinates achieving security through knowledge, by the boss achieving the realization that a change is needed, or by some combination of the two. The most positive result is, the more the boss participates, the more subordinates start solving problems by themselves. Do not forget, the boss is leading others to do what the boss is doing and tens of people produce many more solutions than the boss alone.

Chain Of Command, An Enemy

The fifth and last notable problem to the employee's peace of mind is our chain of command. This is an effective structure for deciding and transmitting orders and for getting things done. Everyone knows who is responsible for what and everyone knows who should be held accountable for any error. But chains of command are notoriously weak for sending information in the up direction because filtering out is universally practiced. The effect is the person at the bottom converses only with the lowest levels, people who are only slightly more powerful and knowledgeable than themselves. Filtering stops their pleas from being known upwards and access to that someone, the proverbial "they" with sufficient power and knowledge to resolve the issue, may not be possible.

In addition, as discussed in Chapter 1, over the past forty years society has changed dramatically in its view of bosses at the top of the chain. The old norm of considerable respect and occasional reverence has been replaced by open distrust. Disrespect and disdain for seniors became the norm in the mid to late '60's and was characterized by a general suspicion that the goals of bosses were self-centered and not of benefit to juniors. The effect of this increasing distrust of the chain has been to magnify its inherent tendency to suppress upward information flow. Often, people at the bottom are so distrustful and suspicious of bosses that they will not attempt to make their problems known. For the same reasons, middle links in the chain have a lesser tendency to report problems, further exacerbating the problem.

The result?? Gaining the good will, trust and loyalty of subordinates, such that they will commit themselves to gaining and maintaining the excellence of their company, has become a much more demanding and time consuming job.

Encouraging subordinates to bring their problems up through the chain is not an effective solution. Those who respect their bosses will and have been using the chain without any encouragement or instruction. For those who do not use it, exhortations to do so sound like a threat or a challenge. "If you don't go through your boss and give him a chance, you can't see the next one on the list". Middle managers generally order their subordinates to do this. What the juniors hear is that no one really cares about the problem, only that the chain is to be protected at all cost.

The Open Door

So how do we get our people to tell us their problems, the ones that turn them off and cause poor productivity et al, so we can help with resolution. How do we gain trust and loyalty and overcome the inherent weakness of the chain of command? Easy! Instruct your employees that you don't care how or to whom they bring up a problem, just make certain to bring it up to someone. Tell them you understand they might be reluctant to use the chain and openly admit that it is better for orders down than information up. Tell them you don't want them to suffer with their problems in any case and will be happy to hear their problems as you are walking around or during group meetings. Tell them you have an "Open Door" policy; anyone can make an appointment to see you privately, during or after working hours, and they need not tell their immediate bosses the nature of this discussion.

Tell them you require intermediate levels to do likewise, so if a customer is not satisfied by, or doesn't want to use one Open Door, they can always try another. Encourage them to use the other available mechanisms as desired; corporate, city or state EEO, union representatives, National Labor Relations Board, going over your head to your boss, the Human Resources group, ombudsmen, the courts and others. Encourage them to be strong and independent, to do what they think they must. Tell them you yourself are prepared to use any mechanism available to solve your own problems and you certainly want them to do likewise. When the going gets tough, the tough get going!

The above is an obvious attempt at 5Star development, to get the employee to actively participate rather than grumble or complain. This extremely important management tool must be backed up by action:

1. While the lowest levels think Open Door is great, their supervisors and other intervening levels will view it as an invasion on their control. You must totally explain the conditions I have just covered in order to gain their understanding of the need for Open Door. At the same time make clear you will not brook any insubordination. You must also assure middle and lower management (be certain to be good to your word) you will not take any action on the basis of a complaint without first gathering information from everyone involved and permitting all levels of supervision to play their appropriate roles, as if the problem had surfaced at the lowest level. Your forthrightness and "do unto others as you would have them do unto you" will hold you in good stead. The possibility of an unfair decision by a boss with less than half the facts is the supervisor's only valid concern with Open Door.

2. Producing results, addressing and hopefully solving the problems are a must to give this process of gathering problems any credibility. Gathering without correction only serves to conclusively prove management's disrespect for employees. Management must be elephantine in keeping track of every problem, tenacious in achieving resolutions and absolutely accurate with respect to getting back to the person presenting the problem. I highly recommend good notes and ticklers.

3. During problem correction, protecting the source may be important. But be certain the need is valid. Confidentiality is inappropriate if the information will in any way be used against another employee. In addition, if the supervisors do not know the source, they might not be able to determine the appropriateness of corrective action. But if knowledge of the source is not relevant to

problem understanding or correction, confidentiality is possible but not encouraged. This means that in healthy, productive groups, protection of a whistleblower may not be necessary because retribution will not be forthcoming in any event. But in all other cases, protection may be a necessary evil. The closer to 5Star one makes the group, the less the need. Once the norms of a slight majority of 5Star take over peer pressure, the old "whistleblowers" are accepted as being "positive contributors" or "team players" and no protection is desired since they will want their accolades. Refer to the Public/Private rule in Chapter 4 under forthrightness.

4.   I have used Open Door with 1,000 employees effectively, but how much higher this number could go I am not certain.

Gaining Peace Of Mind

Always ensure that trying to resolve the problems people have is actively pursued. Resolution is gained by use of Open Door, Go Out To Your People (GOTYP) in Chapter 8 and Group Meetings in Chapter 9. All of these require that bosses be good at listening, Chapter 7. There will be much more information given in this book about the techniques involved. In fact, these techniques will fulfill all of the boss' needs for leading people.

SUPPORT CONCLUSIONS

If, in spite of the power you have over their paycheck, you expect people to tell you what's wrong so you can have it fixed, to be open with you about their own errors, to ask for what they need, to be creative and aggressive in performing work, and to work to high standards, you had better do a lot of "what can I do for you". You had better make them know they are more important than you.

Fixing your support systems to a high standard is the fastest way to bring your people toward 5Star. Dramatic changes take place in them once they begin to follow your new high value standards. They start to realize you have not only taken away most of their excuses, but have made them feel indebted in the process.

Training is a real KEY. <u>No other</u> single investment has such a fast and long-lasting payback.

Discipline, fair and simple, is essential to gaining the good faith and respect of your people. Discipline for rule infractions is the only action which pays back those people who did make the extra effort required to comply with those rules.

Providing high quality support to your people demonstrates great respect for them which they return many fold in their work performance. Once again, <u>you get what you give</u>. I like to view support as a great de-motivator of people when it's below a standard of 5. As it rises above 5, it provides less and less excuses for poor performance, and at the 8-10 level leaves them totally <u>to their own motivations</u>, whatever they are. <u>Since they are like us, driven by identical values and similar hopes/fears, their performance will begin to match their own values</u>. They eventually will eagerly look for higher standards to meet as they go farther toward 5Star and away from any tendency to use the excuse box.

Many workplace jobs are menial or repetitive and haven't much pizzazz to them. Serving customers sometimes feels demeaning as well. Negative feelings from these sources will disappear if subordinates are the boss' customers. "If the boss can do it, why can't I?"

The success or failure of this journey is largely dictated by management's view of its role relative to subordinates. If bosses view themselves as <u>suppliers of services to their worker customers</u>, excellence is possible. <u>If the view is the workers are the servants of the bosses, excellence is quite simply NOT possible.</u> This is a cause and effect relationship wherein bosses err by not recognizing themselves as the cause. The decision is always unilaterally made by the boss. My advice is not to be your own worst enemy. Always remember, <u>working level people will treat their external customers as they are treated by the bosses.</u>

Because of its size, the support function of direction will be discussed in the next chapter. However, the understandings and whys of support given in this chapter are completely applicable to direction.

CHAPTER 6

SUPPORT THROUGH DIRECTION

Direction consists of four basic elements: orders, a vision, goals and coaching. I shall also discuss responsibility, authority and control as related concepts.

In the previous chapter, the boss was a supplier of support functions to subordinates or in essence, subordinates became the boss' customers. The highest quality support was crucial to the subordinate's success in two ways; in the support itself and in the value standard messages which, once conveyed, would be used by the subordinate as standards in "how to" perform the work (quality, attitude, industriousness, excellence, safety, cleanliness, etc.).

Direction is just one more element of support and it too sends value standard messages which constitute the boss' leadership. However, because of the human traits discussed in Chapter 2, direction by its very nature can produce negative reactions in subordinates which are far more serious than those from providing too few or low quality tools. The good news is that a set of simple, straightforward actions exist which will prevent these problems.

My Own Development

For my first 12 years as a boss, I believed my most important job was to give the right orders. I believed it was my responsibility to determine what needed to be done and then to give the necessary orders to achieve those ends. Needless to say, I devoted a great deal of time to figuring out what my next order would be. I certainly was convinced giving orders was a good act. Oh, how wrong I was!

After my conversion in 1970, I learned through listening that many subordinates were willing to take charge if only they were given a reasonable chance to succeed through adequate support. By listening, I also learned my better trained juniors already knew most of what was needed and, if given small amounts of help, could learn how to develop most of what was lacking. I also learned no one enjoys taking orders, rather they enjoy being totally independent of them. With this knowledge, I placed more emphasis on training while beginning to realize that giving orders is actually a small part of every boss' job.

My last breakthrough about direction concerned followers. I worried that people who had been made into followers would always be followers. This meant if a good leader was replaced by a bad one, the natural law dictated that the performance of these subordinates would deteriorate to the level of the new leader. By this time, I also understood the strengths of 5Star people and that they actively <u>resist negative influences</u>. So I began to work to make everyone strong and independent. Slowly but surely I learned people were able to change, to become independent of what others do such that they would use only <u>their own values</u> to determine their own actions. The more avenues I used to assist this change, the more change occurred.

The success of this effort exceeded my wildest dreams, not only because so many changed, but because these strong and independent people produced far more output than I had expected. Much later, I confirmed that once a person gains independence from using the value standards of others or "what others expect of us", this human condition is so appealing, so in tune with our nature, that few will give it up. <u>If a new boss projects low value standards, these people do not follow.</u>

In the process of the above effort, I learned that direction as commonly perceived is truly the worst enemy of the "strong and independent" trait. <u>Helping juniors to be strong and independent is releasing them from the bondage of following to the dictates of their own motivations</u>. Stated another way, it is <u>helping them to take charge of their workplace</u> and this is the underlying issue of the remainder of this book.

ORDERS

Bosses naively believe that giving orders, more orders are better, is what they were hired to do. "Wait 'til I'm in charge and I'll change everything" with lots of orders. Ignoring some obvious exceptions like fire emergencies, giving orders to subordinates constitutes the weakest and potentially most destructive action which any boss can take. It leads toward turned-off, <u>robotic behavior</u> and creates distrustful people who have plenty of excuses for their own poor performance. It is contrary to the goal of 5Star self-directed people who are strong and independent, have their brain turned-on and fully functional, and do not need our orders. Since everyone has a natural aversion to taking orders, many will <u>turn off their brain, their only source of creativity, innovation, productivity, motivation and commitment.</u>

Bosses who over-direct condemn their company to having a large number of weak and dependent employees, robots. Those affected require plenty of direction since they lack commitment, initiative, risk-taking and creativity. The increased costs of more workers to make up for this lost productivity and more supervisors/managers to watch after, prod and correct their errors are significant. Adding the increased costs associated with their training, health care, absenteeism, etc., we have more than enough justification to quickly replace the associated boss.

Intimidation is the most severe case of over-direction because a large number of people literally stop using their brain. Once the brain stops, little gets done without the intimidator stepping in to give orders. Since most observers distrust people in general, the intimidator boss appears as a hero amid the many who don't know what to do or don't seem to care. For those observers who understand the natural law, that 90% of us are followers who only follow the leads of the boss, it is easy to recognize the intimidator boss as the real problem and his/her subordinates as victims.

With the above understandings, over-direction can be defined as any direction provided by the boss which a specific subordinate or group could have self-developed if given the chance. The only alternative is for the boss to ask the subordinate what he/she thinks should be done and follow-up with leading questions and additional facts, values and principles as appropriate. If the junior knows very little, the boss conducts a training session and then asks, "Now what do you think should be done?". This prodding, plus erring on the side of giving less rather than more direction, will cause subordinates to practice:

1- turning on their brain
2- applying their values
3- developing their commitment
4- making decisions
5- being creative and innovative
6- becoming strong and independent

All of the above are moves toward 5Star, character building of the best sort. With plenty of practice caused by the boss, these subordinates will use their new habits and new turn-on for a myriad of targets, well beyond the boss' capacity to micromanage. The boss' initiatives will become a small portion of the total being undertaken by the group as the boss' leadership gets more followers moving toward independence.

I mentioned using values in decision-making. Recall that most people only use their own value standards to judge others, not to design or critique their own behavior. But they will joyously embrace the use of values for this purpose so long as everyone else does likewise, <u>especially the boss</u>. So the boss forces the use of values by <u>asking</u>, not telling, juniors what standard they are shooting for and why. And how about a high standard for knowledge in technical decisions, training programs or conversing with customers? How about forthrightness, humility and integrity when dealing with each other or with customers? How about efficiency, cleanliness, positive attitudes, quality, cost and timeliness? Every value has a place. Their regular use in brain-storming sessions is habit forming, building a new and better culture each person carries into everyday actions. To create this better culture, bosses must get in the habit of preparing for their interactions with subordinates, particularly as concerns which values apply and how to get them into the decision-making process.

The boss' leadership is prerequisite to having a culture based on values. If you have been asking your customers (juniors) to give feedback on your performance in providing support and how you are doing in meeting values in that support, and if you have been correcting problems in a timely fashion, you will have led your people to improve their own performance.

How To Proceed

<u>Stop giving orders to subordinates!</u> When you are about to give one, <u>try to find an alternative</u>.

For instance, you are quite sure the office copy machine needs replacing. Since you probably are not an expert in copiers, you do not know the technology, costs, reliability, usage rates and the like. You may even be wrong about the necessity, while some user out there may know that a certain repair or modification is the least cost, highest quality choice. You could give an order, but the message would be that you don't care what the users think and it is your office and only yours. <u>A big turn-off!!</u>

The turn-on approach is not to give an order, but to pick an alternative such as:

1. while walking around, ask a person at the machine how it's performing.
2. while walking around, remark to a person at the machine you are amazed that they are able to put up with such a poor machine. This approach of criticizing the machine permits the person to say what they really feel.

3.   at a group meeting relate how a little bird told you the machine was having problems and it may be time to replace it. Ask if there is any truth to that.

4.   at a group meeting talk about efficiency and how sometimes spending $'s saves time and if the cost-benefit indicated a healthy payback, we should seriously think about committing the $'s. Bring up a past example and ask for any new ideas. This approach encourages ideas as compared to "Dollars are scarce, but --" which turns off ideas.

Each of the above are first steps which require a careful drawing out of subordinates. As concerns moving to execution, the boss functions as a facilitator who ensures use of high value standards. Fairness requires that everyone affected be afforded the opportunity to agree/disagree with and rework the solution <u>before</u> implementation. Excellence requires that all relevant policies and facts, administrative and technical, be considered. It also requires that affected people be committed to the course before attempting to implement. Respect requires that the boss not ram something down the throats of fellow team members. Timeliness requires that the action be taken soon enough to create a good feeling in all concerned, rather than sorrow that we waited too long. Etc., etc.

<u>So don't give orders which relieve others of taking charge</u> when they should have. Take time to cause the appropriate subordinates to define a necessity and to carry it through to a satisfactory resolution. Cause them to <u>practice</u> highly responsible conduct so they will know what to do the next time. The action may be using a tool, formulating a plan, buying a machine, changing the organization or modifying policies. But get your people to practice what they should do at the lowest possible level. <u>Help them to take charge of their destiny, of their workplace</u>. Make them know it is just as much theirs as it is yours and that <u>their rights to taking charge will be protected by you</u>. If not this, why should they attempt to change?

Beyond the task of facilitator, every boss has knowledge, experience and a point of view not found in subordinates, all being relevant to decision-making. Bosses by virtue of their position have access to day-to-day knowledge not available to subordinates. They also have a better understanding of relative priorities and urgencies. This knowledge should be provided during the investigative phase. Experience and point-of-view should only be provided <u>after</u>

alternative actions have been formulated. This prevents exclusive robotic use of them as "what the boss really wants us to do".

In addition, stay away from telling anyone what you prefer or would like. "How would you like it?" questions to the boss may seem innocuous enough, but they support <u>yes men</u> and your responses will often be interpreted as orders. The only thing which every boss should want is for juniors to create excellence in compliance with high value standards. So the boss must answer these questions with "What I like is irrelevant! What is the right thing to do is the issue. I am sure you can figure it out. Give it a try." or "What help do you need to make a decision?". <u>Refuse to permit yes men and robots to exist</u> and refuse to allow people to waste time thinking about what the boss likes. If it is their job, let them do it, help them to do it, but <u>never do their thinking for them</u>.

Let's expand on this point:

1. Beyond averting yes men, no organization should be run on the basis of the likes or dislikes of anyone, including the boss.

2. None of us are able to read someone else's mind.

3. Bosses who say they are upset over something or who believe we should do a certain thing, cause juniors to wonder what the boss wants - in order to please. Release your people from this form of bondage to the power of <u>self-control</u> through use of what they do have, the objective criteria of value standards and principles. This is an order they sorely need.

Anti-Robot Rules For Bosses

Since giving orders quickly produces robots, first line foremen probably have the biggest challenge. They often use the invalid excuse that there isn't enough time for anything else. I suggest a rule that only permits foremen to assign jobs. Think of a mechanic. Being assigned a job, the mechanic would then tell the foreman how he/she will go about doing it. The foreman then provides questions and comments, as was done above, and gains the mechanic's commitment to some method. The worker would then state how each part of the job will be handled from a safety consideration, with the foreman fulfilling the facilitator role again. Some training may have to take place to fill in any knowledge deficiencies if the knowledge cannot be found in the mechanic.

This procedure turns on the mechanic's brain and proves whether the mechanic knows what to do. After all, he/she is the only one who really needs to know. It also gives the mechanic a chance to <u>talk back</u> to the boss about support issues and results in a better job done to the best standards of at least two brains. If the mechanic is new or has forgotten or is preoccupied with family problems, this will be evident to the foreman. Under the robot approach of giving orders, these unfortunates often go to the job not really knowing what must be done, but trying to get by while not daring to tell the foreman of the problem. Or they go as a safety hazard in a mentally pre-occupied-by-family-problems state. Events like these demoralize workers, reduce self-esteem and often have worse results than low productivity (safety accidents or equipment failures).

When An Order To Subordinates Is Clearly Appropriate

1. To avert failing to meet adequate value standards. Hopefully, it will only be necessary to stop them and allow realization of the problem to carry on from there. But if they are unable to do so, explicit "do it this way" orders may be necessary. Make this a learning experience so they will be able to meet standards the next time.

2. To perform a task that only the boss could have foreseen or that only the boss understands fully and that is not a part of the subordinate's function.

3. To a group after they have designed a course of action, to support execution of that action. Although they collectively agreed, a specific order may be necessary to ensure that everyone hears exactly the same words and can therefore have no doubt as to the exact course of action. This order is for clarity only.

4. In a situation where time is of the essence and discussion is not possible.

NOTE: We have been discussing orders to subordinates related to their direct responsibilities, orders that turn off their brain. There are other cases in which the boss' orders may be essential to success, orders which do not turn off brains. Orders to major external suppliers fall into this category, primarily because the boss's authority is such a key factor to meeting high standards. Since these orders are beyond the scope of this book, I'll not say more. I'll only note that <u>orders are not bad things</u>. They are only bad when they serve to <u>turn off subordinate brains</u> and thus 5Star.

PREACHING TO THE CHOIR

We all know what it is when someone does it to us. But that, unfortunately, does not stop us from doing it to others. Preaching to the choir is telling a person something which that person believes he/she already knows.

Preaching can be applied to values such as "I want everyone to pay more attention to detail. We always get in trouble when we miss a detail like a bolt left out or a test not done. I get the idea we aren't spending the time to ferret out the little details. Etc., etc.!" Since each of us has the same good values, we each think we understand the value and think the boss must be talking to someone else who doesn't. Or we might have heard too much of this preaching from our parents and teachers with the result that we are offended when the boss preaches about values. Or we might disrespect the boss over values in general because of the boss' poor support. For such reasons, when preaching starts the brain "turns off" and the person stops listening.

Essentially, the same process occurs when we are given on-the-job instruction or training in an aspect of the job we believe we know. It matters not whether we really know, only that we think we know. This is an important reason why the Anti-Robot rule above must be followed.

Preaching is disrespectful and demeaning. It is a holier-than-thou approach that has bad effects, never good. It fills the air with negative leadership messages that set examples of egotism and arrogance for our followers. It accomplishes the exact opposite of what was intended.

Preaching is unnecessary if you are forthright. This is true because you can be forthright only by discussing each and every question or problem your people have. In the course of these discussions, why one thing is wrong, a second is right and a third is more right will be determined by measuring them against value standards. By this method, everyone learns more about values and how to achieve them in everyday work, including the boss. These discussions render preaching unnecessary.

In fact, helping to solve workplace problems offers every boss more than enough chances to present outstanding leadership in values. For one-on-one or group discussions, techniques based on the anti-robot rule will keep everyone's interest and maximize knowledge gained while averting the negatives of preaching. This process will become clear and straightforward in Chapters 8 and 9.

VISIONS AND GOALS

A vision and corporate goals are elements of direction that the boss must provide, but not create. (Another name coming into vogue is mission statement.)

Everyone needs an over-arching goal or vision, something to which we can commit ourselves. As members of a team, we need a common goal so that we can enjoy the good feelings of comradeship as we link arms and move forward together. As individuals, we need a sense of direction and a clarity of purpose in order to discern for ourselves that actions will be supportive and that will he detrimental. These needs can be met by a carefully chosen vision articulated by the boss. An appropriate vision would therefore serve to heighten morale, unify diverse groups, create a measure against which to judge all actions and gain individual commitment.

A vision can only achieve these effects through the power of its idealism, through its appeal to our sense of values. Human beings are value-conscious, attach great importance to them and are thus able to identify with them readily. For example, their great respect for quality causes willing support of any efforts designed to improve it and this is a big reason for general acceptance of Total Quality Management programs. In order to be effective therefore, a vision must be simple to understand and must appeal to human beings at a Gut level.

To be powerful, a vision must also take into account that everyone truly wants to be a superstar in their own right. If the vision does not require each person to excel at whatever job they might have and to expend considerable effort to achieve the vision, it will not gain wide acceptance. Therefore, including every employee, from cleaning attendant to CEO, and invoking a <u>clear message of excellence</u> are minimum requirements. Do not think that the charisma of the boss can sell just about anything to the troops. Charisma is only good for the short term. What is needed is a solid form of excellence that each employee can respect and feel that striving for it every day is worthwhile.

Whatever the vision chosen, such as "being the best ------------- in the world", the boss must vigorously articulate it. The boss must also use it as the primary judgment criteria for all actions. "How can we expect to be the best ------------- in the world if we -----------?" must be heard again and again. All subordinate bosses must likewise apply this standard as a routine until every employee both understands and uses it. If it passes all of the criteria above, it can become a powerful force for excellence. If it doesn't become a rallying cry, get rid of it.

Goals

Having too many goals negates success by severely diluting focus and concentration. Bureaucratic staffs love to have them numbered in tens if not hundreds, but these always spawn a large number of reports. Reporting, tracking and looking good in these meaningless paper reports become the real goals while substance and reality suffer. I suggest a limit of five company goals and these must be significant initiatives that require more than a little discussion and coordination by diverse groups.

Beyond these five lie literally thousands of little goals tied to the critical need for continuous improvement. If success in business is your thing, continuous improvement aggressively pursued is the surest path. It should be a lifelong commitment by everyone and 5Star people are not only receptive to its message, but on their own will pursue it doggedly. <u>Do not squelch these initiatives by written reports. What is on paper must be only that which those directly involved have decided to use for control.</u> Bosses must encourage efforts to improve through questioning and suggesting, "What if we ---- ", but rarely ordering. In addition, bosses must serve as conduits of lessons learned through credible on-site observation (not through paper reports) and personal transmittal to other groups. Never require the burden of written explanations to fall on originators as it is a turn-off. These originators are more than willing, however, to show off their improvements to interested parties.

The major tenet of continuous improvement is if you are doing something today the same way it was done yesterday, you are probably wrong. The old adage of "if it ain't broke don't fix it" represents far too low a standard for today's competitive world.

Continuous improvement to be successful must also include getting out of our own plant or office to assess what the rest of the world is doing. Consultants have their benefits, but get out with your people to look at it. First hand experience is crucial to understanding something that is different from what you have. This must be a considered strategy, consciously pursued forever.

Similar to a vision, continuous improvement strongly appeals to everyone's value standards and can become a great source of pride. Any other strategy will be less respected by your people and less inspirational. It will also be less profitable to you in the long run.

COACHING

Whether it is helping people to run machines more effectively or to make better practical use of values, coaching is what the boss is really doing. It is a cooperative effort by the boss to team up with subordinates to aid in their becoming the superstars of their dreams, in gaining the pot of gold at the end of their own rainbow. Coaching is applied to their performance with things such as machines and paper, and with people such as customers, bosses, peers and juniors, to every facet of their life at work.

Recall the discussion in Chapter 2 of forming behavior before understanding value standards. And keep in mind, <u>each person believes what they did was right</u>, whether with the aid of excuses or not. Do not forget for a second that <u>they know themselves to be good because their values are good.</u> Do not act surprised that their behavior does not meet value standards, rather act surprised and grateful if it does. If it doesn't, act happy that you have another opportunity to help a budding superstar and prove that they are lucky to have you as their boss. Because most bosses concentrate on managing "things" and not people, you shouldn't be surprised that no one has helped this person. But you can <u>apologize</u> for it.

Coaching Tone

Can you feel the tone that the above two paragraphs set? If there is a key to coaching, beyond the procedure provided later in this chapter, this tone is it. The tone is that the subordinate is superior to and more important than the boss (refer to "humility" in Chapter 4). <u>This is the tone that overcomes the natural fear subordinates have for anyone who controls their paycheck.</u>

Without this tone, distrust and defensiveness will strangle moves toward 5Star. This tone is prerequisite to success in managing people and achieving excellence.

The Coaching Process

The coaching process itself is a simple and obvious one. If a boss hires a new engineer, accountant, or production worker, there is a process that must be followed to make use of and augment the person's skills. The start would be to indoctrinate the new employee in the company's procedures, policies, values and vision. The next step is to assist the person in adapting to the special needs of the new workplace. As work is assigned, the person is asked how they will go about it (the Anti-Robot Rule for bosses). This discussion permits the boss to find out exactly what the person expects to do and to correct or add as appropriate.

Then while the person works, the boss watches to ensure proper techniques and a high quality output. The boss provides instruction where needed to increase the subordinate's knowledge and provides the opportunity to practice using that knowledge in order to increase skills. The instruction could be weeks of school and the practice could be over some period of time.

Coaching is a trial and error, try a new tack or come-in-the-back-door process. A person's self-esteem, confidence and progress toward 5Star cannot be sacrificed to any effort to gain speed. 5Star is far too important and the brains of followers turn off too easily.

A successful process depends mainly on the boss' attention to detail, degree of perseverance and use of high standards. This is true for every person and every discipline. No subordinate has all the knowledge and skills needed. The boss works with the person to adjust, augment and adapt as necessary to the work.

Whatever else it is, coaching can only be successful as a team effort. In this context, the boss as leader, teacher, standard bearer and supplier, allies with the subordinate as customer in order to aid in a superstar development program that is the customer's goal. To better understand this, let's look at needs.

Needs of Juniors and Bosses

First, life is a continual test and we are all striving to pass it. While life consists of family, community and work, our level of success at work has a significant impact on our success, or lack of it, in the other two. This is true because we gain our livelihood from work and because we spend the most productive hours of our lives at it. Our success at work depends upon our knowledge of the possible alternative actions we could take and the criteria that should be used to evaluate these alternatives. Since we all, juniors and bosses, want to be superstars at life and recognize that achieving it would be heaven on earth, our challenge is in knowing the hows and whys of doing it (the knowledge of this book).

Second, of subordinates it is said that they never want to know what the boss cares about, they only want to know if he or she dares. This pearl of wisdom is worthy of careful thought. People who believe themselves to be numbers do not think the boss cares about them and will not waste their cares on the job. This is a Gut level issue. We all want to feel important to the task, to be a valued member of the team and to be worthy of consideration if we have a problem, suggestion, complaint or, most particularly, a day in the barrel. We can detect instantly when we are not treated like team members and we pay it back in kind. What's fair is fair! If the boss cares about us, we respond by showing great care about work. This side of the coin is much closer to indebtedness than to excuses and gets the boss our extra effort.

Third, every boss needs profits, productivity, innovation, creativity, acceptance of change, admission of error, reports on problems and the like to succeed in today's competitive environment. While the boss also needs to be a superstar, his/her success can only be determined by measuring the sum of the quality and quantity of each subordinate's production and comparing that to standards. <u>Success for the boss cannot be measured by the boss' output, only by the output of his/her people.</u>

Looking at the above three needs, we can conclude that <u>the needs of juniors are perfectly compatible with those of the boss.</u> Achieving each of these needs will be greatly assisted by coaching the subordinate. In fact, there is no other way for the boss to fulfill all of the above needs. So long as the boss is willing to personally uphold high value standards, coaching will be a big step in the right direction for both.

Why Should Subordinates Change In Response To Coaching?

As frail human beings, we all have many things that could use some improvement. Most of us do things that hurt ourselves as well as others and that reduce the productivity or quality of our work. But before we become willing to make a change, we must be convinced that change is warranted by reasons that appeal to our sense of fairness and other values ("what's in it for me?").

Most managers believe performance change can be justified by corporate needs. Profits, lower cost products, efficiency, productivity, or a better corporate image are good choices. Surprise, Surprise! Don't ask where they learned it, but most subordinates don't believe that company goals will serve them fairly. They suspect that what is good for the company may be bad for them. There are a few forces that make management and labor appear as bitter enemies locked in a classic struggle of good and evil. The truth is, <u>whatever truly serves the best interests of the employee is also best for the company. So why bother to discuss corporate needs?</u>

An example might help. If a junior wants a pay raise, the boss' corporate judgment criteria are used in order to <u>justify any change</u>. On the other hand, if the boss wants the subordinate to improve his/her performance, would it not be fair to use the subordinate's personal judgment criteria in order to <u>justify any change</u>? Before deciding what's fair in this case, let's look at a set of personal judgment criteria based on human values, criteria that could be applied to anyone's performance, boss or junior. These criteria are actually rationales for changing what ails us

SIX RATIONALES FOR CHANGING PERFORMANCE OR BEHAVIOR

1. CHOICE

An example of coaching a person with a bad attitude follows wherein the boss focuses on our inherent ability to choose. The words below would be said with plenty of tender love and care, with humility and compassion, not with derision and scolding.

> "Why choose to hurt yourself? Does having a bad attitude make you feel good? Why did you decide to feel unhappy? So what if your boss chewed you out when you didn't deserve it, or your fellow worker said you were an ugly no good person? You admit they were wrong to do those things and then you chose to become unhappy to boot? Why cause yourself mental anguish? How come two wrongs make a right? Why not choose to be happy? Aren't you a human being and not an animal? Why not choose your responses rather than automatically responding in some animalistic fashion?"

The above message is that each of us may make a choice, a decision, over everything. We may choose; to do a thing correctly or incorrectly, to learn from errors or not, to react to something or not and if reacting how, or to accept whatever automatic reaction occurs, good or bad. That we have the power to make these choices is something that was decided by our Creator. How we exercise this power to choose, or whether we even use it, is entirely up to each of us individually and cannot be decided by anyone or anything external to us.

Most importantly, we can choose our attitude, our approach, our perspective. This single choice in large measure determines outcomes for us, whether we are our own worst enemy or our own best friend. We can decide to feel eternally fortunate just for being in the United States of America and not in Somalia or Bosnia, or we can feel unfortunate to have to go to work today in America. We can choose to be unhappy about having a problem or happy about having a challenging opportunity to excel. Choosing negative attitudes and unhappiness dooms us to mediocrity at best and mental illness at worst.

Knowing the above choices exist is powerful, but not sufficient. <u>Bosses must cause their subordinates to define and evaluate alternative choices before acting.</u> When confronted with a problem or a stimulus, whether it be a bad boss, technical difficulty, bad health, a rainy day or a natural disaster, the first step is to determine the possible choices and then to evaluate the consequences of each. Don't react first, but step back and take a breath. All known and unknown principles must be disclosed and for the unknowns, some path to enlightenment chosen such as referring to experts, studying books or whatever. This process can easily be related to handling technical difficulties encountered by the affected person in their work.

Once all alternatives and their consequences are clearly understood, the choice often becomes obvious. The great majority of people never get out of the reaction mode in their day to day dealings with other people and with life's problems. That people can choose to be strong and independent and take charge of their own lives at work or at home, rather than choose to be weak and dependent, is a truth that can only be learned by doing. There are excellent books and audio tapes available from Drs. Norman Vincent Peale, Denis Waitely and Robert Schuller, to mention a few, that cover this subject and provide useful knowledge. <u>But the key in the workplace is a boss who takes the time to cause people to develop their innate ability to choose.</u>

<u>Think and choose.</u> Use the power of being a human to make things good for you! Strive to realize your full potential as a 5Star Superstar. <u>Everything you are or ever will be is up to you.</u> You are the primary creative force in your life and it all starts with a choice.

2. WHO IS #1?

Who is most important to consider when evaluating any choice? Better, who is number 1? Everyone knows the answer down deep inside while many will not admit it to a boss. They think he/she expects them to say the boss or the company is #1. The boss' job is to convince each person that #1 is him or her self.

The issue involved is quite simple. If we keep ourselves mentally and physically fit, give ourselves a positive attitude and the other assets needed to succeed at our chosen endeavors, we will have done very well by #1. And what is truly good for #1 is good for everyone else. Taking Care of #1 is not an egotistical, selfish or self-centered principle. It is the way in which we meet the obligations incurred when we have family, friends, community and country. So the first obligation for each of us is to invest in and take good care of ourself; body, mind and soul.

But if we choose a different path, we become our own greatest enemy rather than our own best friend. If we choose bad attitudes, stress from whatever source, lack of knowledge or laziness and use excuses to justify this sub-standard behavior, how can we be proud of #1 or be happy? If unhappy, we are damaged goods, less capable, more susceptible to sickness, living one more day the brain wants to forget and probably wasting one more day that could have been used to good effect. Nothing is good and everything is bad that comes as a result of this wrong choice for #1. Good excuses are never good for #1.

Doing the "right things" extremely well really turns on human beings. Choose to treat #1 well by turning yourself on rather than off! Through diligent efforts to meet the highest possible value standards and by becoming well trained and strong and independent, you may reach "the impossible dream".

3. WHO ARE #2 AND #3?

And besides #1, are there any others whose circumstances are important for us to evaluate? Most of us have other people who are very important to us, who are right up there with #1. For those with families, #2 may be our spouse and #3 may be our children. For some, parents or other family members get very high on the list. Many of us have very important outside interests such as church or community functions.

The first point to this discussion of who are #2 and #3 is that our job may be well down our priority list. Yes, the job provides your livelihood, but one should not dedicate one's life to a company or a boss. Besides, your goals may change and may not be compatible with your job. Give the job more than it pays you so that you are never indebted to it, but don't make it your life.

In addition, dedication to a specific company or boss may stop you from making the right decision/change at the right time for #1, or #2 or #3. And conversely, a company cannot be dedicated to you when product orders dry up and layoffs are a must to keep the goose alive to lay at least a few eggs.

The second and more important point is while incorrect behavior on #1's part mostly damages #1, the next most extensive damage is experienced by #2 and #3. Don't kid me that you love your spouse when you bring home the bad attitude that you blame on your boss or the bad feeling that nags you from doing wrong things. And bring it home you will! That damage is better described by the word hate than by love. And the children? They should be so lucky to learn that going to work is so terrible, that bosses are so bad, or that the traffic is so frustrating. I'm certain it will cause them to do worse in school and to try to figure out how never to go to work.

And how about fellow workers, the company and the boss? All losers, but far less so than #1, #2 or #3. At least the company has termination as a possible out. For #1, #2 or #3 the only way to improvement is for #1 to get rid of all those excuses and make the choice to be happy and industrious, to be 5Star so that all of life will be full of good flavor for the person and family. If you are 5Star, everyone will want to hire you. If not 5Star, I wish you luck.

4. DO UNTO OTHERS AS YOU WOULD HAVE THEM DO UNTO YOU!

This Rationale is the <u>Golden Rule</u>. It is the cornerstone of life. Understanding it is the solution to all of life's trials and tribulations. The world of business, being just a subset of life, is perfectly served by this Rationale.

This Rationale is not an admonishment, not a threat like "If you don't eat your vegetables you will never ---------". This Rationale is a great gift to each of us because of its promise. Doing unto others as you would have them do unto you assures you of having the most enjoyable, most happy, most fulfilled, most rewarding, most satisfying and most "everything is very good" working experience possible. This promise implies that each of us has the tools by which to decide what you would have others do to you. How true! Our own value standards and our own Gut are those tools.

The Rationale also implies doing good to others has a positive payback for the doer. The biggest payback is in our own good feeling about ourselves, a heightened sense of self-esteem and pride at having done something good. We are also paid back in kind by the other person, good for good and bad for bad, your choice as to which.

As concerns bad for bad, if you disrespect another person, you should expect to be disrespected in return. So the Golden Rule is not "do unto others as they do unto you". The rule is to return Good for Bad so that you are Good to both #1 and others. Getting back at others is never good for #1, #2 or #3.

This Rationale can effectively be used to evaluate incorrect behavior and generate some analysis of alternatives. Does the person's choice to be unhappy, or to revert to some basically bad behavior, make sense against the humane concepts of loving your neighbor, doing unto others as you would have them do unto you and turning the other cheek? Would anyone support your having a bad attitude or having any right to cause others to feel bad? Loving your neighbor is giving him/her a smile and a cheery "Good Morning", not the reverse. Does a smile turn people on or off and that should we do?

Do we have the right to turn someone else off? Haven't each of us enough of our own problems to confront without having to accept those of others? Who has the right to force their own problems on others so they can be turned off as well? Is this the way to make the workplace better or worse? Does the boss hire people to come in and mistreat others, or should he/she expect everyone to work in a loving, respectful way as concerns others? What gives you the right to damage other people? Do they have the right to damage you? Should the boss permit this?

In the workplace, people are frequently unhappy about something. What should they do with their unhappiness? Too often the answer is to pass it around to fellow employees. While each person is capable of withstanding the frustrations generated by their own life, their morale cannot normally withstand the frustrations associated with two or more lives. An easy way to wreck a marriage is for each spouse to dump all of their frustrations and unhappiness on the other. Now they each can feel twice as bad. What if they only shared the good things in their individual lives, never the bad unless something good could come of it or when help is needed by one or the other? This could be what they are doing about correcting a problem, or how sad it is for the person at work who is causing a bad situation.

The message is, sharing frustrations or unhappiness is a bad thing to do to someone else and complaining only produces more bad things. If you follow Rationale 4, you will not turn off fellow workers with what bothers you, but turn them on with what's good about your circumstances.

It might appear that asking for help when it is your day in the barrel would violate the Golden Rule. This is not the case since asking for help is not complaining or sharing complaints. In fact, it is a turn-on for those you are asking since it is a chance for them to do a good deed. And those with their heads on straight will appreciate the opportunity.

The Golden Rule presents a further challenge. Some people contend it is incompatible with discipline or even with requiring superior service from product suppliers, internal or external. The answer is that the Golden Rule doesn't sanction bad acts. Rather it assumes that good people expect to pay for their errors and not have others suffer from them. Returning parts or materials that turned out to be partially defective and demanding reimbursement is not a Rule violation, unless it is done in a very demeaning and arrogant manner.

Likewise, discipline fairly executed in a humble, compassionate but firm way is good for the person disciplined, for peers and for the company. While neither of these actions is something we'd rather have to do, if done well we have every right to be proud of them. In fact, only by doing them can we fully comply with the spirit and intent of the Golden Rule.

5. ACCEPTING WHAT WE CANNOT CHANGE - THE SERENITY PRAYER

> **"God give me the strength to change those things I can change, the courage to accept those things I cannot change, and the wisdom to know the difference."**

There are a multitude of events going on in the world. While modern communications have brought more of them to us, we have no more control over them. Life was much simpler when we had at least some control over the events of which we had knowledge. Today there are literally hundreds of events that have the potential to make us mad, frustrated, sad, or unhappy. Besides routine events such as traffic, rain, parents, children, bosses, fate and neighbors, we also have earthquakes in Mexico, drug wars in Columbia, starvation in Somalia, discrimination in South Africa and ethnic cleansing in Bosnia-Herzegovina. The list grows longer and none of them are under our control. If they were, we wouldn't be frustrated, mad or sad about them.

Unfortunately, each of us has only a finite amount of energy to expend each day. Negative emotions or feelings take up a certain amount of that energy resource in thinking about all of these events and since we are not able to control them, this energy is totally wasted. In addition, negative feelings reduce the effectiveness of our remaining energy. The choice to expend energy on being frustrated results in a significant decrease in our personal ability to work or help our family or invest for the future, so much so the good flavor of our work and home life can be lost to us.

Why decide to feel bad about things you cannot control? Why not choose to accept them and not let them affect you? Why not look at the bright side, the silver lining in the cloud? Why bother feeling frustrated that something is the way it is when you can't change it? Don't you live in one of the finest, if not the finest country in the world? You could have been born in Somalia and then you'd have a big problem, starvation. You could have been born in Russia,

Yugoslavia or China. Do you really believe your problems are so big that they justify damaging yourself, your family and your fellow workers?

Let's analyze the choice of feeling badly about our boss. If you work for 30 different bosses over a lifetime, how many great ones, bad ones and mediocre ones will you have? Don't you deserve your fair share of each, or are you such a weak person you can only work well for the best? Why are you better or more deserving than the rest of us? In the meantime, why not accept that you are not hired to change your boss. Only his/her boss has that job. Advise if you can, but otherwise forget it or change jobs. It's a free country.

The above analysis can be done for traffic, parents, the weather, starvation in Somalia, you name it. You have no right to be frustrated at the way the world is. Only a God could have such a right and we humans are definitely not Gods. If you decide starvation is a very important issue, get involved and make an effort to start controlling it in whatever way you can. But under no circumstance ignore the Serenity Prayer. This <u>Rationale</u> is a road to mental peace and enables each of us to make the best use of our scarce energy resources.

So why don't you just accept what you can't change and be happy you have what you have? Are you just going to curl up in the fetal position and head back to the womb, or will you when the going gets tough, get going like the tough ones always do? <u>The true measure of a person is how they deal with problems, not what problems they have.</u> Why don't you use that prayer to tell you what being tough is and stop wasting a lot of heat and effort?

6. A SENSE OF PERSPECTIVE

Rationales two through five are just common sense ways to use our inherent human ability of choice, the number one Rationale. Our last Rationale, "a sense of perspective", is one more way to look at the human condition in order to <u>choose</u> actions that meet high standards.

This Rationale refers to picturing our own difficulties relative to those that other people are experiencing. The problem that perspective addresses is the trap of "oh, poor me". In feeling sorry for ourselves, we destroy our most effective weapon to combat difficulties, our positive attitude. This error causes us to violate Rationales two through five and everything turns bad for us.

Keeping our positive attitude, our high morale, is greatly assisted by analyzing what's happening or has happened to other human beings. This evaluation process should be undertaken at least semiannually in order to prepare for the next of life's problems that is surely on its way. Evaluate diseases and other bad conditions and their effects on people. Try to visualize other environments. Evaluate what others have done to overcome all sorts of problems. In the process, yours will either pale to insignificance or show up as being no worse than many others that could have come your way. In any event, you will come to realize yours are opportunities to excel and to show your love for others by <u>bearing your own cross in a way that will make everyone very proud to know you</u>. Don't make them sad. It's your choice.

Evaluation of the actions of other people convinces us that living by high value standards during tough times is the only reasonable and correct response. All others cause hurt to those we hold most dear and serve to turn us against ourselves. Regularly gaining this insight prepares us to recognize when we are about to fall into the "oh, poor me" trap.

THE BOTTOM LINE OF RATIONALES

When discussing a subordinate's performance or behavior that requires change, the boss must use whichever Rationales apply and then add values in order to help the subordinate to understand the need for change. The reason for this approach is, as previously discussed, that employees have trouble viewing their problems solely through the boss' window of increased productivity and lower costs. Although corporate needs are certainly valid reasons for change, they are nowhere near as powerful to the employee as the Six Rationales. Besides, what is truly good for subordinates is good for everyone, including the company and the boss. Subordinates who think the boss only cares about himself or herself, or just likes to be critical, will be disarmed by these Rationales.

In addition, Choice, Who's #1, Who's #2 and #3, doing unto others, accepting what we cannot change and Perspective are down to earth, easy to touch concepts. They are very close to how each of us wants to deal with life and thus their power. Everyone will embrace these Rationales since they always hoped it would be this way in the business world. These Rationales alone constitute compelling common sense that become very good habits, better with more use.

When using these Rationales, be prepared with stories about your own errors. Relating what you did to change serves as a constructive example and makes the correction process an accepted part of life rather than a cause for anguish and anxiety. Changing our behavior must be considered a normal task that no one can evade since we copied most of it without consideration of value standards. We are all in the same boat on this and what's more, we all make the same errors. The only difference between us is how often we make a specific one. Telling about your own makes you infinitely human and humble, saves you once again from the error of arrogance and converts your coaching from an offensive confrontation to the caring, greatly acceptable act of helping another team member.

Now that we understand Rationales, without which coaching would not be effective, let's get back to coaching.

MORE ABOUT COACHING

Before we can proceed with the details of how to coach, we must understand five additional considerations:

1- types of human errors
2- error is our best friend
3- widely held errors, culture, may require a different tactic
4- there are a set of hazards inherent to coaching
5- small doses may be appropriate

Types of Errors

When machines develop small problems, we shut them down and perform repairs. We try hard to find little problems and "nip them in the bud" before they get bigger and cause failure. Repairing total failures costs far more than repairing little problems. In addition, we conduct overhauls of very big machines in order to return them to an almost new condition. Bosses devote considerable time and effort to repairs and overhauls. Small machines are analogous to individual people and large ones are analogous to groups. Thus, coaching individual people is repair while coaching at a group meeting is an overhaul (see Chap 9). Both require time and effort.

Bosses must be prepared to deal with three types of people errors:

1- in technical/work performance
2- in dealing with workplace conditions
3- in personal behavior

Machines such as lathes or computers and work functions such as assembly, sales or purchasing, each have characteristics that dictate a specific set of rules or guidelines for achieving success. The better these characteristics and rules are known and understood, the better the person can perform. Thus the need for coaching in work performance (#1 above). Great benefits accrue.

Not so obvious is the fact that the employee must learn to cope with and react properly to workplace conditions (# 2 above). There are many of these conditions. They could be one of the fifteen "Conflicts" in Chapter 3 or discipline, value abuses, training, overtime, rules, or one of the conditions addressed in Appendix A; bosses, bureaucracy, peers, change, unions, customers, priorities, competition, discrimination, communications, relief of the boss, committees and life's problems.

Unfortunately for bosses, little knowledge of normal workplace conditions has been gained prior to our entering the workplace and learning them is by trial and error, hit or miss. For the most part, we are guided by peers who rarely have the best solutions. This process causes considerable consternation and unease to ourselves as well as to our peers, juniors and bosses. These can all be considered identical to the peace of mind issues of Chapter 5. Like machines, each of these conditions have whys and hows, rules for success, which meet all high value standards.

Bosses must be prepared to coach subordinates by providing the Six Rationales for behavior change and the knowledge of how to successfully handle workplace conditions in accord with high value standards. Through coaching, bosses can change the stress of making errors into the pride of successfully dealing with conditions. This coaching pays big dividends since the same solutions become the accepted norm for everyone, bosses and juniors. Appendix A gives the whys and hows of those conditions that I could not logically include in the main parts of the book. I suggest a brief look at Appendix A right now so you'll understand what I have provided.

In #3 above, there are eight personal behaviors; personality, likes and dislikes, ego and prestige, assumptions, bad morale, bad attitude, stress and emotionalism. Appendix B provides an understanding of the hows and whys of successfully dealing with these eight. Most importantly, Appendix B explains exactly what behavior is and provides two easy to execute, powerful methods to alter behaviors that appear hard to change. Bad morale and stress are perhaps the most prevalent personal behaviors and require the most emphasis. These eight are more prevalent in management than working level people.

In order to coach people issues, the boss must be equipped with criteria (Rationales and values) and with solutions (the hows and whys of principles) that are in accord with the criteria.

Error Is Our Friend

Error or failure is our best friend. From it we can learn much, all of it good if we want. While there is nothing like success for our morale, self-esteem and take-home-pay, we can turn success into a bad learning experience if we become arrogant and egotistical. Conversely, making errors is not a good feeling, but it presents a great learning opportunity. It is the natural process given to us so that we can learn and develop. Besides, each of us wants to be a superstar and wants to learn not to make errors.

Bosses must help us to make our behavior meet the standards of our values. They must therefore embrace our errors joyously and coach well so subordinates get on with learning and achieving excellence, rather than stopping for finger pointing, defensiveness, remorse, politics and competition among supposed team members. Learning from errors is an investment in the future and every error is a chance for the boss to support the person through detection, correction and turning-on. Each is an opportunity to demonstrate great respect through the supplier role. Without errors we would need no bosses, but the choice is always the boss' as to how to handle them. The "What the hell do they think they're doing" choice will always be a loser.

Culture

Some behaviors in reaction to workplace conditions, including those of Appendices A and B, are so widespread as to be considered reflections of culture rather than of individual, isolated problems. Poor customer service, poor attitudes, distrust, stress and negative reaction to change are examples of cultures that are most effectively coached at group meetings in front of everyone (This very important forum is discussed at length in chapter 9). Cultures are often easier to change than isolated cases, but when they are part of an overall response to negative leadership, progress will be slow until subordinates begin to think that the boss cares. This will not occur until the boss has made good progress toward improving the quality of his/her support and has established the supplier role for bosses. Both of these are crucial and neither can be done without the other.

Hazards of Coaching

The hazards associated with coaching come from two sources. First, the boss may appear to be looking down on, disrespecting, criticizing, berating or otherwise demeaning a subordinate. Second, the subordinate may be inexperienced at correcting personal behavior and/or be unaware of the paybacks. The boss' weapons against these two hazards are knowledge that:

1- people do what they think is right, whether in truth it is wrong or not. Excuses supplied by the boss may have played a role.

2- people view themselves as being good because their values are good and this bubble needs reinforcement, not bursting.

3- the boss needs them as much as they need him.

4- humility, praise and apologies go a long way toward decreasing negative reactions and setting the correct tone.

5- errors are normal and Rome was not built in a day.

6- turning on a person is more important than instructing.

7- admission of error is an emotional event unnecessary to problem correction.

8- problem correction always has a positive effect on the person while failure to correct is always negative.

The first hazard of appearing to demean or disrespect is overcome by setting the proper tone, one of supplier to customer and of helping a good person who we know wants to do good things and improve. The proper tone also helps to overcome the subordinate's natural fear of dealing with someone who controls their paycheck. The second hazard of inexperience in learning from our errors is overcome by patience, by admitting to your own errors and what you did to correct them through use of Rationales and value standards, and by persevering in a firm but unthreatening manner. Without these tactics, coaching by most bosses is an impossible task marked by anxiety and lack of significant success. As usual, the level of effectiveness is up to the boss, his/her choice.

Small Doses

While the need for coaching is quite obvious, how much of it is really necessary? The answer is it can be as simple as providing a little knowledge or a Rationale that leads toward a solution. Since success is only gained through action by the person involved, little bits of help may be more valuable than large doses. In addition, just taking the time to be a sounding board or offering a shoulder to cry on is more therapeutic than most of us realize. Think about Mother Nature's process of creating a flower - cultivation, seeding, watering, sunlight, weeding, watering, weeding and suddenly a flower. High quality coaching includes these elements from the day the person is hired.

But for bigger problems beyond how to operate a machine or "I'm unhappy with ---", for which the boss does not want repeats or for which little bits of help are not getting results, I will now provide a full-fledged, large dose procedure. This can always be shortened to handle minor cases since it has all the elements so necessary to not turning off a subordinate. I have used this on both bosses and workers for; personality clashes, extremely bad attitudes that damaged innocent bystanders, bosses who gave too many orders, fear of responsibility, over-reaction to taunts by peers, racial and sexual confrontations, stress and others. The understanding and two methods of the 3x5 card principle in Appendix B aided this process, but the basic procedure is that given below.

PROCEDURE to COACH Subordinates

1- Find an action that could be improved, big or small.

2- Review the characteristics and solutions needed to understand and fix it. Review applicable values, Rationales and principles.

3- Meet with the subordinate.

4- Praise and say how badly you need this person and how much you appreciate his/her efforts.

5- Bring up the action with kid gloves.

6- Apologize for any excuses that you may have provided (whether you did so or not). Then learn why he/she believed the action was right.

7- Provide facts you have that the person did not have.

8- Ask what criteria was used to arrive at actions (values or whatever). Ask if the values that you consider relevant were used. Ask if the person looked out for their own best interests and discuss these along with any Rationales that are applicable.

9- Help the person to postulate alternative actions.

10- Help the person to choose the most correct action.

11- Help the person to commit to improvement.

12- Praise again and thank sincerely. Wish good luck.

Step 5 requires some preparation in order to evade the two hazards of coaching. Some bosses are naturally better at this than others, but making errors is of no importance. Gaining proficiency is critical and can only be done through trial and error, lots of practice and self-criticism. Your errors are your friends. Turn them to your advantage by going back to the person, admitting to your errors and then repeating the event correctly. This is powerful leadership. How else can our subordinates learn how to do it. Besides, there is nothing to hide because what you are trying to do is good for everyone. Above all, be a good listener (covered in chapter 7 in detail).

In step 6, the boss first apologizes for whatever the boss may have done to cause the error, directly or indirectly. <u>After all, if the boss had done his/her own job of making the person 5Star, the error may have been averted or be of less impact</u>. In other words, <u>the boss-junior team has screwed up, not just the junior</u>.

Then the boss draws out the facts and logic that were used to arrive at a "right thing" that turned out to be incorrect. Relieve pressure through telling stories of your own errors when doing what you thought was "right" and make clear that mistakes are our friends, routine for everyone including the boss. We want to minimize any consequence and learn how not to repeat them. Ask discreet questions to flush out all facts such as the involvement of others, past practice, worry over family problems, or actions by superiors. Be open to the possibility that the person's performance is a habit that was copied without supportive facts and reasons.

If excuses surface, apologize again. Seize every opportunity to relieve pressure. Do not become involved in the no-win game of questioning the validity of the facts associated with an excuse. <u>If you apologize for them, excuses will lose their force as an issue.</u> Doing otherwise makes them the issue. You do not care if the person is trying to get off the hook or believes that two wrongs make a right. You are trying to improve future actions. Listening to the excuses, getting them all out on the table so that they will not prevent future improvement is a necessary step <u>before</u> we can proceed to the fix. You might bring out some of the excuses that you have used or been tempted to use and admit to that error. At the end of these, thank the person for disclosing all of this.

In step 7 the boss brings out any relevant facts that the person did not disclose. Use questions to find out if the person knows them before just providing them. The boss must first find and then fill in gaps in the data base, such as understanding the decision criteria of Rationales, values or the principles with their hows and whys as given in Appendices A and B or other sections of this book. While the hows are very important to short term progress, the whys are far more important to long term improvement. If the whys are powerful, they become the culture, a <u>value-based culture</u>.

Facts must also include knowledge of the consequences involved, positive or negative. The effects on fellow employees, customers, #1/2/3 and the results of progressive discipline must all be discussed in a matter of fact, why they must occur, manner. These effects are "facts of life" that we may not always like, but they occur and have valid whys. For instance, some acts become serious with repetition and could lead to termination. These possibilities and their reasons must be thoroughly and openly discussed. <u>These are not threats</u>, only facts about the whys and hows of consequences that the person can choose to use or not. It is, after all, a free country and everyone gets to make their own choice.

In step 9, the boss should cause the subordinate to design several performance alternatives and to evaluate each against the facts and criteria discussed (values, Rationales and principles). In step 10, the subordinate chooses the best of these and in step 11 commits to making this improvement. Conducting this exercise also equips the person with an effective process to support future improvements, something the person can do on his/her own. If the person is a subordinate boss, they also now know what they should be doing with their subordinates.

Note that in the above, we have not asked for an admission of error. It is unnecessary and may be too emotional an event to accept. The idea is for the boss to help the subordinate to look for reasons and ways to improve. The wisdom is, asking people to admit to error about an already known condition, such as dealing incorrectly with a peer, is unproductive.

The actions of subordinates in response to coaching are major signposts that clearly point out your best, most valuable people. Do not get caught up in what they said or what their mistakes were. <u>Judge them by what they do to move toward 5Star.</u>

Additional Comments On Coaching

The original behavior may have adversely affected or caused mental anguish to one or more other employees. They deserve an apology. After step 11, the boss should question the person about this need and gain commitment to it as a matter of basic courtesy. If the person is not willing, order it since only this action will demonstrate that you value courtesy, cooperation and teamwork highly. Follow up with any victim to ensure that a proper apology was made. If not, cause it to be repeated until it is acceptable to the victim. This is necessary leadership.

Particularly in large organizations, many behaviors cannot be corrected without an effort by several bosses in the same chain. This effort must be coordinated, not fractured, and those involved must make the need for improvement known and not be seen as disagreeing, either actively or passively. Bosses need not say everything exactly the same way, particularly for the correction or the seriousness, but they all must be striving to change the same behavior. Written evaluations must reflect the same need. If any of these appear disconnected, the person will be more resistant to change. Isn't this coordination between different levels of the chain the same approach we use for problems with machines?

Coaching is the only proactive way to cause improvement in a specific performance. It puts the boss squarely on the subordinate's team for their mutual benefit. Learning through errors and improving our behavior are lifelong processes that must be mastered and revered, not feared. Coaching is a boss' mechanism to support this change. To appreciate the extent to which change is possible and to lend credence to the procedure presented, one need only review what occurs in a United States Marine Corps boot camp or in an Alcoholics Anonymous rehabilitation center. The AA approach through the 12 steps is readily available and worthy of thorough analysis by any boss who is eager to succeed.

Coaching Subordinate Bosses To Be Bosses

With "things", it is reasonably straight forward to ask a person to try a new approach or use some different knowledge and see how it works. This request will normally be honored and given a fair test. Over people issues however, the request will be met with disdain if not with outright rejection and a fair test may never occur. Why? For a myriad of reasons, most of which add up to "if I can't believe in it, I won't be able to do it, so don't ask!

If such a resistant stance was applied to learning a new sport, no one would ever learn to like tennis, Ping-Pong or golf. The same would be true for every work vocation. "Believing in it" before we do it cannot be a valid prerequisite.

In light of the above, bosses who attempt to get subordinate bosses to change their methods to those of this book must discuss this wisdom with the subordinate up front. <u>Make clear believing in it is unnecessary, but carrying it out as designed, without changing the basics, is required.</u> Explain that success will surely come and only success generates belief.

This completes coaching and leads us to the related principles of responsibility, authority and control.

RESPONSIBILITY AND BEING RESPONSIBLE AT THE LOWEST LEVEL

<u>The most important level in any organization is its lowest level, the people who are responsible for daily creation of products and services to provide to customers. The reason for this is, any business will only be as good as the quality and quantity of the sum of the outputs of these people.</u>

Now that we know what the lowest level is responsible to do, we also know what their immediate supervisors are not responsible for doing.. Because of the way people are, attempts to perform the tasks of subordinates, whether it be making their decisions or performing their actions, will cause those subordinates to become less responsible. In fact, the more authority and influence subordinates have over the production process, that only they carry out, the more responsibly they will act when doing it. (Influence is through someone else's authority as compared to our own.) The boss' function is not to do the subordinates job, but to provide whatever support the subordinate needs to achieve excellent performance. This support includes discipline and thus accountability since without them subordinates will not act responsibly. This extremely proactive, not passive, role requires your full understanding, so let's examine it. An example follows.

Admiral Rickover, father of the Nuclear Navy, was testifying before a committee of Congress. His record of outstanding training programs was noted as he was asked what could be done to improve training in the entire Navy. The Admiral respectfully declined to answer stating that since he was not responsible or accountable for training in the entire Navy, anything he said would be "irresponsible". The Admiral knew the law that people will act irresponsibly, without meaning to do so, if they believe they cannot be held fully accountable for what they say or do.

Since this is such an important point for bosses, let me be more specific.

1. If I am responsible for 100% of a job, it is uppermost in my mind that I could be held accountable for its final outcome. This state causes me to act more and more responsibly as time passes.

2. If I am only responsible for 10% of a job, and my boss, and possibly my boss' boss, is likewise only responsible for 10%, I believe that I cannot be held accountable for the job's final outcome. This causes me to act more and more irresponsibly as time passes. Think about bureaucrats and how they are members of this group.

3. If I am only responsible for 10% of a job, but report directly to a boss who has 100% responsibility for its final outcome, it is again uppermost in my mind that I could be held accountable for my 10% or more. This causes me to act more and more responsibly as time passes.

The law of responsibility above could be restated as "Followers will act responsibly only to the extent they believe they will be held accountable or will suffer the consequences of any negligence on their part". Bosses who do not observe this law will suffer many negative consequences.

As for 5Star non-followers, they hold themselves more accountable than any boss could. This does not mean their boss should not discipline them for negligence, only that they have a built-in control system that drives them toward acting more responsibly than most.

In view of the above, the boss' strategy is to:

1. grant authority over a person's work to that person, as much authority as possible.

2. grant protected rights to that person to influence all aspects for which that person does not have authority.

3. hold that person accountable for the entire job, to the maximum extent possible.

RESPONSIBILITY AND BEING RESPONSIBLE AT THE BOSS' LEVEL

Now let's look at responsibility from the boss' perspective by tracing the process of making a small company into a big one.

John Doe starts a company in his home to produce "widgets". He starts by doing everything needed himself; from production to quality control, from book-keeping to sales, from pension plans to purchasing. It is clear that John is responsible for every task because he is the only employee. Let's assume John is successful and starts to expand. At some point he must hire another person. Assume that each year brings more success and he ends up ten years later with a thousand people. What has happened to John's responsibility?

Let's say John started with a bag full of marbles, each marble marked with the name of one of John's responsibilities when he started his company. What happened to his bag when he hired his first person? Did he give away any marbles? No! What he did was make a duplicate of some of his marbles and give those to the new hire. And after increasing employees to 1,000? The number of marbles in his bag remains the same. Hiring someone to do a job that John once did does not change his own responsibilities one iota. It removed the necessity for doing what the new hire does, while increasing what he had to do to support and oversee people, and on and on all the way to 1,000. So what John must do to meet his responsibilities changes markedly from when he started his company, but his responsibilities don't change.

Therefore, any boss has the responsibility of ensuring that his/her own actions and those of everyone below him/her in the chain of command, meet high standards for all good values. This means subordinate actions are no different than the boss' own from the reference point of the boss' responsibility. This is the responsibility that each boss assumes when accepting a position of authority over others, whether the boss knew it at the time or not.

It should be obvious that ignorance of below standard actions by subordinates is simply a case of "irresponsibility" by the boss. "No one told me" is an excuse voiced by a boss in an attempt to escape being held accountable by his/her boss. Thus, a boss can only act "responsibly" by knowing both what is being done and whether that meets acceptable standards. Accepting measurements made by juniors or outsiders without routinely and personally checking their accuracy or credibility is just one form of "irresponsible" action.

Once you as boss have the correct knowledge, you can still be irresponsible by not holding people accountable for unacceptable standards or by attempting to do their job for them. Thus, while acting irresponsibly is as easy as doing nothing, acting responsibly will require effort and knowledge on your part.

Failing to praise can be just as damaging as failing to hold accountable. Either will make people believe the boss doesn't care and either will be used by followers as excuses for future errors and derelictions. The concept of acting responsibly requires the boss to take actions that help to make better products for the customer and at the same time ensure that the machines and people under his/her control are cared for properly. Sacrificing people or machines for customers always constitutes a shortsighted and irresponsible action.

More Issues Related To Responsibility

Knowledge is therefore a prerequisite to being responsible. As a boss, responsibility requires accounting for an entire business or part thereof and distinguishing between right and wrong for all facets of your own actions and those of subordinates. The functions of accounting and distinguishing cannot be performed responsibly without having considerable knowledge of what the people assigned must do in order to succeed at their jobs, whether in making actual products or in supporting others to do so. Achieving this knowledge will require not only a substantial upfront effort, but an ongoing one to keep up with the continual changes occurring in the marketplace. Lacking this knowledge, the boss will be held accountable for something that he/she cannot assist toward excellence.

Promotion up the chain does not reduce our responsibilities, only adds to them as the number of functions for which we are responsible rises. The process and guidelines to high quality solutions, however, do remain the same; getting to the high ground of 5Star. Some would maintain that higher level bosses must be more concerned with corporate strategy than their lower level subordinates. This is not true. Apart from the fact 5Star is the way to a secure future, if everyone is not concerned about strategies for the future and how best to respond to a changing business environment, the company is in trouble because of a lack of good leadership.

As indicated by the John Doe example, responsibility cannot be delegated. No matter how many subordinate bosses and/or workers the boss chooses to hire, his/her responsibility for any particular aspect of the world does not decrease. Bureaucrats have expanded their empires by hiring more subordinates in the belief that they will be held less responsible for errors and can always find a scape-goat. Although it worked for many years, I do not recommend this path now since it is definitely the road to higher costs through more turned-off people and will result in losing to the competition.

The last comment is that subordinates are unable to affect the boss' responsibilities. Juniors cannot reduce them since they are a characteristic of the boss' job and are assigned by his/her boss. Neither can they make the boss more responsible since that would require action on the boss' part, not on the part of the junior. However, they can cause the boss to be irresponsible by failing to report problems and thus preventing the boss from taking corrective action. This violates the "most important management rule" of reporting all problems. These reasons must be used by bosses when explaining this rule and responsibility in general.

NOTE: This book delineates how to proactively manage people in a "responsible" manner. It does not cover how to proactively manage 'things' such as production, accounting, sales and the like. The general concepts of responsibility given above are, however, equally applicable to 'things' as well as people.

AUTHORITY

Authority is an ingredient necessary to success in any endeavor of more than a few people. The difficulties associated with authority stem from too much use or too little use and/or misplaced use. Each of these cases has bad effects and choosing between them is a waste of time when it is so easy to choose the road to 5Star superstars.

Authoritarianism, Too much Of A Good Thing

Those who err through too much use of authority are termed authoritarians because they tend to emphasize absolute obedience to authority, the message that the boss knows best. This form of imbalance leads toward robotic "yes" people who dare not use their brains to challenge the boss and thus destroys 5Star. By its arrogance, it offends and turns off followers, thereby resulting in lowered productivity levels, lost creativity and increased exposure to competition.

Authoritarianism pervades American society to such an extent that erring in this direction is the norm by a wide margin. Being told what to do by our parents, teachers, media, churches and bosses has a profound effect on over 90 percent of us. Not only does it change us from non-followers into followers, some more and some less, but we then copy this authoritarian model when acting as a boss or parent. Authoritarianism is therefore a strong habit that can only be broken with a concerted effort and aid from our boss.

Egalitarianism, Too Little Of A Good Thing

Those who err through too little use of authority might be termed egalitarians since they give everyone the freedom to do as they please. This is the "help only" solution discussed in Chapter 5 under "discipline". "Help only" fails just as surely, but more so than authoritarianism. If bosses are <u>unwilling to back up high performance standards, with effort and force as needed</u>, subordinates will become convinced that since the boss doesn't care, they shouldn't either.

No workplace will perform effectively with a democratic or consensus management style. Encouraging people to put in their two cents, make up their own orders and pursue excellence on their own will only be effective if the <u>boss serves as the bearer of high standards</u>. Not using authority to ensure that subordinates achieve high standards, in the name of democratic, participative or consensus management, is just one more unacceptable excuse for poor performance, another case of irresponsible behavior by the boss. Where consensus management has appeared to be successful, I contend that a more informed inspection would reveal such a well balanced use of authority as to render authority itself a non-issue.

Understanding Balance

Clearly, the use of either authoritarianism or egalitarianism as a management Principle fails to achieve high productivity and high performance in general. Instead, we should rely on a values-based culture where authority is utilized to cause use of and provide back up for high standards of all good values. Using this as our guiding principle, along with the tools of this book, will help to keep us from suffering the results of too much or too little use of authority.

BUREAUCRACY - A Case Of Misused And Misplaced Authority

It should be clear that for a group of 5Star people who naturally believe in teamwork and in control through values, authority is not an issue. What they do will normally be decided on the basis of values, not authority. But where 5Star are a minority insufficient to gain control over all aspects of work, authority or "who gets their way" could be a way of life. If so, the workplace has arrived at rule by politics and/or rank rather than by values or merit.

Unfortunately, there are many more agendas beyond values that are vying for control of the workplace, most being enshrined in authoritarianism and its offspring bureaucracy. High level bosses in large companies usually grant their authority or power to staff people in an attempt to introduce and control more programs in more parts of the company. This results in bureaucratic rule by process and, as you will see, is a case of misplaced authority.

Specifically, bureaucracy is a world wherein "doers" must gain the concurrence or the action of a centralized support function before they can get to "go". Similar to a game of Monopoly, there are many hazards along the way. Unlike Monopoly, getting to "go" may be impossible. Bureaucracy can be likened to a condition wherein many can say "no", but only a very few can say "go". "Doers" waste considerable time and money gaining concurrence (actually not getting a "no") from many, and/or action from few. The decision-making process grinds to a crawl. The internal result is that frustration and de-motivation become a steady diet and take a heavy toll on "doers". This is the first of four negative results of bureaucracy.

For our second negative result, external customers become pawns in this power game. Their needs take a back seat to the rules, policies and procedures of the bureaucracy. Bureaucrats impose one set of policies, "one size fits all", on everyone for all sorts of superfluous reasons beyond the fact they have the power to do so. Meeting the differing needs of customers is something only expected of line management, not of the bureaucracy. Lack of timeliness or responsiveness to external customers is the most obvious result because no one can give sufficient attention to the customer's needs while struggling with an internal bureaucracy?

The third negative result is in the process of this struggle, line management finds compromising value standards to be a much faster and easier route than doing battle with bureaucrats. Moreover, complaining to bosses only brings various counter-charges or new bureaucratic systems that make the old ones look like child's play. So whether it concerns a centralized engineering or purchasing function, the line starts to "work around" this very frustrating, tiring and unproductive struggle. There are a myriad of methods, but they all come down to avoiding correction of the real problem and doing something that, while not meeting high value standards, at least can be done without all the hassle and delay.

Many organizations encourage these work-arounds since everyone knows the bureaucracy will not be responsive. These become a dangerous form of heroism because some of the work-arounds are themselves serious breaches of value standards and hazardous to the very people who were only trying their best to please the customer. And what of the external customer's desire for high quality? And don't the negative leadership messages emanating from this entire situation constitute a real and present danger to the boss' goals?

The fourth negative outcome is the damage sustained by the bureaucrats themselves. They often become irrelevant, unnecessary to any goal unless it has something to do with power or politics. They practice doing many of the wrong things and they are rarely turned-on by the next challenge. Lack of professionalism may become a way of life and their group may become a dumping ground for the sick and lame. And who can be turned-on while doing something that causes harm to so many others? Isn't theirs a service and if so, who is the customer? (more on Bureaucracy in Appendix A)

The Fix

The above four outcomes need not be chosen by the big boss. It is not bad to centralize and doing so for some procurement or engineering or information processing functions can be a considerable gain from all standpoints; cost, professionalism, responsiveness to customer needs, et al. However, to prevent occurrence of the four outcomes above, the boss must choose to give the full rights of being a customer to those who are being provided this support. Suppliers who dictate to customers cannot survive in today's marketplace and it is no different inside a company. The necessity of having to please internal customers, and being held accountable by them, will cause the support to become professional and timely, and will make all actions more compatible with external customer needs. This choice by the big boss realigns authority so that the law of responsibility on page 106 is no longer being violated.

This decision in its simplest form is one of who gets to complain. In the bureaucratic choice, bureaucrats spend no time complaining since they get to write the rule book for their service. In this case, only the user has reason to complain. In the just described fix, of placing the authority with the line, the roles are reversed. The only complainer will be the supporter who will at first be upset at having to satisfy their internal customers individually rather than make one set of rules for everyone. But choosing this fix also best supports the external customer for two reasons; their needs will no longer be sacrificed to the desires and rules of internal support groups, and the line will be far more able to serve external customers without the old frustrations and delays. And the staff will soon stop complaining as they start to feel proud of providing products that have real value to their customers. In fact, everyone wins and your external customers will be happy customers.

Once authority is placed within the line for everything that directly impacts their ability to service external customers and the line has no reasons to complain, at what level in the line should this authority be exercised? If you have a reasonably flat structure with very few levels in the chain, this will not be a problem. For others, a plant manager would probably have sufficient knowledge and be high enough in the chain to achieve fairness. This is really the technical question of how to gain excellence in everything, 5Star and timeliness included. Each case requires some careful analysis, but err on the side of placing authority lower in the chain in order to protect 5Star.

One more issue of authority/bureaucracy is worthy of mention. Problems that appear to have organizational overtones often fall within the authority of more than one group. Ignoring these organizational issues and holding each group equally accountable is the wisest course. This precludes having them attempt to so carefully draw the lines of authority that there is no overlap and something falls through the crack. It will also inspire the different groups to realize that they all sink or swim with the outcome and therefore should work harder to cooperate. To do otherwise may convince them that the big boss doesn't believe the groups must act as a team.

Two More Observations On Fixing Bureaucracies

There are two more equally important conclusions. First, the existence of problems that result from misplaced authority can be found by bosses who diligently search for heartburn at the troop level (accurate Gut level responses). Second, solutions that compromise one or more good values need not be accepted. Too often, bosses fall into the trap of believing business can only be conducted through compromise and some bad results must be accepted. The truth is, we may not be able to achieve 8-10 standards in all cases, but we never need to accept something that reflects a bad versus good value. Stated another way, we need never lead in the wrong direction.

A Replacement For Bureaucracy

Hopefully, you now believe the new management theories of acting through bureaucratic, shared authority schemes do far more harm than good. But what process should we use to adopt new computer technology or techniques such as Re-engineering, Total Quality Management or others? The answer can be found in the boss' role as a supplier.

Without knowledge, no boss can properly serve. So the boss must <u>first</u> gain knowledge through books, consultants or other sources. <u>Second</u>, as a supplier the boss makes subordinates aware of what is being done and why. This gets their juices flowing while allowing them to contribute. <u>Third</u>, the boss needs a first hand look at the use of this new "thing", sufficient to understand why it might be valuable and how to implement it. <u>And last</u>, the boss must provide this same learning opportunity to subordinate bosses and some if not many of the work force.

As knowledge is gained, brainstorming sessions are conducted to elicit everyone's opinions and ideas. All subordinates are kept informed and allowed to add their Two Cents. At some point in this process, there are enough people convinced that this new "thing" would make a valuable addition to the company or group involved. If the bosses have done their part in keeping subordinates informed of the necessity for change, answering their questions and addressing their suggestions, the group may proceed with making an implementation plan. When the great majority of subordinates are committed to the implementation plan, only then should it be placed into effect. (For this process of achieving everyone's commitment, Chapters 7-9 provide additional insight.)

For bosses who have many similar groups to which the new "thing" is applicable, making a pilot program at one site to work out all the bugs is prudent. A few very experienced line managers and workers would be chosen to assist this change and later to carry it to each of the other groups. At the end of the process, they would be returned to their original groups.

There are cases where assimilation of the new technology will require producing a whole new system such as a computer-based airline reservation system or a complete maintenance management system. By virtue of size and degree of difficulty, these productions are too time consuming for line management. The logical course is to select a very successful senior line manager who is intimately familiar with every aspect of the business. Allow this person to become educated in the new "thing" and give him/her the resources necessary to achieve the goal. The process must still include the same aspects enumerated above for handling the process using line management.

For "things" that are more cultural in nature, such as diversity, the method is top down education and commitment through leadership. Staffs can aid in education, but because of the natural law, <u>only the boss' leadership can effect the change</u>. Any use of staff personnel must be closely controlled in order <u>to avert confusions of authority</u> and to ensure that the staff acts as a supplier to an internal customer in need. However, if the boss hasn't made subordinates feel the need for help, what the staff has to offer will fall on deaf ears.

The above is a brief sketch of a process meant to supplant bureaucratic staffs while meeting all high value standards.

CONTROL

Shouldering accountability for subordinate performance and responsibility for support of their work will cause any boss to yearn for an adequate control system. A simple system would measure actions and results. The information gained would then be used to generate direction that modifies future actions in order to achieve improvement. Follow-up inspection to ascertain the effects of modification and design/re-direction would be conducted until results came in line with expectations. The system sounds simple, but clearly implies that directing depends totally on the accuracy and credibility of the measurements. This truth determines, to a large extent, the design of an effective control system.

While retailing, auto manufacturing and computer software development are quite different, they all use people. Admittedly, the technical knowledge requirements vary greatly and success is dependent on professionalism in these "things", but since people are common to each of these, people rules should fit every environment.

Human beings are so marvelously capable that simple techniques for measurement are unable to portray what's really going on, and thereby lead to inferior decision-making and direction. Humans can effectively deal with a large number of variables and in so doing create an associated set of complex interdependencies that defies understanding by other than extremely experienced observers. Paper reports and numerical evaluations never capture the real picture. Well-meaning actions, or even questions, based on these information mediums will not only fail to improve quality or productivity, but will have negative effects.

The real picture of "what is" exists only in the workplace, never in the office. "What is" is a group of interrelated facts whose dependencies and importance can only be understood in the workplace. Each can only be misunderstood away from it or when isolated from the other relevant facts. Viewed through reports, the realities are totally lost. The analog is a one way written communication that, without tone or body language, loses 93% of the message. Being able to discern "what is" requires several years of experience down in trenches tied with more years spent trying to manage them from a local office. So the watchwords of any control system are credibility and quality before quantity.

SELF-CONTROL

In view of the above limitations, a control model based upon authoritarian or bureaucratic methods will fail to meet high standards. Superior performance can be achieved by causing individuals to self-control through value standards. Self-control requires that relevant measurement information be provided to each employee and their immediate superiors. This supports self-direction by juniors and coaching by their boss. Self-control also requires that the lowest level be able to ask bosses for better support or whatever they need in order to excel. Subordinates must "Talk Back to the Boss" and bosses must be responsive to these requests in a timely fashion.

The boss' role is therefore not one of running the workplace but of improving self-direction and support, and thereby outcomes. Higher bosses must consult both the working level and their immediate superiors regarding any measurement information that they deem worthy of action. Subordinates must fully understand and agree to any need for change or improvement and be fully prepared to implement it before they, not the boss, make the decision to do so. This constitutes Leadership through respect for others wherein the high quality of the message elicits a positive response from budding superstars.

The last major rule to this control system is you get what you inspect. Attention to detail by subordinates can only be infused through attention to detail by the boss, the details of the boss' leadership. Those details are out in the trench waiting to be inspected, not back in the office, and can only be addressed accurately in direct contact with the details and the person(s) involved. In addition, subordinates will accurately learn of the boss' expectations when face to face.

So the only effective control system/model is self-control by each individual person supported by accountability for and coaching in value standards and principles by the boss.

REPORTERS AND REPORTS

Outsiders unfamiliar with the workplace often make interesting observations. But they are unable to read or understand most of the important signposts. Only extremely experienced observers, ones who have successfully served in the trenches and succeeded in meeting the highest standards as its middle and upper level bosses, are able to accurately detect "what is" and determine "what's wrong". Use of inexperienced staff personnel who have a narrow focus can be effective only when they report directly to an experienced senior who <u>personally controls all of their actions and reports</u>.

As concerns reports, get rid of most written ones. There is one area that is fair game for reports since it doesn't inconvenience those in the trenches who are doing the really important work. This area is the information that must be recorded by juniors in order to properly control production and support local decision-making. This information is recorded by their own choosing and it is fair for bosses to require submission of a copy. Note that while quantitative data is valuable, written qualitative reports are virtually useless, especially when compared to <u>highly credible on-site viewing</u>. Stop them. This policy reduces the time spent on paperwork and allows subordinates more time to be with their people.

ASSOCIATES

Call your subordinates "Associates", not employees. This name makes it "our" company and puts everyone on the equal footing required for high performance and teamwork. This name is truly compatible with the concepts expressed in this book, of service by the boss and of attempts to make everyone a 5Star superstar. The image that the word Associate conveys is a powerful one embodying the principles of unleashing the full potential of your people and control through self-control.

CONCLUSIONS

The most useful purpose direction serves is to cause subordinates to take charge of their workplace and their lives. Direction that meets this test will foster 5Star development and will be best for the company's bottom line. This course can be set by any boss through repeated articulation of the orders below in association with and as solutions to specific workplace problems.

ELEVEN VALUABLE ORDERS

What to direct all subordinates to do or believe:

1. Live by your own value standards and in their use be strong and independent. Do not think of what the boss might want.

2. Everyone should be well trained and bosses will do everything they can to help.

3. Use the six Rationales of this chapter in determining your own actions.

4. The 10 most important things to bring to work are attitude, attitude, attitude, attitude, attitude, attitude, attitude, attitude, attitude and attitude.

5. Bosses are suppliers whose job is to supply high quality support to their customers (subordinates).

6. Bosses must use the Anti-Robot rules.

7. Talk back to the boss, ask for whatever you need to achieve excellence. Use the Open Door for access to higher level bosses.

8. Self-control by each individual is the only control mechanism that will achieve superior results.

9. Self-control will be backed up by Open Door, GOTYP and Group Meetings to ferret out conditions not supporting excellence.

10. We shall be the best ------------------. (Vision)

11. We are all on the same team. We are all Associates. Cooperate and treat each other well. Let's be superstars together.

I suggest that you commit the ELEVEN VALUABLE ORDERS TO MEMORY.

WHERE ARE WE IN THE BOOK?

At this point in the book, you have all the basic knowledge and understandings needed to be an outstanding boss. Converting these into leadership actions reflecting high standards will take time, but once you start your effectiveness will change quickly.

In order to greatly shorten the conversion process and for the sake of clarity, I shall provide in the last three chapters just how one goes about applying this knowledge through leadership. First I shall present the real do's, don'ts and whys of listening since it is so central to the issue of success. After that, I shall present the two most important mechanisms for the boss' leadership. These two are so powerful that even fair performance in them assures success from the day you start to use them. They also permit simultaneous detection and correction of all support deficiencies, including the bureaucratic ones. Each stone kills many birds, not just one. They are Go Out To Your People (GOTYP) and Group Meetings.

CHAPTER 7

LISTENING

Let's step back from the book for a moment, long enough to refocus on what managing people really is. It consists of two distinct yet intertwined efforts. The first is to repetitiously communicate high value standards through support to followers so they will use these in the performance of their work, the main thrust of Chapters 3 through 6. The second is to free these followers from the bondage of following and thereby release them to their own motivations and direction, the true 5Star state.

The reason for doing the first is a significant rise in productivity. The reason for doing the second is a more significant rise in productivity and creativity through the power of personal commitment. The first produces a group that can be led back to a state of mediocrity or worse. The second produces a group that will actively and forever resist any movement away from excellence, away from doing the right thing.

Though dependent on the first, the second effort is more important for the long run. While the remainder of the book provides more details of how to pursue both efforts, bear in mind 5Star is always the real goal. With that said, let's proceed with listening. I shall first cover its hows and then provide some compelling whats and whys.

Up to this point in the book, I have placed several requirements on the boss that can only be met through interactions with subordinates. Success in these rests largely on the boss' ability to <u>listen</u>. There have been six of these requirements:

1. Finding deficiencies in support, formulating corrective actions, taking those actions and determining if they were effective.

2. Deciding what direction (particularly the Eleven Valuable Orders) and knowledge need to be provided to subordinates.

3. Finding out what excuses for poor behavior are being used.

4. Discovering whether subordinates believe that you and other bosses care about them, are their suppliers.

5. Learning what values, Rationales and principles are in use, and what the culture of the workplace is.

6. Ascertaining the status of 5Star and the extent to which self-control is in use.

Satisfying the needs of subordinates, any boss' most important function, must start with finding a real need. The means to this end is effective listening since it permits the boss to accomplish all six of the above <u>each and every time</u> he/she interacts with one or more subordinates. Fully 5Star people need little aid, but a good listener can still assist them by hearing a need for knowledge gained from a different perspective or for information to which only the boss has access. For those not 5Star, listening is a first step to a better tomorrow, to making a contribution that only the boss can make, to helping another person to be a superstar.

What Is Listening? What Are Its Guidelines?

Listening is the gathering of information for the purpose of determining appropriate future action. Success in gathering depends upon how well the boss; sets the tone of the interaction with the people involved, understands possible future actions and questions the people relative to the six issues above. Guidelines for setting the tone and determining possible future actions (the principles of the main Chapters and Appendices A & B) have been explained in the previous two chapters. So let's proceed to those for questioning.

Case 1

Assume you have had few, if any, previous interactions with this person. Start with something innocuous like "How's it going?" or "How's life treating you?" or "What can I do for you?". A few will grab this opportunity to get right to some nitty gritty, but most will want to talk about generalities or that life isn't so great. With a wide open field, people will pretty well do what they want and will display their tendencies, their approach to life or work or whatever. Pull on any thread given <u>gingerly</u>. "That's too bad. What's getting to you?" Whatever the thread, it was offered for a reason that you will not understand until you find out exactly what lies behind it. In the process, you will learn a lot about this person. The goal is to let the person direct where the conversation goes and for you to nudge it along and listen for information related to the six requirements above.

This starts a relationship. Don't let it be one sided. Put something into the pot, some experience or hope or problem that is somehow relevant to the subordinate's thread. This is sharing and team members do it. Don't be in a hurry, but make good use of the time by carefully choosing the experience you share. It could be a problem that didn't meet your value standards, but shows you are trying to improve. It could concern an issue about which you want to know people's opinions. "I've got some of those. I'm worried about the current union-management situation. Maybe the company is doing the wrong thing." Or if trying for better treatment of customers, "I really got upset the other day over what one of our customers is doing. I'll bet you get a lot of those frustrations."

Note that these openers contain possible violations of values, Rationales, or principles and demonstrate openness and admission of error. Since none were great success stories, each provides an opening for the subordinate to enter. The junior's response tells volumes, whether very little is said or out pops the fully 5Star response "I keep thinking of the rule that our customers are always right and what I must do to help them, and I don't let myself get upset at what they do".

The person may move toward some support deficiencies. These still tell volumes, but also permit you to demonstrate being a supplier by apologizing and admitting to error, and leading through correction and value standards. So for someone you want to know more about, getting him or her to lead the discussion while you respond is the most effective gathering technique.

Case 2

For the case in which you know the person well and have a specific goal of wanting to determine if their execution of a certain function met all value standards, you can proceed directly to the issue. What should be gathered? All of what they did and why they did it. Have the person relate in chronological order exactly what the other person or machine said and did and all of the reasoning used to determine the next step. Gather every detail. The boss can now address each deviation from standards by questioning the person as to why he/she believed it was right and what improved alternatives exist. The boss provides missing facts and judgment criteria. This coaching is valuable because subordinates find out what is expected and to what extent they met the mark. Praise for compliances and ask for a commitment to fix any incorrect actions. Questions derived from listening are the key.

Note that for any form of coaching to be successful, bosses must stand on firm ground as to what has been done incorrectly. Most of the time, the boss was not on the scene and has only indirect knowledge of the event. Therefore, the most solid ground is whatever the person believes happened and why. Objections of "Hey, how do you know, you weren't even there", whether expressed or not, won't occur because of the credibility of using the person's own facts. Remember, all people are basically honest, so bringing out the details is strictly a function of the boss' skill at questioning.

If you are worried a certain error may have occurred but was not brought out, ask leading questions about it. If nothing is admitted, talk about it to send the "never get caught doing this" message. "I am certainly glad that you didn't -----. I never want any one to do that because ------. People who do that really hurt our results!" These clear warnings will make the person think twice about ever repeating this error.

Other Guidelines

In between Cases 1 and 2 lie a number of variations. The boss should start these as in Case 1 and proceed to wherever the subordinate's response leads. Let's assume after an opener by the boss, the person brought up a support deficiency. In this case, the process of questions remains the same, but the need for credibility can no longer be satisfied by the person's own data base. Questions must delve into other instances past and present, actions to gain correction through other bosses, what peers think, etc. But the facts disclosed will rarely be more than a very small proportion of those needed to validate a problem or choose a fix.

Also spend time gauging the level of discontent and checking for other support failures (is this the straw that broke the camel's back?). These will indicate the level of apology you must give for being a poor supplier and how much you should discuss the value standards violated. These also indicate the speed and level of attention you should use in pursuing correction and in getting back to the originator. Keep in mind, gathering this information is crucial to your own success, to the message that your own response will send and thus to your leadership.

Listening permits us to recognize support deficiencies the person accepts as a way of life. For instance, in the process of addressing the main issue of machine breakdowns or objections to policies or not getting the part on time, you may learn of tools that are not readily available or supervisors who will not answer questions or a tortuous procedure to get the requisition to the

Purchasing Department. Near the end of the interaction, those support deficiencies must be mentioned, an apology given and the item recorded by you for corrective action. This will help the person to be more demanding through following your leadership. Go out of your way to lead when an opportunity presents itself. The lead can be very short, but it must reflect a high standard.

Some interactions with subordinates create more questions than they answer. What's been left out? Is this a cause or an effect? Who was really involved and what loyalties exist? What if the tone of voice and body language negated what was said and if so, what is really true? Is some agenda other than getting the work done at play here, perhaps power? Is the person objecting about the straw that broke the camel's back? These issues do not complicate gathering, but the information itself may not be worthwhile in deciding how to improve support. Hipshooter bosses really get in trouble over these, while the deliberate gatherer patiently searches for reliable data.

Another guideline is not to ask leading questions if they lead to the right answer. Lead away from it or be neutral and alternate between these two. The exception is for people with whom you have regular interactions. For these, use all three cases randomly so that they will never be able to predict your opinion from what you say. Your goal is to make it very uncomfortable for yes men or any tendency in that direction. Removing that safe haven forces every person to think independently.

Your questions should be general at the start and move toward specifics in a series of steps, closer to the details each time. Responses show how tuned in to what should be done, how problem correction oriented and how close to 5Star your subordinate actually is. Level of independence and training become obvious. People who have trouble finding the bottom line or who jump to it so quickly that they miss relevant factors are in need of help. Do not foreclose gathering this data by starting with details. An example of the exception was given in Case 2 wherein the boss already knew the person well. However, most of our interactions are with people we need to know better.

The last guideline is bosses always have specifics that they want to know and if the person provides no threads or has no agenda of their own to prosecute, the boss can then pursue one of his/her own. Just do not forget that the supplier's needs always come second to the customer's. More about this under Chapter 8, GOTYP.

We have now seen how gathering data or listening depends on gaining answers to carefully designed questions. Since questions are naturally threatening to people, they can cause defensiveness as well as anxiety. Just being in the presence of a boss increases our anxiety and the higher the boss the greater the anxiety (non-5Star only). Therefore, a major goal of any questioning process must be <u>to relax fears and prevent anxiety</u>.

In view of this, I have chosen to present to you the procedure a boss should use to receive a problem report, certainly a most challenging situation loaded with pitfalls. Since reporting problems is our most important management rule, the procedure must certainly not shoot the messenger, but must welcome the bad news as another opportunity to excel. Done correctly, messengers will not be terrified to make the report and some few may even feel glad to do so. The boss will have made problem reporting something for which no one has a valid excuse not to perform. So here's the procedure.

DON'T SHOOT THE MESSENGER

1. Train yourself to physically <u>clap your hands</u> for joy and smile warmly as soon as you realize that standing before you is a messenger of bad news. Add a few words of welcome to reduce anxiety. Clear your brain to concentrate on listening.

2. Then allow the reporter to continue without interruption while you <u>smile warmly</u> as if you have heard some of this before (you probably have). Perhaps you can start to take some careful notes. Note taking always keeps us occupied, keeps us from missing anything and permits us to slow down the reporter.

3. At the end of the person's report, ask <u>very politely</u> if that's all there is or if there is more. Send the clear message you are in no hurry and that quality in getting all the details is your only desire.

4. The reporter may be ready to discuss corrective action and if so, take it now before you start asking questions. You might desire to reverse this, but remember we are far more worried about the <u>reporter's feelings than yours</u>. So do whatever the reporter wants. When the reporter stops, ask if there are any more details worth knowing. Do not assume that the report is complete until there is a definite statement to that effect. Then worry that some details have been left out.

5. Now <u>give thanks</u> for the information and appreciation for the person's effort to tell you. Perhaps a reference to your reporting rule can be made and how important that is to your being able to do your own job. "Well, that's quite a load, George.

Thanks a lot for bringing it. You know I've got this rule about reporting all problems, so I am really grateful that you brought it. If you don't report the problems, I'll never be able to do my job. This is really important to me and I appreciate your report".

6. Only now can you ask questions. At this point, you should have been able to gain composure and prepare yourself. You have had plenty of time to mentally note what's not been said, what's been implied that needs amplification, what the reporter's body language gave you that was missed in words and what was said but not clearly enough for you to understand. The reporter's body language should have sent relative importance, degree of hazard, whether there is more to the story and the like. You have also had time to compare this event with others in your experience so that you may now apply previous lessons learned.

7. So go back over the problem carefully with your questions, even to the extent of full repeats. <u>Do not be accusatory</u> or in any way place the reporter on the defensive. Remember, the person is on your team and vice versa so the questions must be professional, unemotional and matter of fact. You set the Tone. You might even explain this fact and that you want to ask some questions so you will fully understand the nature of the problem, and after all, making things worse by taking inappropriate actions is not your intent.

8. Beyond the problem itself, there are root causes that are the people problems of this book. Your questions must probe for these possibilities. Frequency of occurrence, similarity to other problems, association with particular groups or individuals as well as the reporter's tone and body language can be great signposts. "I don't want you to criticize your peers (or boss), but what do you think, George, about how the problem got started? How can we do better?" Careful, circumspect probing that begs for possible answers is the rule.

9. Any need for fixing people problems will slowly become apparent as problem understanding and its solution are developed. People problems can only be understood after some detailed discussion. The wrong order, miscommunication, the wrong goal, the wrong training or tool or procedure are so pervasive that laying blame on a people problem is not possible

until the very end of the process. Do not attempt it in the beginning as it will really shut down the problem report.

10. . Ask if the reporter has any recommendations as to how we should proceed, if not already provided. Ask questions to get all the details and the reasoning. People who spend time using their brainpower to figure out actions must be recognized and praised.

11. So the careful, <u>not aggressive but firm</u> questioning is done. The quality of the report will dictate the number and variety of the questions. There may be just a few. A by-product will be an understanding of the reporter and perhaps some practical training for the reporter to the extent his/her own homework was not completely done. After the above process, rest assured his/her next report will be of higher quality and will require less questions on your part.

12. Now ask if there is anything else that might be important to know in designing what we do from here.

13. At the very end, thank and appreciate once again, and <u>with a smile and a lilt to your voice</u>, let the messenger go. "Thanks again for bringing up the problem. I know it is not easy for you, but it is very important to me. Thanks especially for bearing with my questions and being so open with your responses (whether true or not, because this makes the next time better).

I recommend blind adherence to the above and a solid attempt to have your body language exude the positive, bright and cheerful tone intended. Every boss should welcome the tough problems with open arms because without them <u>you would not be needed</u>. Bosses can only truly earn their pay in times of great difficulty. If they get tough when the goin' gets tough rather than get unhappy or vengeful or rattled or reactive, what a great example, what great leadership!

Did I say leadership? Did the script above pass all of the value standards with an 8-10? Check it for positive attitude and enthusiasm and smiles and cheerleading! Check it for humility, fairness, forthrightness and "do unto others as you would have them do unto you"! Do your own evaluation!

Please make one important observation. The boss gave <u>no answers, opinions or conclusions</u>, choosing to concentrate on getting every possible input that the reporter could provide. The boss paid close attention to the reporter and not on thoughts, conclusions and whatever inside his/her own head. Most bosses are so busy with their own thoughts and deciding what they will say that they miss half or more of the communications emanating from the reporter. This is interpreted as being egotism or selfishness and leads in the wrong direction, away from selflessness and fairness. From such, reporters learn they will not be heard.

If the boss consciously uses the above procedure for receiving any problem from anyone, whether initiated by the boss ("how are your tools?") or not, it removes all pressure on the boss to somehow perform as the provider of all answers and all knowledge. It also allows the boss to concentrate on listening, questioning and not missing anything. Besides, after you have completed pumping everything possible out of the reporter, time for thought on what to do will be available. Many other people may need to be involved and should have a chance to provide input before proceeding. Do not jump to conclusions or make quick decisions or pronouncements. You only have one report, one of many sides. Be careful to get all sides covered before you err by trying to manage something that needs more facts to reach a conclusion or should be decided at a lower level in the chain of command, etc. Many possibilities exist and most of them indicate that keeping your mouth shut is the best policy until careful thought is possible. Don't be a loose cannon.

Bear in mind that the previously covered value of quality is a real key to the above. Taking a chance on providing guidance or direction or judgment that is of less than the highest quality, when there is no emergency or other condition that requires immediate response, is unnecessarily chancing poor leadership. Lack of quality always comes back to haunt us and using the wisdom of "anything worth doing is worth doing well" will pay you back many fold. Do not be pressured into being a hipshooter. Deliberately stop and show respect for the gravity of the situation, for the needs of leadership in general, and most of all, for the people involved. Take the time to do it right. This is termed "attention to detail" for bosses.

Coaching After Getting The Report

Listening often discloses an opportunity for coaching and this should be seized at the time. Let's look at the process.

Besides probing the problem and then probing for root causes, how about collecting signs about the reporter? What violations of value standards, Rationales, or principles became apparent? For instance, if open criticism of a boss or peer occurs, make note of it and come back to it after handling the main issue. Start with some careful probing -- "sounds like you get that pretty regularly" or "sounds like that really bothers you. Is there more to it" or "I can understand how you feel. I'd certainly tend to feel that way. What else happened?" Get a good handle on the problem.

Since the one who has the problem is right in front of you, it would be remiss of you not to take time at the end of the report to address a problem and coach before it gets bigger. If you are prepared to coach, it is very effective while the problem is fresh to yourself and the reporter. For instance, "While you are here, let me hand you a pearl of wisdom that has helped me. I can sense that you are fairly critical of your boss, for what you think are good reasons. I criticized my own boss in the past. I have since learned that it was an error and how to avert it. Having noticed you tend to do that, perhaps providing you with my own experience and what I have learned will be of real help." Then give the knowledge in Appendix A. Throwing in do unto others, choice, the serenity prayer about change (recall the discussion of having 30 different bosses in a lifetime), and the value standards of loyalty, respect for authority and humility gives you an overwhelming argument.

As a second example, postulate that Bob showed he was really down in the mouth about the problems reported. You start off with the same approach for this case. "Bob, while you are here, let me give you some advice about -------- . I've often felt down in the mouth over ------. Although it took me years, I finally realized that having a bad day over workplace problems is a bad choice and completely unnecessary. Why not enjoy it and have a good day? Each day is over at midnight and we never remember the bad ones. We aren't animals and as human beings we get to choose ---- (insert prepared speech on choice). Besides, my morale is not only very important to me but to ---- (insert speech on morale and effects on #2 and #3). Besides, when I feel bad I treat others poorly and ---- - (insert speech on doing unto others). Besides, when the going gets tough, the tough get going! Bob, you must take control, put a smile on your face and take charge. Why not ----- (remarks from Bob with appropriate answers, Rationales et al by the boss to any excuses like the moon was blue). Good luck and hit'em hard! Don't let anything get you down and remember to be good to #1."

Coaching from essentially pre-prepared speeches covering problems that reoccur regularly in the workplace because people are always the same is very valuable and greatly promotes 5Star. These 5Star development opportunities must be seized with great joy and not wasted. In addition, mention the bottom line of being strong and independent, taking charge, acting in accordance with his/her value standards, and that you want only what is best for the subordinate. If you smile and laugh at your own recounted errors, then smile at the reporter's error and keep a very positive tone throughout, the reporter will leave the interaction all charged up because of being coached. Coaching done correctly is very uplifting because it shows that the boss really cares about this person.

Anyone who is not uplifted by coaching such as above either has a serious problem or the coaching was of poor quality. Both require perseverance to achieve a solution.

The Key

The key to the listening procedure lies in your concentration to the tasks of Listening to and recording what you heard verbally and sensed from body language and tone. Concentration prevents you from shooting or otherwise turning off the reporter. As concerns the information received, make notes at least until you become proficient and afterwards for the longer stories. Equipped with this knowledge, you can later decide on courses of action to achieve your goals. Do not hurry yourself. It isn't important that anything be decided during the event with the messenger. It is terribly important that you don't shoot the messenger!

Appropriate action can always be determined afterwards when you are alone and can think without interruption. Then you can go back and modify any previous statement and/or correct errors of both omission and commission. With people, it makes no difference that it is done later so long as you admit to your error or oversight and apologize before giving the correction. Besides, the person will be impressed you took the time to think about it. This tactic takes the pressure off you to perform perfectly in the heat of battle, so to speak. And you will be more proficient when the next reporter or messenger arrives. After practice comes excellence.

UNDERSTANDING THE TRUE POWER OF LISTENING

PUTTING IN OUR TWO CENTS

(a stimulant known to cause brainstorming)

Now that we understand how to listen, let's attempt to grasp what we are really trying to accomplish.

First off, problems and difficulties occur in any work group with a predetermined regularity dictated by the 5Star rating of the group and the difficulty of the work. The lower the rating and the higher the difficulty, the greater the number of problems and the longer each remains before resolution.

Being 5Star can be viewed as a commitment by the employee to continually strive for excellence. The more committed they are, the more they act to find and resolve problems. The less committed (non-5Star), the less energy and thought they devote to correction and the more time they spend causing problems.

Secondly, I have heard many, many employees in the midst of a bad workplace say all they want is for someone to listen to them once in awhile. They state how great that would be even if little is ever done. That's real hunger! The obvious question is why should anyone turn on their brain in the morning if no one will listen? Why try to be creative to make improvements for the sake of productivity or quality, or make suggestions to reduce cost if <u>no one listens</u>? The answer is it would be dumb to try if <u>no one will listen</u>. "To hell with them! Why make any effort if they don't care what I think?" Leave your brain at the door!

The sad thing is many bosses, high and low, are so busy giving orders and direction that subordinates do in fact decide to leave their brains at the door. People with suggestions are viewed as trouble makers or complainers. "Shut up and get back to work." In this mode, no one can participate, be involved or use their brainpower. They can only be a number or a pawn, and <u>they know that no one cares</u>.

WHAT IF people could put in their two cents any time they chose and management would always Listen and get back to them with possible actions and/or answers?

WHAT IF they were allowed to add their two cents again on this response and the process would continue until management had decided on a course that seemed reasonable to everyone?

WHAT IF management only changed things after conducting this dialogue?

WHAT IF in response to questions, our bosses were forthright and provided the real answers and their whys?

WHAT IF management took this one step further and went out of its way to provide information relevant to job, company and anything that might affect or be of interest to each employee? (This would be the 52 Card principle in action, Chapter 4 under forthrightness.)

WHAT IF the working level could get in on the ground level with work plans and policies before they turned to cement, get in on what work and how it was to be done before starting?

Would You Want To Work In Such A Workplace?

GAINING COMMITMENT - This is really BIG!

To be committed, one must have ownership. To have ownership, one must be able to influence. And to influence, one must be heard and be reasonably answered. So when management does the "what ifs" above, subordinates are in reasonable control or ownership of their workplace. When nothing is done without their knowledge and all useful knowledge is shared with them, using their brainpower to figure out everything becomes a worthwhile effort and they are suddenly released to their own motivations, otherwise known as being turned-on! In this mode, control is rationally effected through self-control and commonly held value standards since they are the only criteria used to decide what is "right", by bosses and juniors alike.

The above is also a considerable part of the answer to the question of trust. With <u>protected rights</u> to knowledge, reasons and planned outcomes before execution, subordinates <u>own</u> the outcomes and can freely trust all because they themselves did it. The question of trust becomes less important and peace of mind prevails. There may be threats of external competition, but with knowledge and rights of ownership everyone will get behind slaughtering the opposition.

Note that in this mode, the boss provides information and assistance in moving toward 5Star so each subordinate can take charge and come to their own conclusions rather than sit around and Follow. In this mode, the boss has faith that people will effectively resolve issues on their merits and believes that authoritative declarations are self-defeating.

But too often direction gets in the way of ownership and this preempts commitment and 5Star. This is a "cart before the horse" error common to many management techniques and styles. The most basic reason may be that bosses have no faith or trust. They don't trust juniors to arrive at reasonable conclusions and thus deny them information, Rationales, value standards and listening. These bosses are being slowly but surely weeded out by the free enterprise system. I believe that a change to the above tactic will stop you from being considered a weed. <u>Leadership is trusting your subordinates to provide valuable input</u> and it is rewarded by their trust in you and their commitment to the job. It has <u>significant positive bottom line implications to your company</u>!

RELEASE THEM TO THEIR OWN MOTIVATIONS,

DON'T MOTIVATE

People can make good decisions if provided information and the decision criteria by which to judge it. In addition, they can be encouraged and cheered on to bigger and better things. I am not, however, a believer that they can be motivated. Motivations are within us and no one can gain full access to them. Most of us don't fully understand our own motivations much less those of another person.

This principle permits us to stop focusing on motivating people and start focusing on those actions that are easy to understand and implement. Cheering, encouraging, supporting, coaching, informing, directing, disciplining, leading and listening <u>must become practiced skills</u>. In the process, our people are freed from the <u>bondage of following</u> and handed over to their own values and their own motivations. When they march to their own drummer (5Star), their motivations will never cease to amaze you. Spend your time making conditions such that these flowers can bloom. The blooms are always of such surprising quality and variety that we wonder what it was we thought we were doing back in the days of motivating with carrots and sticks. While they have their place, carrots and sticks are only a very small part of gaining commitment through 5Star.

Following Up After Two Cents

Listening to complaints and suggestions is worthless <u>without follow-up action</u>. The desire to be heard includes this second aspect. If no appropriate action is taken or if no reasonable response is forthcoming, we become turned-off and will not bother to put in our two cents the next time. Why even turn on our brain to think about suggestions if no one will act upon them?

A response will not be considered reasonable unless it is timely and of high quality. As concerns simple issues, one or two days is enough. The remainder should never go beyond 1-2 weeks, although the timely response may only be a status report of what's being done and when a full response may be available. Bosses need to use their own common sense and value standards in deciding both timeliness and quality. "Do unto others as you would have them do unto you" is your guiding light, your Golden Rule.

With respect to quality, do not make a pronouncement of a new policy or of "the" solution. Make it, "this is what we are thinking of as a possible solution and these are the alternatives" and keep the door open to discussion and change. Extremely complex issues may require several discussions before attempting to design alternative solutions and then several iterations of alternatives may be appropriate. Keep quality before quantity in mind, but don't allow issues to be stretched out beyond the time your common sense would accept if you were the complainant or persons making the suggestion.

Allowing subordinates to put in their two cents fits perfectly with the most important management rule of reporting all problems. Timely and high quality responses will demonstrate high standards in forthrightness, humility, grit, fairness and just every day respect for the dignity of other human beings. These actions will speak far louder than words. This is <u>leadership in the caring values</u> at its best and sets standards that all subordinates will apply to their work. And it all starts with the boss being able to listen.

PROTECTED RIGHTS?

If creating commitment through allowing people to put in their two cents has tremendous value, what should be done to ensure its general use?

As followers, we spend an inordinate amount of time trying to discern what is expected of us. If some bosses listen and some do not, or even if all do not, we tend to accept that status and make no objection. If, on the other hand, we are told that being heard and receiving a reasonable response is the big boss' requirement, we will not want to accept less and will tend to press harder before giving up to have our two cents accepted into the pot by immediate superiors.

If someone takes this <u>right</u> away from us, we will also tend to make our displeasure known to higher authority for correction by them. This <u>natural control system</u> can only be placed into effect if the boss gives the process the status of being a <u>requirement</u>, a subordinate <u>right</u>, that the big boss intends to enforce upon sub-bosses. (This policy is, to my knowledge, the only one compatible with self-control by the individual through values.) Your Open Door policy is, of course, their safety valve for objecting to a loss of their <u>rights</u>.

Without clear guidance and without <u>frequent reinforcement,</u> foremen and middle managers will consistently place the needs of production above the needs of individuals. These bosses are trying to do what they think the big boss wants since most of them are Followers. In facing general responsibility for getting the work done, they are subjected to the considerable pressures of meeting schedule and cost requirements. As such, taking time out for people appears to them to be in conflict with productivity. If you recall the Support section on training, the answers to this discussion are the same as given there. Allowing people to be heard is similar to training, in that, without considerable attention and direction by <u>the biggest boss</u>, few below will have the grit to justify time spent on this endeavor. But as with training, the payback is far, far greater than the total costs.

As usual, exhorting sub-bosses to do better for people, to "do unto others as you ----", will be like preaching to the choir and will not achieve the goal. Success is gained by setting forth the rules as if they are subordinate Rights, providing mechanisms to conduct the process and collecting/addressing deviations. The boss must personally set the example and enforce compliance by others, be the <u>protector of rights</u>. The mechanisms for accomplishing this are GOTYP and Group Meetings, covered in Chapters 8 and 9 respectively.

Who Are Your Best People?

Our listening skills are particularly important to this issue. First, each person needs coaching in order to improve their own performance and each responds differently to coaching. Second, our subordinates become involved in the process of correcting support deficiencies. If the boss could know what a specific person had done for all of the events associated with these two functions over a period of time, this knowledge would provide an accurate picture of that person's capabilities and present status of technical development and becoming 5Star.

This knowledge can be gained through <u>patient questioning and listening</u>, through probing our subordinate's understanding and use of values, Rationales and principles and their execution of planned actions. Faking answers is very difficult with a boss who listens and whose questions rarely lead in the right direction. Faking the results to a boss who often takes the time to ask for all the details and who gets out of the office into the workplace, is simply too hazardous and thus will only infrequently be attempted. So our listening skills, including for tone of voice and body language, provide accurate answers of who our best people are.

Responses by subordinates to coaching and support correction reveal overall attitude, ability to change, willingness to accept criticism, level of respect for subordinates, creativity, status of being 5Star, effectiveness in creating 5Star people, leadership talent, attention to detail, technical aptitude, standards for all values and almost anything else you would want to know. These are always on display if we want to see them, to draw them out and listen to them. After gathering this data, we should be able to decide who to rely upon when the going gets tough, who needs what help and who to promote. But only if we use values, not our likes and dislikes (see Appendix B, Likes and Dislikes).

CONCLUSIONS

Listening is the door through which bosses learn about support deficiencies, needs for knowledge or direction, excuses provided by the boss, values or Rationales not understood or in use and the 5Star status of subordinates. Listening is thus the door to improved leadership for the boss.

From the junior's standpoint, listening by the boss is their door to commitment. If the boss answers questions forthrightly, is always reliable in following up with juniors concerning action, takes no action without their reasonable input and concurrence, and causes the use of values and Rationales as judgment criteria, subordinates can understand and gain influence over everything in the workplace. They now have nothing to distrust. Their new-found influence grants them a sense of ownership that in turn gives them commitment. All of this releases them to their own motivation and frees them from the bondage of following. They then will march to their own drummer using self-control through value standards and Rationales.

Listening is our most important managerial skill and only by its use can we start the process of providing high quality leadership through support. Too often bosses complain that their people do not listen when it is the boss who should do precisely that, a better job of listening. Only through listening can bosses cease their irrelevant preaching and hand control of the workplace over to its soon to be committed members.

Listening requires concentration and a conscious effort to record, analyze and compare the information received to other knowledge and then to ask the next probing question in order to fill in the blanks. Don't ever think about what you plan to say while others are talking and don't be distracted by something. Apply 100% of your brainpower to JUST LISTEN!

WHAT'S NEXT?

Where do we put to use all of the elements of managing people; of listening to gather data and turn on brainpower and morale, of coaching to generate 5Star and of demonstrating our leadership through support? The answer is that we must use them in everything we do; discussions, small or large meetings, one-on-one or one-on-few interactions, while walking down a corridor or in a plant, etc., etc., etc.

I shall address these opportunities as belonging to two mechanisms: the one-on-one mechanism of Go Out To Your People (GOTYP) or the one-on-many mechanism of Group Meetings. These mechanisms of the boss' leadership will be the subject of the last two chapters. These are where it all comes together.

CHAPTER 8

GO OUT TO YOUR PEOPLE (GOTYP)

GOTYP is one of the two most important mechanisms through which the boss demonstrates leadership, the other being Group Meetings. GOTYP is the boss going out of the office to find out directly from the people involved what problems they are having. Although the great majority of these problems are caused by deficiencies in the support that the boss has supplied, there are many others as we have previously discussed. The boss' leadership becomes clear through what he/she <u>does</u> and <u>says</u> about these problems. Since actions speak far louder than words, let's discuss the "<u>do's</u>" first.

WHAT THE BOSS "<u>DOES</u>" ABOUT PROBLEMS

Because businesses use human beings and errors are quite human, incorrect actions and the problems they cause constitute a steady stream. Problem correction rate can be equal to or greater than the stream only through strong leadership by bosses. Each of these leadership acts must consist of the boss finding a problem, something that violates value standards and adversely affects one or more people, and pursuing that problem to correction. These problems may involve technical and/or people issues. Finding a real problem affecting a specific person, fixing that problem to high standards and getting back to that person have a large positive effect; from the good feeling everyone has in knowing the boss cares and from the leadership that causes everyone to do more <u>problem solving on their own</u>.

Properly executed, these "do's" of leadership set the highest example for others to follow, show great respect and caring for people, and reinforce high value standards. If these examples are demonstrated with sufficient Repetition, subordinates will follow by correcting problems on their own and will overcome the stream. If not, the stream overcomes the people and the level of problems rises to a point where drowning may occur.

How does a boss know when enough of this form of leadership has been provided? For starters, there is no such thing as enough, but there is a number of leadership examples per week that may be sufficient. In order to gauge the number, don't bother to look at problem levels because the accuracy of any measurement system will make such data invalid. The answer is to measure the level of 5Star. If 5Star are in a majority and rising, you may be doing enough. If 5Star are in a minority but rising, you may not be doing enough. For other cases, you had best do a lot more and also find out if subordinate bosses are doing their share. The real guideline for quantity of problem finding and correction is overkill, doing more than enough to set and continually reinforce the highest standard.

WHAT THE BOSS "SAYS" ABOUT PROBLEMS

While in the process of leading in problem correction, time must be spent discussing the problem with the person(s) involved. This discussion includes the incorrect action(s) that led to it and some possible solutions. During this process the boss will be leading through what he/she "says", whether intended or not. To lead in the right direction, the boss must use values (Ch 4), Rationales and the Eleven Valuable Orders of Chapter 6, and send the message that the "boss is your supplier". Other principles such as the understanding and solutions given in Appendices A and B may also be necessary. These criteria as a whole provide the wherewithal to determine why a particular action was incorrect and what the correct action would be. Applying these criteria to a specific problem brought up by a specific subordinate sends the powerful message that we can each find solutions if we rely on our own values. The solution is within us!!

I am not proposing an exhaustive, all encompassing discussion of each problem. The requirement is for leadership; leading juniors to use these criteria to determine and control their actions rather than copying whatever happens to be in sight. The boss effectively leads by applying two or more of these criteria in a detailed manner to the problem at hand. This leadership will only be effective if what the boss "says" matches his/her future actions (the "do as I say not as I do" test) and considerable repetition is achieved. The rules for deciding how much repetition is sufficient are the same as were stated above for the "do's" of corrective action.

Leadership by what the boss "says" is an effort to reduce the significance of the problem stream created by people. If they use values and Rationales and become more 5Star, the consequence of their errors is reduced, if not the number. The overall effect is very positive and is synergistic with the "do's" of leadership through problem correction.

ADDITIONAL GOTYP GOALS

Beyond what the boss "does" and "says", Going Out To Your People (GOTYP) is also necessary in order to achieve the following:

1.   Show people the boss cares through finding out what support deficiencies exist and correcting them. This is also the important task of removing excuses (Chapter 2) for substandard behavior and leading through support toward 8-10 level standards.

2.   Determine if what people are doing is the "right thing" to do.

3.   Find problems that no one else is addressing.

4.   Gain real knowledge of "what is" such that the relative importance/priority of all problems can be understood.

Looking at the list above, it should be obvious the requirements of <u>doing and saying</u> can be met while executing goal #1 above. Likewise, determining if the repetition of leadership acts is sufficient by measuring 5Star can be satisfied in the same process. By correctly performing goal #1, the boss fulfills the most basic subordinate needs; to be cared about, to be respected, to be a full member of the team and to be able to put in their two cents. This is clearly a case where one stone kills many birds.

APOLOGIES

Since achieving goal #1 involves correcting support problems and all support is the boss' responsibility to provide to juniors, <u>knowledge of an error demands an apology</u>. Of course, there would be no deficiencies, only accolades if you were doing your job to a very high standard. If the person is complaining much about a very little thing and shows non-5Star characteristics, you owe an apology for not having done a better job of getting this person to be 5Star.

An apology is always warranted for one or more reasons. The most important reason for apologizing is to set the <u>proper tone</u>. Recall the previous discussions of humility (Chap 4), of supporting customers (Chap 5) and of coaching hazards (Chap 6). An apology by the boss meets all of these requirements <u>and thereby encourages 5Star performance by subordinates</u>. How else to get 30 to 300% productivity gains?

As with any apology, do it 3-4 different ways in the course of the discussion so as to leave no doubt that you mean it. This form of admission of error is very highly respected. Other than being what is expected at an 8-10 value standard for courtesy to others, apologies reinforce the subordinate's status of being the boss' customer and <u>leads</u> them to be more willing to bring up problems. Of course, if the boss takes no corrective action, they might never again bother to bring up problems.

But assuming your actions are reasonably effective, subordinates become even <u>more willing</u> to report and are <u>led to do the fixing on their own</u>. Since our goal is to conquer the naturally occurring stream of problems caused by human errors, we need action by everyone in an environment of few excuses, if any.

Apologies should cover almost everything.

1- If the person has been turned off over something done by their immediate superior, apologize for creating the turn-off. Since you were not there and don't know all related facts, you can't apologize for what was done, only for what the subordinate felt. "I never want you to feel bad and I apologize for whatever I did to cause it."

2- If something was supposedly done by the company or bosses that would definitely be bad if true, apologize. Say how you would have felt had you had that experience. Commiserate! State that if the person is correct in what they are saying, you can understand why they are upset. State that you will investigate and get back with whatever you find. Then do it in a timely fashion.

3- If lack of support originates from a group not under your control, apologize for not having gotten that group to respond. Never be critical of other groups as this encourages disrespect, discourtesy and a failure to cooperate. Take the opposite tack by saying you are certain they are trying to do their job, but you yourself will have to do better in working with them. Take the blame on your own shoulders, because it surely is your fault, and thereby avert creating a we/they atmosphere of distrust to exist. If you have already been trying to no avail, share that, apologize for your lack of effectiveness and ask the person for any suggestions or help they could give. In short, if it is bad news or good news, the 52 Card principle demands that you share it, but in a positive, constructive "what can we do better" manner. If the person is openly critical of the other group, you must change that by shifting to a discussion of compassion, humility, Rationales 4 and 5 of Chapter 6, and how to treat peers.

Think how you would feel and how you would respond if you were treated as above by your boss. All of the above constitutes respect, forthrightness and teamwork in action. Apologizing sets the proper tone, reduces the fears associated with talking to someone who <u>controls his/her paycheck</u> and makes the person a respected member of the team. Sharing the applicable information reinforces the apology and sets a terrific example. Note: the boss has not been critical of others and has not agreed, before knowing all sides of the problem, to anything except investigative action.

Opening gambits

Now that we understand apologies, the most important action to take in addressing support deficiencies, here are fifteen opening gambits for the boss to use to encourage subordinates to bring out those deficiencies.

1. What can I do for you? This is very powerful because it sets up the supplier-customer relationship. Since the first thing anyone discusses is more important than others, the junior learns that achieving high standards in the boss' support performance comes before the subordinate's performance. Talking about your own performance deficiencies first makes subordinates much more receptive to discussing their own performance.

2. Have I caused you any problems lately? This question moves closer to the nitty-gritty, again making clear your purpose.

3. Did we provide you the right tools?

4. Were you well-trained for your job?

5. Are the correct spare parts or materials immediately available when you need them?

6. Is adequate planning provided to you?

7. Do our disciplinary actions give you any heartburn?

Questions 3-7 may only get a weak one word response. If so bring up some specifics or ask why they believe "yes" or "no" is the answer. Since people are inherently honest, the great majority will give the real details if prodded and the boss will probably find a problem beneath the surface. The boss must be assertive to be successful in disclosing problems. Fortunately, this simultaneously supports measuring 5Star since in order to measure you must get the subordinate to do a majority of the talking.

8.   Are the corporate or normal human values in use? Honesty? Teamwork?

9.   Who decides what you do?

10.   How did you get your job assignment? (probes Anti-Robot foreman rules.)

11.   How do you rate your bosses?

Questions 8-11 probe the quality of leadership and direction provided. Is the person over-directed and how do they respond? The answers may tell more about the person than about the bosses.

12.   Where are we wasting time or resources?

13.   How could we improve quality?

14.   How can we improve?

15.   What opportunities are we missing?

5Star people respond easily to the 12-15 questions. They want to make things better and always have ideas. 5Star only have a problem answering if they believe the boss doesn't really care or doesn't accept 5Star people. They are not complainers since they are appreciative of whatever support was given. They don't make excuses since they have no excuse box. They may not complain about not having the right tool since they would make it or get it on their own if necessary.

Non-5Star are the opposite and would rather complain about everything. Bosses must not waste time complaining about the complainers or of seeing a classic battle between good and evil. <u>Bosses must be 5Star themselves, thankful for what they have and figuring out what to do to make it better.</u> Of course, the answer is to fix the support, remove the excuses, project high standards through high quality support, and then almost everyone will make a significant move toward 5Star. Peer pressure will then be on the 5Star side.

Now we have learned we cannot rely on our best people to tells us about the little deficiencies that make our support sub-standard, below 8-10. Not to worry, the complainers will be more than willing to do so. <u>Fix the problems that they report as quickly as possible since the payback is so large on a cost-benefit basis.</u> When the complainers have to really dig for a complaint, you know your support standards are in the 8 range and you are not providing many excuses. So don't waste your time complaining about the complainers, but take advantage of them to really improve your support. There will be far fewer complainers after you fix your support deficiencies.

The hazard to the above process is that bosses may listen too much to the squeaky wheels and not enough to their best people. This is easy to avert since <u>your best people are the most valuable ones to consult before making any changes required to correct problems</u>. They are the ones who must be given the opportunity to mull it over, discuss it, investigate it and change your first proposal, iteratively,_before implementation_. If they are made a part of the change process, <u>most problems will be resolved before they occur</u>. We shall see how that works when we discuss the corrective action procedure for deficiencies found during GOTYP.

COACHING DURING GOTYP

In the course of asking questions, a problem dealing with workplace conditions or a personal behavior problem may appear, or one of the conflicts (Chapter 3) or an "I'm unhappy with ---!" not associated with work. Take the time to do a little helping and coaching. You must, <u>at a minimum</u>, openly acknowledge the problem and show sympathy for the bad effects on the person; commiserate, empathize, share the emotions, <u>don't criticize,</u> <u>don't preach!</u> As time permits, discuss the applicable values, Rationales or principles and the solution. In short, demonstrate how one analyzes and goes about solving personal behavior problems. Then make a note to decide on future action.

The above completes "showing that the boss cares" through handling GOTYP support deficiencies. Since knowing the status of the 5Star goal is important, we now turn to it.

MEASURING 5Star DURING GOTYP

By measuring 5Star, the boss can identify people who need help to become superstars. A person who is less than 5Star needs help, but may be just one of many belonging to a subordinate boss who needs help in basic leadership techniques. If a boss' performance has been excellent, the majority of his/her subordinates will be closer to being 5Star than those of other groups. Therefore, measuring the extent of 5Star in people is also measuring the effectiveness of their boss' leadership.

There are degrees of being 5Star, actually a full spectrum from weak and dependent, non-5Star, to strong and independent, fully 5Star. Every boss must define the spectrum by choosing the left side, the right side and the middle position for each element of 5Star. The definition consists of what each person would be saying (words) and looking like (body language and tone of voice) if he/she was in front of you talking about a certain subject. So choose a subject and determine three points that would define the left, right and center of its spectrum.

When actually measuring, more than one subject must be addressed before the boss will hear and see enough to obtain a valid measurement. No person operates at the same point in the spectrum for all of their actions. If a person's average is 66% of the way toward 5Star from Non-5Star, their worst action may be 15% below the average, their best 15% up. A plus or minus 20 percent band may be a normal workplace deviation. Narrow, plus or minus 5 percent, deviation bands centered well above the midpoint of the spectrum are the 5Star goal. Young people generally have wider deviations than their elders because of being less mature. Wide deviations, especially for your better people, are signs of severe leadership deficiencies by the bosses.

How a person reacts to problems is the surest way to measure their 5Star status. As already explained, fully 5Star do not complain. The more "oh poor me", the closer to non-5Star. Are little problems a source of frustration? 5Star either fix them or do not worry about them. non-5Star leave fixing to others and are busy complaining and using an excuse box that 5Star don't have. Non-5Star look to the boss to decide and shun responsibility. 5Star don't believe responsibility is an issue.

There are many other signs. Here are a few:

1. Fairness. A big non-5Star issue that never gets on the 5Star priority list. Non-5Star may exaggerate while 5Star understate.
2. Team playing. 5Star are constructive and critical of very few people while non-5Star may be destructive and critical of almost everyone.
3. Values. The extent to which people use them to create action is another measure. 5Star use them to guide their actions, but non-5Star use them only to talk about others and criticize.

4.	Industriousness. 5Star are industrious and seem to be striving to work harder, more effectively. Non-5Star defend why they do not work or do so slowly and ineffectively.

5.	Strong and Independent(SI). 5Star are SI self-starters and as such supervisors are of little concern to them. They are also active initiators, but this may only be apparent if the boss looks at the details of their work to find the extra little things that they do to meet very high standards. They will barely take credit for these acts preferring "Aw, shucks". Non-5Star start nothing and are very concerned about supervisors who actually supervise. SI people are always industrious, but perhaps not for assigned work. In this latter case, the person has decided the company is not deserving or some other goal is more important than the work (Hitler was certainly SI, but use of his particular set of value standards had bad results for the rest of us). Newly hired SI, since they are also industrious, will almost on their own become well trained.

6.	Attitudes. A positive attitude may not mean a person is 5Star. Effective yes men always appear to have positive attitudes. Conversely, a quiet and almost unenthusiastic attitude does not mean the person is not 5Star. Non-5Star normally demonstrate a negative attitude in their bitching about everyone, especially those in authority.

7.	Timidity and meekness. Do not confuse it with non-5Star. I have more often than not found a tiger in their tank waiting to be released by the techniques of this book.

8.	Nouns and Verbs. 5Star use them to talk of problems while non-5Star use adjectives.

So when looking around for problems to solve and opportunities to demonstrate your best leadership, measure your 5Star problem, the effects of your leadership. In addition to "What can I do for you", ask about the most contentious issues (union-management relations or contract, policy changes, corporate profits, employee benefits, promotions, safety, or whatever). These are valuable for two reasons. Firstly, since they are often emotional, the real person tends to emerge and presents an accurate view of 5Star. Secondly, bosses cannot be seen evading these tough issues, hiding behind a tree, unwilling to discuss what the lower level really wants to know. "Bosses want to talk about their own issues, but never ours." Don't be two-faced or fearful. Leadership requires getting out there to find out what concerns your team members and giving your view of why the company is right. Besides, it is a great test of your policy or reasoning and <u>if your best people cannot support it, you need to move toward a change.</u>

Never forget that all cases of non-5Star can be assumed to be <u>the boss' fault</u>. These people need your help and they are your responsibility.

COACHING TO 5Star

As to improving 5Star, the big picture solution is for the boss to assiduously carry out the hows of this book. One of these is to address as many individual non-5Star problems as you can when they appear. The approach is always the same and the rules for getting on the person's team are those under coaching in Chapter 6. Below is a brief example for lack of industry.

1.   Is it good for you (#1) not to be industrious? Why? (Talk about job security and how the person's income is at risk since no boss wants people who hardly work.)

2.   Besides, what is there to be proud of and don't you take this lack of pride home to wife (#2) and children (#3)? Don't they get turned-off? What about your family if you lose your job?

3.   How about your fellow workers who are industrious? Can you expect them to always accept doing more to make up for you? What's fair about you taking home the same pay even though you don't do as much? Should you be asking for a pay cut?

4.   How about if everyone slowed down to your pace? Could the company survive? How about our customers and our shareholders? You think you deserve a free ride, but it's not OK for every other person?

5.   How about the plumber who comes to fix your sink at home? I'll bet if you saw him goofing off or working slowly, you would kick him out or refuse to pay half his bill. But for you, we should do differently?

6.   What are your excuses for not being industrious? They must really be good. How come you have chosen not to be industrious? Why can't you just choose to change? Maybe you owe all your fellow workers an apology for the way you have treated them. I'll

apologize to you for all of my support errors and will pledge to remove all of these excuses. How about you making changes for your own good?

The approach above is only slightly different than that given for attitude in Chapter 7, Listening (the second example under "Coaching After Getting The Report"). We get big dividends from taking the time to confront these problems, and where they are more numerous, by training subordinate bosses to confront them. As we shall see in the next chapter, Group Meetings also provide a terrific opportunity to demonstrate values and Rationales in action and to spread the good word of 5Star.

This completes discussion of our #1 "Additional GOTYP Goal" of showing people that the boss cares. This was the place where the boss was able to demonstrate all of the values covered in Chapter 4. This has been outstanding leadership in action and only through it will our subordinates learn to care about their work, their customers and each other.

The Last Three "Additional GOTYP Goals"

The last three, #2 of determining if people are doing what is right, #3 of finding problems no one is addressing and #4 of gaining knowledge of "what is", can only be done in the workplace. Even if the people are not physically there, the workplace reflects what they are doing and not doing. Neatness, cleanliness, care for machines and tools, safety and many other attributes present themselves to the careful observer. Things that are adrift, the same things looking different and deterioration are problem signs. Everything has a message attached waiting to be read, people included. Even the level of industriousness and training cannot be hidden. Bosses must get out there to see, hear and feel these messages because there is no other way to get a credible view of a workplace.

The #2 goal is of obvious importance to the first line supervisor who must gain personal assurance that the quality and quantity of today's production are up to standards and the steps to support tomorrow's are complete. But each level of the chain needs the perspective of all three goals so their actions can support the most pressing needs now and address the others thereafter.

Do not passively receive what you see and hear in the workplace, but ask the people why it is the way it is and if they think it is right. Probe them because they have been there and because you need to know what they know and what their Gut level judgments are. Besides, just showing interest may be enough to spur them to find solutions. And you need to hear 5Star status and reinforce teamwork.

So these last three goals are adjuncts to the #1 goal of showing that the boss really cares about other team members and will support them always.

MESSAGES SENT BY THE BOSS DURING GOTYP

Whenever any person can be seen or heard by others, messages are being sent and received. What those messages contain can only be controlled by the sender. For any boss, their significance to corporate success justifies making them positive.

A few smiles, eye contact, uprightness and neatness tell others the boss is confident we are doing what should be done. We may be in the midst of a terrible problem, but we can all take heart. Looking harried, slouching, a stern face and the like, all loudly proclaim a lack of confidence in the troops and a fear for the outcome.

In the process of discussing problems, praising accompanied by smiles for improvements or meeting high standards, loudly proclaims confidence that we will overcome. Without it, doubts will arise and constructive effort will be degraded. Praising with smiles provides subordinates a higher octane gas that gets their spirits up so they can charge up the next hill.

Our facial expressions, eye contact, body motion and tone of voice can either back up what we say or negate it. They do tell of our sincerity. They thus modify what should have been carefully chosen words and their effect may be as much as 93% of the message received. Just walking by another person without looking and smiling is dangerous. A look but no smile is negative. Make the time spent walking from one place to another work for you, not against you.

So choosing the right words is only a small part of sending messages and bosses must apply effort to making proper use of these other transmitters. It makes no difference that you "didn't mean to ---" or that you "intended to ----" because these are excuses that, like all other excuses, are invalid.

PROCEDURE TO ADDRESS CORRECTIVE ACTION AFTER GOTYP
(a procedure to avoid leading in the wrong direction)

Now that the boss has found what appears to be a problem, he/she directs an investigation to verify its existence/extent and to determine its solution. The approach is to involve all affected subordinates and whichever superiors are necessary to gaining the appropriate authority. In order to do the leg work, form a group from the lowest level affected with perhaps one interested person from management. Use the rules given in Appendix B for Committees. The size of the group depends on the size of the problem, but two people are enough for most problems.

The underlying goal is to gain commitment and <u>not to destroy any that already exists</u>. Because of the nature of commitment and its reliance on being able to add our two cents after totally understanding the change and its reasons, <u>commitment must be gained before implementation</u>. Waiting until after implementation is self-defeating and hazardous.

The person in charge of the effort should be the lowest boss having authority to approve the fix. If this person cannot afford the time, pick the next highest one who can. This person assures that the group accomplishes the following:

1. the problem is analyzed for validity, nature and extent. If not valid, the process stops.

2. everyone's rights to put in their two cents, up and down the chain and at the very bottom, are protected. See "<u>protected rights</u>" of Chapter 7, Listening.

3. the facts disclosed are all those needed in order to be convinced that a real problem exists and to develop a solution.

4. alternative solutions are determined, possibly through looking at solutions used by other groups or companies.

5. once a proposed solution is chosen, it and its reasons are circulated to all affected employees. This solution must include a plan for implementation with dates and responsibilities.

6. everyone's right to comment on the proposed fix and plan are <u>protected</u>. This is an iterative process.

7.   once the proposed plan is chosen, it will be pursued and follow-up action taken until such time as it is a part of the culture. Keep everyone advised of progress.

If the problem is a very minor one, some of the above steps may be combined, but <u>none may be omitted</u>. There are three reasons for this.

First, what may have appeared to be a problem may not be one after all and the real problem is something else. When people make an objection over something, the only certainty is that they have some dissatisfaction. The real cause may take some searching and may have nothing to do with the target chosen.

Second, anyone who was unable to be knowledgeable of the entire process and the reasoning behind the fix, and to vote/add their two cents will not be committed to making the fix work. <u>"Without influence there is no ownership" is simply another law</u> and without committed involvement by those concerned, no fix will work no matter how well designed. Therefore, only discussion of possible alternatives can be allowed until general agreement exists that the problem needs fixing. Once that light is shining, we may proceed to the actual choosing of a plan. The comment phase is also the phase of gaining commitment. If the plan is placed in cement before getting everyone convinced of its value, they fail to continue to think about it or develop commitment since they know that their two cents will not be welcome. So only after an iterative comment phase and general agreement on the plan, both the fix and its implementation, can we proceed to execution.

Third, lower level bosses in the chain are human beings too, no different than anyone else. Senior bosses cannot afford to find a supposed problem and simply give orders to fix it or to effect a particular corrective action. By so doing, they tend to destroy lower level bosses as well as people at the bottom. The alternative is to have these people assess validity and proceed from there.

BRAKE NOT ACCELERATOR

The boss serves as the brake in this process, never as the accelerator. Accelerator bosses cause stress and feelings of "its being rammed down our throats". They also cause the process to lose good judgment and brainpower.

Brake bosses allow subordinates to be the impatient ones who are trying to accelerate/convince the boss to allow the Indians to proceed to the next step.

In this way the boss, who supposedly has the best business judgment, can sit back and use it on every step of the process. Holding up the process long enough to gain commitment is the best use of the boss' authority and judgment.

In a perfect world, the bottom would be told of the supposed problem and then they would carry out all steps of the procedure. They would be advised in this effort by their seniors who would serve to ensure quality. Bosses would pay most of their attention to being facilitators and protectors of rights as well as of values such as quality, cost, respect and service to customers. In this way, each and every brain on the team is in use.

This completes the corrective action discussion except for two relevant comments. First, recognizing problems without persevering to a reasonable success rate in solutions breeds contempt of the boss. Second, since the act of GOTYP is one of leadership, quality is far more important than quantity. Get a quality product first and know what that looks like, feels like and tastes like. Only then attempt to increase the number performed while maintaining quality.

CONCLUSIONS

Armed mainly with values, Rationales and principles, the boss goes out of the office to be with the people in order to help with problems, personal or work related. The main points of GOTYP are:

1.   GOTYP is a major effort to resolve all types of problems through leading others to recognize and correct them in a high quality way.

2.   GOTYP is also a major effort to cause a reduced consequence of problems through leading others toward self-control and taking charge of their workplace while using values, Rationales and principles as the criteria to determine their own actions.

3.   The boss accomplishes 1 and 2 above by providing very clear demonstrations of each, particularly through apologizing for and correcting his/her own support errors. He/she chooses a leadership repetition rate and the targets of it by gaining knowledge of the effect of his/her leadership, i.e. by measuring the status of 5Star.

4. By performing the above, the boss demonstrates true concern for subordinates, real caring through listening. In turn they become willing to care about the workplace, their customers and each other.

5. GOTYP makes the boss a fallible human and creates teamwork through jointly solving problems.

GOTYP is recognition by the boss that information does not flow up the chain easily, that the chain can never fulfill the boss' need for knowing "what is" and that written reports must be eliminated. "What is" includes finding out what messages are arriving at the lowest level as compared to what the boss believes was sent. Similarly, GOTYP permits a boss to find out if his/her Eleven Valuable Orders are being carried out or sabotaged.

GOTYP gives bosses a first hand knowledge of what's going on in the workplace, without which they haven't a snowball's chance in hell of making the right decision or issuing the right order.

GOTYP is a one-on-one or one-on-few tactic for which there is no alternative. Its complement is the Group Meeting of Chapter 9. These two are the boss' most important mechanisms for leadership and neither can be totally effective without the other.

CHAPTER 9

GROUP MEETINGS

(our most powerful leadership mechanism)

This is the last chapter, the place where we put to use all the parts of this book. Group Meetings are the boss' most powerful leadership tools, but they rely upon a full understanding of all that has preceded this chapter. Keep in mind that <u>the science of managing people is the science of leadership</u>.

To get in the right mindset, think about GOTYP for leading through correction of support deficiencies, Listening during GOTYP for leading our subordinates to gain commitment through ownership and influence, and coaching during GOTYP to lead our juniors to use value standards, Rationales and principles. Can we visualize the positive impact of GOTYP on costs, productivity and quality?

What if we did GOTYP in front of 40 people? If GOTYP can lead people to solve more problems, to use their value standards to create less problems and to care more about the work and their customers, then doing the same with 40 people at a group meeting is over <u>200 times</u> more effective. If GOTYP can lead people toward 5Star and commitment, taking the same actions before a group produces an almost irresistible influence on subordinates to move toward them. Think about this and chew on the effectiveness of this kind of leadership.

The reasons for the over 200 times effectiveness are two; there are 40 people simultaneously being affected for each action versus one for GOTYP and your credibility before 40 people rises over 5 times. While the first reason is obvious, why does our credibility increase? One-on-one in GOTYP, individuals will not attempt much testing of what the boss is saying or doing, will not challenge or fight back even through body language. Because of this, subordinates can't be sure of the boss' intentions or if he/she really means it. <u>Fortunately for bosses</u>, in 40 person groups the dynamics change completely in favor of challenges, to the extent they are numerous and may even be abusive. In 40 person group meetings, each person can see 39 sets of other body language signals that either support or reject what the boss says. Either way, attendees become sure of the boss' intentions.

If the boss accepts these challenges using Don't Shoot The Messenger rules and takes the other actions recommended herein, he/she will pass these multiple tests with flying colors. In fact, a great majority of the audience will be

185

totally convinced; that the boss Cares, that subordinates should live by their own value standards and be 5Star, that the boss will protect their rights to add their two cents and receive reasonable responses, and that the boss will him/herself live up to high value standards.

They also begin to throw off the yoke of following in favor of being strong and independent (5Star). In a group meeting where problems and the criteria for judging them and solving them are openly discussed, a process in which the boss facilitates and guides participation, people practice using their brainpower and their own value standards. Repeated practice is exactly what is needed to convert followers from conforming to being 5Star non-followers.

Conducting this process in a group is the only way bosses can cause sufficient practice backed up by real credibility. GOTYP cannot achieve either sufficient practice or credibility. Group meetings remove all doubts and cause far more practice for the same time expended. For these reasons, they are an irreplaceable management tool.

So the boss conducts him/herself at group meetings as in GOTYP, making each one good practice for the other. But since people will say things one-on-one they would not bring up in a group and vice versa, and since meetings lack the physical reality of the workplace, the enormous power of group meetings cannot be fully tapped without the boss' knowledge through GOTYP of "what is". GOTYP prepares a boss with issues that will soon be brought up at a group meeting and serves as an investigative mechanism for issues brought up at past meetings. While being extremely similar, these two mechanisms of leadership are truly complementary and neither is capable of reducing the need for the other.

WHAT EXACTLY IS A GROUP MEETING?

The stated purpose is to provide a forum in which subordinates may bring up complaints, suggestions and questions about anything of concern to them and be provided with high quality responses at future meetings. This is a meeting for subordinates, a chance for them to put the boss on the spot and to question every aspect of the business in a relatively relaxed atmosphere away from the workplace. In a group the individual subordinate feels a sense of security, a sort of shield that permits each to be more openly critical of the boss' policies or whatever. As a group they can all gang up on the boss.

A group meeting is also their chance to interact with bosses higher than their immediate supervisor, to get answers not readily available to them in the course of the workday. It is also their chance to practice the 5Star trait of taking charge. Sufficient opportunity will exist if these meetings are conducted weekly or no less frequently than monthly and the group size is limited to about 40 people.

The basic procedures for the boss to follow during the meeting are that of Don't Shoot The Messenger under listening (Ch 7). After a meeting and all that listening, the boss uses the corrective action procedure of GOTYP in order to gain resolution of the issues that arose at the meeting. In this process, a boss simultaneously accomplishes the two GOTYP leadership functions of doing and saying, the first of the four Additional GOTYP Goals and important directions. That is, he/she can:

1. demonstrate the way to go about correcting problems.
2. demonstrate the use of value standards, Rationales and principles in problem solving and as performance guides.
3. show he/she cares by apologizing for and correcting support deficiencies.
4. provide the direction of the Eleven Valuable Orders listed at the conclusion of Chapter 6, Support Through Direction, in order to advance 5Star development.

All of the above can be provided in the course of addressing the complaints, suggestions and questions of subordinates at group meetings. All of it is leading by helping fellow team members to improve and providing them what they need in order to take charge of their destiny and their workplace. Being in charge is a promise inherent in our values and Rationales. The boss' function is to cause us to practice taking charge and applying criteria (values, Rationales, principles) to thereby prove this promise can come true.

What Can Be Accomplished at Group Meetings? - COMMITMENT and 5Star

Every employee wants to put in their two cents, to influence their environment and make it better. By listening and responding in a timely and high quality manner to complaints, suggestions and questions, the boss meets these needs and shows that he/she really cares about subordinates.

If the frequency of these opportunities is sufficient to more than meet their needs, subordinates will become extremely committed to the job and everyone reaps the benefits. The needs of all people include reasonable control and influence over all aspects of the workplace that can affect them. The foregoing must be the primary goal of regular group meetings and <u>must **never** become secondary to any other purpose</u>. In other words, don't have an agenda to which they must listen before they get to voice complaints. Bringing up an issue to get their juices flowing may be appropriate, but only to get things started. To do otherwise would jeopardize commitment.

Direct subordinates to talk back to the boss. The policy is to tell the boss when he/she is wrong, when anything is wrong, and almost demand that it be fixed so that work may proceed properly. "After all, don't I tell you when your performance isn't good enough?" Tell subordinates that to do otherwise is failing to stand up for relevant value standards and will always be a turn-off. And in order to succeed as a team, <u>whoever finds the problem must point it out so the rest of us can get to fixing it</u>.

This policy should be brought out in the course of discussion of some problem. Yelling and screaming about serious problems is acceptable, but yelling and screaming at the boss is unacceptable. Advise them not to be insubordinate or to swear at their boss rather than at the problem, but encourage them to stand up for what's right and to be good to (#1).

"But talk back! Bring up the problem. Be loud. If you are right, we will fix it. This place is everyone's place to earn their livelihood, no more mine than yours. We all sink together. Take ownership and don't let it get away. Talk back so that it doesn't happen. And if anyone holds that against you, that person is my enemy as well as yours."

At the same time, make clear your policy that the boss is the supplier of his/her subordinates and provides whatever support they require at a high standard. Explain this so they will know what to expect. Use your <u>forthrightness</u>.

And don't worry that a very few might misread your words. They will, but the tremendous gains of people taking charge of their workplace will make these few problems insignificant. <u>Instead, worry about not doing enough to unleash the power of your people.</u>

At these meetings, the boss will be demonstrating exactly how to listen and respond to subordinates <u>in spite of any abuse</u>. If the entire management team was present, wouldn't they learn how to give juniors real satisfaction rather than a brush off? And wouldn't subordinates also be encouraged to ask more questions and raise more complaints and suggestions, both at meetings and at other times during the work day? And wouldn't subordinates tend to ask their immediate superior, who is more available, knowing they could always ask the boss if that person did not satisfy them?

The answers to the above are all yes. In addition, everyone needs to learn how to listen and respond to abusive customers as well as to each other in a respectful, objective way, rather than in a defensive, emotional manner. In this we sorely need the boss' good leadership. If the boss can withstand being talked back to <u>and still listen and respectfully respond in spite of abuse</u>, the rest of us can certainly do it. This is leadership at its best in caring values. This leadership in how to treat customers will become more obvious in the discussion of "Agitators" later in this chapter. But it is a powerful way for a boss to demonstrate handling external customers.

Other than about the work itself, subordinates will have many complaints/questions about a myriad of fairness issues. Age, sex, race and other types of discrimination, unfairness in promotions and job assignments and discipline and overtime, concern over employee benefits and layoffs, mistreatment by bosses and safety on the job all fit into this category. Though personal and contentious, these fairness issues are of concern to everyone and are prone to word of mouth dissemination through the grapevine. As such they are particularly worthy of a public airing where their fairness will shine through the veil of bum rumors. These issues also affect "peace of mind" and can be very disruptive if left to fester.

In return, the boss will receive valuable input by which to correct problems of faulty procedures, policies and even specific acts. If left uncorrected, these constitute festering sores that may individually be of little consequence, but taken as a whole, create the clear perception of unfairness. These excuses to be unhappy and act incorrectly can not only be effectively removed, but the boss will have a truly golden opportunity to demonstrate outstanding leadership in the caring values, including admission of error.

As a single value, admission of error in the workplace cannot be taught, it can only be led by the boss. Bosses must embrace error as the long lost friend it truly is and do so regularly in front of groups of subordinates. Bring up your own errors if no one else will, but be happy for the chance to apologize and to clearly demonstrate the standard. Public admission is far more powerful than private, so welcome every opportunity because all subordinates sorely need understanding of the principle involved. Only this leadership can start them on the road to admitting their own errors.

There are a multitude of other issues over which employees have concern; quality, sales, profits, future plans and goals, expansions or contractions (layoffs), competition, changes in the workplace such as computers or robots or work measurement, new technology and any others that confront the company and its people. The boss demonstrates that we are in this together, all on the same team, by making information about them available. The more involved and knowledgeable the boss makes us, the more responsible, productive, innovative and turned-on we become. Dissemination of information at group meetings destroys the rumor mill and enables constructive criticisms and suggestions. Meetings are an opportunity to correct misunderstandings or miscommunications down the chain by hearing it "straight from the horse's mouth". All of this is the 52 Card Principle in action and it signals to subordinates that they won't be wasting their time if they turn on their brainpower.

Detractors

Ignorance of what is really happening makes people susceptible to opinion makers who are conducting anti-management campaigns for whatever reason. While these are present in any sizable work force, group meetings remove the detractor's power by eliminating ignorance. If not raised for airing by a junior, carefully chosen questions by the boss can prod any contentious issue to the forefront. Once raised, the boss unleashes the full procedure of listening, audience involvement, voting, and, assuming preparation, some on the spot information.

In fact, in order to maintain credibility among the troops, detractors are very often the complainant and thus the boss is presented with a golden opportunity to excel. The detractor's power is usually one of "Listen to me, not to them, because they are bad guys". Does the boss lose if a detractor's allegations are totally correct? Not at all! The boss wins by demonstrating 8-10 standards for all values, admission of error being one. A boss wants everyone to know that he/she cares and that value standards are the decision criteria to be used. The boss only wants to be right about these. If this comes out clearly, the boss wins by upholding high value standards and the detractor, who has been trying to run the boss down as a bad guy, is the only loser.

Bosses become losers by getting so involved in "things" they begin to believe they can be "right" about "things" as well as values. Arrogance like this always loses.

5Star Instruction

Every discussion of problems contributes to the accomplishment of management's most important goal of making everyone a superstar, a 5Star strong and independent person. value standards can be woven into the analysis of and response to every complainant's problem. The Six Rationales of Chapter 6, many of the principles and that the boss expects everyone to work in compliance with their own value standards, independently of others or of what they believe the boss wants, must also be woven into solutions. That everyone should be well-trained can be disclosed in problem discussions. industriousness can be demonstrated when responding to complaints and suggestions, but should also be discussed in association with an appropriate problem as a secret to success in life (Chapters 1&4). Success is an element of problem solving that the boss declares on a regular basis so everyone gets to share the good feelings that it always brings. It is participation in this problem resolving process that trains people to become 5Star.

The boss must at some point be explicit about 5Star. After several meetings and various uses of value standards and Rationales, and after everyone has begun to understand bosses are suppliers to whom they should talk back, the boss discloses the real goal. The boss explains that each person should be well-trained, industrious, strong and independent, and that the boss will support people with whatever is needed to achieve this goal. The boss must explain the reasons for this goal; it is the best for each individual, it is best for their fellow employees, it is best for the company and with it we should always be able to out-compete the competition. This is the essence of the Eleven Valuable Orders at the end of Chapter 6.

If juniors were previously provided a reasonable understanding of the pieces, putting them all together will be a real turn-on. This explicitly releases people to their own motivations and is a good time to explain that the boss cannot motivate and why. This admission by the boss makes all the pieces fit together and places self-control and 5Star at the top of everyone's priority list. Subordinates will begin to question, explore and implement these concepts. "It sounds like the bosses want me to use my own motivations, my own self-control system and be my own boss." Try your best to have all subordinate bosses play the same game.

Those people who are 5Star, or are close, show the most positive responses. They suddenly and individually realize their way is what the boss just described and non-5Star is the wrong way. No one knows who the 5Star are, but some of them will now individually attempt to exert more influence in the workplace. And as they do, they learn about each other and together begin the effort to gain control over peer pressure. If the boss is good to his/her word and perseveres, 5Star will become the new standard. If the boss doesn't make 5Star an explicit goal, he/she denies the group a very powerful vision, one that like all effective visions provides a standard against which to measure all future actions. With this clarity of purpose, a boss greatly augments the process of turning on people with self-control through values and of commitment through influence and listening,

The boss can further assist the 5Star move by addressing a few very positive aspects of taking charge of one's own destiny. In the course of discussing an appropriate problem, a person will show great frustration or anger. This is your cue. Explain the proactive approach to problem solving that is a positive attitude and getting your own way by using constructive solution techniques.

"We all have problems, you and I. We shouldn't let them worry or bother us. Don't waste your time bitching. Get your attitude up and when the goin' gets tough, get goin'. And there are many ways to kill a cat; talking back to the bosses, Open Door, EEO, Union Representatives, the National Labor Relations Board, OSHA, the courts and other state and city agencies. I have often gone three different directions at once to get mine resolved, hoping that I would succeed with at least one of the three. I will try my damnedest to help you with yours, but go over my head or wherever else you must in order to get it solved. That is your right and this is a free country. Never live with the bad effects.

Life is too short to permit that. Be strong and independent."

The above speech trains juniors to be strong and independent. It shows the boss truly cares for his/her people. It denies intimidation and releases people to their own motivations. It may appear to be risky, but it is only an admission of truth that anyone could find out on their own. But when the boss encourages us by sticking out his/her neck, it really sounds likes caring. Besides, this approach meets all value standards as well as federal and state laws. Check it for forthrightness, humility, selflessness, attitude and grit.

The bottom line is that group meetings provide a heat of battle credibility not attainable through any other medium and without them the path to culture change is far longer and more hazardous. That the boss really cares and really means what is said are easy to project. If you can reasonably believe the Rationales, value standards and principles in this book, and if you are an average or better, basically honest and responsible boss, being credible as the leader at group meetings will be easy. If, all of the above were attempted in one-on-one sessions it would elicit a question as to whether you really mean it, but when performed "in the heat of the battle" before a group it always receives "I guess the boss really means it!" In front of a sizable group, you are as if shouting from the rooftops. When the boss' message is <u>directly related to a real problem and therefore is not preaching</u>, Group meetings cannot be beaten as a communication medium. These messages are so uplifting and overwhelmingly positive that <u>many brains become turned-on</u>.

This completes the "big picture" understanding of group meetings and their power of leading people to take charge of their workplace. Group meetings are more than capable of changing whatever dysfunctional culture exists into one of highly motivated, creative, strong and independent people who live by high standards for all good values.

There are several more details or guidelines worthy of your attention while you keep the "big picture" in mind.

Specific Guidelines for Group Meetings

1. Reflecting on the first six pages of this chapter, it should be obvious the higher the level of boss conducting these meetings, the more credible they will be. Credibility and an ability to smoothly interject the Eleven Valuable Orders, values standards, Rationales and principles into problem discussions may be the most demanding elements of leading these meetings. I have seen

weekly small group meetings by foremen coupled with monthly large group meetings by a manager two levels above the foreman, with occasional visits by their executive. I have also seen weekly large group meetings run by a third level manager with occasional visits by his/her boss or their executive. Both were effective.

2. To provide everyone adequate time for complaints and obtaining information, do not hold less than monthly group meetings. If there are more issues needing resolution and more action to report back, conduct meetings weekly until caught up. Optimum group size is about 40 people. All employees, including all levels of bosses, should attend these meetings. Do not exclude anyone since that would not be teamwork. Forthrightness and openness are too important and it is equally important for everyone, sub-bosses included, to hear what the big boss has to say so there is no doubt.

3. Logistics? Coffee and danish are a good touch, although having an occasional breakfast or luncheon is appropriate to show you really value your people. Ensure the meeting place is quiet so everyone can hear. You will want a horseshoe arrangement of tables and chairs with the leader able to walk in and out from the open end. Everyone gets to see and hear everyone else and it isn't a classroom arrangement for preaching. This facilitates the process of interaction. Getting up close to people who ask questions, looking them right in the eye, leaning a bit toward them for very intent listening makes for good body language. Make sure everyone hears the question as well as your response. Walking around the tables and touching people is certainly appropriate and of value if it is done to get a response or to commiserate or such. Senior visitors can sit anywhere, but must get up and do some walking when engaging in the discussions. Don't stand behind a podium or behind anything as this creates a psychological barrier. Get close and let them surround you, getting on the same team and being part of "us" rather than one of "them".

4. Agenda? It's always the same; how to get people to object, provide criticism and add their two cents, only to find the boss wants it. Practicing to be 5Star and learning the boss cares are the goals. General information can be passed out, but it should be provided in response to complaints, suggestions or questions. To do otherwise is to waste the power of group meetings. To get things moving, the leader can ask questions of everyone just as in GOTYP. Don't look for what is good, but search out the bad. And ask specific people in the group if no one is offering to talk. You should plan ahead as to who these specific people might be and how to ask a question they won't be able to evade. Most of the time, this will not be a problem. Examples: "Does anyone have a complaint or suggestion they'd like to have answered?" "George, as a union

194

steward, what am I doing to screw you up?" "Barbara, any tool problems down on the floor?" "I know you really want to go home in one piece, Bill. Are there any unsafe conditions I should be fixing?" "I sure fouled up the ----- last week. Have I done any others?"

5. Shooting who? The people are always having to take the boss' orders and take the flack whenever they make an error. Meetings are an opportunity to reverse the process, a time for the troops to shoot at the boss. Let them do it, tell them to do it, encourage them to do it. Tell them they can't embarrass you no matter how tough the question or complaint. The power of bosses is often almost overwhelming to many people. You become far more human, more approachable and more of a team player by clearly admitting that you are responsible for many things (support) that have the potential for making their life/work more difficult. "When you do something wrong it's my fault. It's something I failed to communicate, a wrong tool, insufficient training or planning or what-have-you." Admit they are your customers for these things and deserve excellent, high quality service from you. Tell them that you will not succeed in your job unless you Listen to your customer, so here you are, ready to take your beating, ready to demonstrate positive reaction to criticism so fellow employees will be led toward the high standards. "Shoot away! Talk back to the boss!" Besides being absolutely correct, this admission to them at a meeting has a powerful indebtedness effect, as it does on any customer. They will also enjoy having the shoe on the other foot and you dearly need their input. Thank them for it, apologize for making problems and promise to do your job better in the future.

6. Whatever you do, don't become emotional! You must retain your objectivity and stick strictly to the Don't Shoot the Messenger procedure as modified herein. Take none of this personally! It's only business and someone may try to get your goat. Be ready to receive abuse and prove that you are a big enough person to take it with a smile. It's their turn to shoot at you. Show them how to receive flack gracefully. Stick to the procedure, let them blow while you smile. You are not in a contest of wills. You are trying to prove to an entire group that you care and that everyone can have a turn at putting in their two cents, a full turn but not at each meeting. They can't embarrass you since you are the boss. And you are not going to fight or argue or get angry with them because it's their turn to be demanding of service from you. In this meeting, you are the supplier. So throw yourself in the mud so they can walk over you and not get the mud on their feet. That should set the tone!

7. More on Don't Shoot the Messenger. If you do it wrong in front of a group, everyone realizes you are just like they feared. But do it correctly and

everyone feels encouraged, uplifted, respected and appreciative that the boss will listen. This is indebtedness! Really great! Since the basic procedure for handling each complaint in a group meeting is <u>Don't Shoot The Messenger</u>, please briefly review this procedure in Chapter 7. The complaint, suggestion or question given at the meeting takes the place of the messenger's report. Some tips:

A.   When you get to the questions of step 6 in the Don't Shoot the Messenger procedure, <u>make certain to be unaggressive and unassertive, merely curious</u>. You may want to start by restating the complaint to ensure what you heard is what was meant and to ensure all 40 people are on the same subject. Summaries can be used to gain concurrence and permit you to gain control in order to focus your questions. The person may not want to give more facts and you must accept this so as not to offend or give any appearance of <u>belittling or embarrassing the person</u> in front of others.

B.   After step 7 as concerns complaints or suggestions, and certainly before you put in your own two cents, ask if anyone else would like to agree or disagree with the messenger or want to add anything. Get some discussion going and if no volunteers appear, ask specific individuals. Don't let them be bumps on a log. Cajole them to participate in their workplace. Once they find you are not critical and will not embarrass them, they will want to participate and <u>thus starts ownership and commitment</u>. Ask the group for the solution and the judgment criteria. You are attempting to have people take charge of their workplace so try hard to get everything from them. Once they realize the process is very similar to what they must do in their private lives, they will turn on their brainpower and take charge.

C.   Was the complainant upset or was there reason to be upset? Did management make an error or might they have made an error? If the answer is yes to any of these four questions, apologize for upsetting the person and/or making an error. Don't focus on whether or not you personally made an error. Show concern and caring for their being upset. "I'm sorry I have upset you. I know you don't need to feel bad and believe me, I didn't intend for it to happen. Let's see what we can do to figure out what's needed to fix it." Or, "If what you say is correct, I'd be mad myself (or I'd want it fixed as well). Thanks very much for bringing it up and I apologize it got that way. Let's see what we can do to figure out what's needed to fix it." These will defuse the emotion or anger about management error. These are particularly effective when promising that an error made in the past will not be repeated.

D.   So who's view of the alleged problem is correct or if only one, does everyone agree? Take a vote on the opinions and get the voters to tell you why they voted as they did. Only then tell them who you think is right, wrong or you don't know and why. This is your time to bring in applicable values, Rationales, Valuable Orders and principles. And as you bring them up, get the people to comment on them or state their own opinions. Discussion is a must to get everyone's brain functioning and to practice 5Star.

E.   An Example. One person complains of intimidation by a foreman. After listening and questioning, take a vote of whether feeling intimidated is good or bad for the person. Get one or more of the good and bad voters to explain why good or bad. Get others to explain what the person should do about it. Ask one or more bosses present for their opinions. Then finally provide the "right" guidance as you see it. Certainly include strong words that attempting intimidation of another person is unacceptable and feeling intimidated is likewise unacceptable since it is a bad way to treat yourself (#1). The boss should also say what he/she would like to do to the offenders, management or otherwise. Bring up value standards and Rationales. This is a real live opportunity for explaining how a 5Star person should respond and everyone wants to be a superstar. As best you can, make this into an interactive discussion in order to keep the most number of brains functioning. <u>Don't be caught preaching.</u>

F.   Assume in the above example the person was unwilling to provide the name of either the offender or the victim. Since this prevents coaching of offenders and apologizing to victims, after discussing intimidation the boss should take votes on the reporter's performance. Did it meet the rules for reporting of problems and the values of forthrightness and teamwork? If an excuse was given, was it valid? In this process, the boss presses to gain an understanding of values and how excuses degrade our actions, <u>but does not criticize or berate the reporter in any way</u>. The boss accepts that we all must make a choice about how much to expose ourselves while we take Care of #1. Make clear your choice would be to try to stand up for what is right, but you respect other choices. So discuss all aspects, but <u>don't in any way be critical</u> since that would turn off the brains you are trying so hard to get started.

G. The voting procedure above is used to get everyone into a discussion of whatever complaint or suggestion is offered. It is also used to start discussion on whether a particular action meets standards and why. <u>Remember, the boss is not attempting to solve problems at the time they are brought up</u>. The boss is only attempting to demonstrate a process and lead everyone to practice it. Causing people to carry out the process is the only way. The process uses value standards, Rationales and principles with the boss as facilitator and leader, not as participant, and 5Star as the goal.

H. And how about the professional agitator? You will not get any points from the crowd for shutting up these people. Let them speak their piece. Ask polite questions to draw them out more, but never shut them off. The group will eventually get bored as they berate and belittle and abuse you. If you allow them to continue, listening intently, asking a few questions and taking notes, you make points with the crowd and the agitator loses points.

When he/she runs out of steam, ask for more and you can tell from the group's faces whether it has been too much. With enough encouragement from you, real agitators will go too far and say too much. They will lose the backing of the group and will eventually, after several meetings, be told by the group to shut up. If you handle them without counter-attacking, agitators in general will not want to play this losing game. If they object to something in the past, besides listening you can disarm them by <u>admitting to the past error and apologizing for it</u>, whether yours or a predecessor's.

When the agitator stops, get opinions from other people as to what they think happened or how they feel about it. Other bosses in the room may want to give strong rebuttals, but don't allow much of that unless it would present a viewpoint that the troops do not normally hear. If you allow bosses to give their views, <u>act as a facilitator and do not take sides</u>. Go away and decide what you should do later. <u>Don't Shoot The Messenger and don't be a loose cannon or hipshooter!</u>

Normally, agitators show high negative reactions toward bosses. They appear to be stressed out and extremely upset about the terrible things these bad bosses are doing. You'll never know if they really mean all this or it is a show. In view of their stressed out condition, what you as boss owe is some human compassion. So, after carrying out Don't Shoot The Messenger, you might say "When I see how upset you are, I know this situation is having a terrible effect on your peace of mind, probably your health, and certainly the peace of mind of your spouse and children. If I believed my bosses were as terrible as you describe, I wouldn't hang around. No one could keep me from getting away from such people. We all owe this to ourselves and our family. We must take Care of #1, #2 and #3 and since this is a free country, no one can stop us from doing it. It's our choice. Besides, our action will encourage others to do likewise." This advice is one more way to make people believe you want them to be strong and independent and do whatever is necessary to stand up for what's right.

The only error a boss can make is to get into the fray with agitators, to defend the fort under attack or to launch a counter-attack. You are performing in front of a group and they want to know if you will use your power to help the little people or to crush them. They are watching everything you do and attacks by you are the same as crushing. Being strong about high standards is your bag, but arguing over conclusions with your little people in front of others is a big mistake. Demand equal time for all to express their opinions and don't allow battles in which we win or lose. We should all win and it is up to the boss to make certain we all do by getting our turn to put in our two cents. If nothing is resolved, if differences exist, that is OK. The key is to keep talking, keep holding the meetings, keep trying. <u>There should never be winners and losers on the same team.</u> <u>They should all sink or swim together</u>.

I.   Raising your voice? If done to make a point or for emphasis, good. Done to be heard over someone else in a group would be a bad example for a boss to set. Give other people time to speak. Then take time to give your view. They all dearly want to hear your view, but they also don't want theirs shut off. If you are pressed for time, recall the principle of quality before quantity. Do less with less time, <u>but never short-cut quality</u>. This is leading in attention to detail.

J.   When as the big boss you are attending a meeting conducted by a subordinate, don't be a passive observer. Whatever you allow to occur will be understood as your standard. If your subordinate is making an error, step in before that particular event is over and demonstrate the correct thing to do. If he/she did not listen, you must demonstrate listening to the person affected and then try to hand back control for the answer phase. If the answer given is incorrect or incomplete, step in and redo that portion. You aren't trying to protect incompetence in bosses. You should be trying to convince your employees that you will listen and act, that you care about them. If you allow errors to go uncorrected, you obviously don't care about the people as much as you do the bosses and this is the wrong message for everyone to hear. Besides, subordinate bosses will learn from your bad example and get the message bosses are more important than subordinates. You can discuss the whole thing with the bosses afterwards to ensure they learned the right things from it. Bosses sacrifice themselves for the troops, not the other way around. Besides, aren't we all on the same team?

More Guidelines

Whatever complaint, suggestion or question arises, do a high quality job in handling it. Don't be rushed to get on with the next one. It matters not how many issues are addressed, only that they are addressed to everyone's satisfaction. If more issues exist, hold longer and more frequent meetings. The first might be allowed to go 3-5 hours. Later they can be reduced to 1-2 hours. Play this by ear. The goal is to satisfy your subordinates' needs to be heard and to practice 5Star problem solving.

Prepare yourself to make these meetings be fun. Make people enjoy themselves and have a few laughs. Laugh at wrong votes and laugh at errors, particularly your own. Laugh at them shooting at you and apologize for your support errors. Don't let these meetings get too heavy, <u>lighten up</u>. Admit some of your best laid plans didn't work, even if you meant well, and find the humor in that. Smile. After someone has put a lot of heat on you, step back, smile, say that what you have just heard is too tough for you and in jest ask the nearest foreman to take that one. Break the tension when it gets too heavy. Remember, everyone present shares many common bonds; values, wanting a happy and enjoyable workplace, wanting quality work, wanting a paycheck, wanting safety and the like.

<u>Don't preach</u>. Don't preach to the choir. There is a fine line between helping and preaching. You know what it is when someone does it to you and how you don't like it. Don't do it to anyone else. Think about it. Use your humility. Don't get caught telling adults that way is up or explaining motherhood and apple pie. Bring up a value in the context of fixing a complaint or of answering a question and ask others if that value has been met and why. Get others to discuss its application and provide your own thoughts (given in Chap 4) only when they add to the knowledge base. Rejoice over values and tell stories/experiences that explain them, but if a story or parable doesn't come to

mind, <u>stop and come back to help another day</u>. <u>Don't preach</u> by exhorting people to pay more attention to detail or to be more industrious!!

<u>Think about your non-verbal communication</u>. <u>Don't forget the distribution of 7 percent to the words, 38 percent to tone of voice and 55 percent to body language</u>. Practice making your tone amplify your words. Practice being animated by moving your hands and body in tune with your words. I throw my eyeglasses (plastic) as a punctuation mark. I also throw up my hands, put my head down and/or pretend to cry, clap my hands over my head with a big smile and perform many other antics in order to reinforce the very weak (7 percent) communication from my mouth. Raising and lowering the voice, to a shout or bare whisper, also have their place. Practice makes perfect. Practice one-on-one and practice in groups.

Since the entire management team is present, use them. When an issue arises for which one or more subordinate bosses probably have first hand information of what or why, require their input as part of disclosing facts. If they are right, wrong or in between, admit it. They are just as much in this as you, the big boss, and they should "stand up and be counted" and admit to their errors if that is the case. These actions will make crystal clear; we are all on the same team only with different jobs, excellence and correction of errors is our goal, no one is deserving of special treatment or protection and forthright candid honest responses are requirements on everyone. If your work force at any time thought the rule was "management is a team against the workers", <u>these actions will dispel those fears</u>.

Group meetings for management alone, at least bi-weekly, must also be held. While they have the same needs as the working level concerning complaints and suggestions, they also need to understand answers well enough to be able to play a leadership role. Higher level bosses must therefore devote considerable time to middle and lower level managers in imparting this understanding and knowledge, on a weekly or perhaps even a daily basis, as necessary to meet the need. The knowledge presented in this book is the foundation for this effort, but it must be applied on a daily basis in the course of routine work in order to reap its benefits. Management must function as a cohesive team and only frequent meetings can generate a coordinated and consistent management approach to workplace opportunities. This is your way of respecting the "oink" principle of the need for repetition.

Group meetings can be effectively conducted by any average boss who is not dishonest, overly manipulative of people, or overly lacking in standards for human values. Even the making of errors is advantageous as long as you admit to them at the next meeting and apologize clearly. Proving your own fallibility is a strength and demonstrating you can learn from errors is valuable leadership for subordinates. There are, in fact, no errors possible from group meetings that cannot be turned to an advantage. No special genius is required, only admission, apology and correction.

Votes, Thumbs Up or Down

Group meetings allow the boss to receive Gut level votes on the acceptability of his/her actions, policies and procedures. When your best people vote you down, you know whatever you did was terribly wrong. If they vote up, you have done something pretty well and if sideways, you missed excellence by quite a bit. While the best people don't always know why their Gut reaction is the way it is, bosses must listen to these votes and then work hard to determine exactly what is in need of fixing.

Use of "Don't Shoot the Messenger" permits us to probe and probe and probe, get everyone's input, and then go away to think and analyze. Often it is not the object of the complaint, but how the boss went about introducing or implementing it that caused the negative reaction. Or maybe it's the straw that broke the camel's back. Actions that meet all the requirements of high value standards will always get an up vote. And if you believe this, you can readily determine your own effectiveness by listening to the comments/votes of subordinates.

<u>Finding out what subordinates care about and fixing those as a priority matter will always be more productive than most other initiatives.</u> Don't become defensive and erect higher walls around your fort. Accept that an employee who is objecting believes they have a good reason to be unhappy and your job as boss is to make a solid effort to resolve that objection.

GROUP MEETING RULE

The most important rule for meetings is while discussion is necessary, <u>no final solution or answer need be given at the time of receiving the complaint or question.</u> If you think you are pretty good at providing answers, practice not giving them for a while. Instead, design great solutions away from the heat of battle and then go back and give the really respectful, "yes I value you as a fellow associate" answer that results in a satisfied, happy person. You will get many points for getting back since everyone knows it's always easier to give a quickie at the time and save a trip back.

Most importantly, by waiting until the next meeting to give full answers you will significantly raise the quality of your responses. Eventually you will be able to provide partial answers of the same high quality at the time of the complaint. Remember, the principle is that <u>quality is far, far, more important than quantity.</u> Using this rule stops you from giving brush-off answers like "We've always done it that way" or "But that's the policy" or "It couldn't really be that way since our practice is to ------". Whatever errors you cannot prevent through this rule can easily be detected by listening to the votes of your best people. <u>Attention to every detail of your leadership and correcting every major or minor flaw should be your goal. Isn't this the standard you expect of production down in the trenches?</u>

Two Last Reminders

For taking action on what you learned at the meeting, follow the corrective action procedure of GOTYP. Only through it can we prove the boss will <u>protect subordinates' rights to influence</u> all aspects of the workplace. If their right is not protected, they lose their commitment along with their influence. So do not put a solution determined after the meeting in cement without getting considerable feedback, at the very least some of it at the next meeting.

Group meetings take time away from the job. As with training, middle and lower level bosses will never on their own conduct meetings because of fear of censure for wasting valuable production time. Senior bosses are able to realize the productivity gains alone will be several times the cost, to say nothing of gains in quality and safety. For executives, this becomes one of those times for directing. Direct that group meetings be conducted regularly without fail for everyone, no exceptions. And then enforce this rule and attend at least one a week yourself to help bosses to gain proficiency. Slowly, but surely lower level bosses will learn the gains far outweigh the costs.

PREPARATION

Prior to your first meeting, study and one-on-one practice will develop the necessary skills. Values, Rationales, the Eleven Valuable Orders and the principles in the main sections of the book and in Appendices A and B should be fairly committed to memory. <u>Proper listening is a must.</u> Practice using this knowledge during GOTYP and one-on-one sessions in your office. It won't take long to feel reasonably comfortable, like breaking in a new pair of shoes, since all of these elements are so in tune with our nature.

When you conduct your first meeting, have someone there to critique you against the rules. Don't be afraid to make errors since each will make a great apology for the next meeting. Besides, you will be acting so completely different than what a conventional authoritarian model would dictate that your people will quickly note the change. Once they recognize the change, your people will become very forgiving of your admitted errors.

As concerns subordinate bosses, demonstration and coaching by you as well as the same preparation steps above will be more than sufficient to overcome any hesitation. The great feelings and results that accrue after doing it right make the entire effort seem too small a price for gaining such outstanding results.

WHEN ARE WE READY TO START GROUP MEETINGS

The troops are ready for group meetings any time. At first, they will suspect them as being the next management gimmick, but if you follow my guidelines, they'll quickly become very thankful.

However, management levels between you and the troops may not be ready. For them, group meetings are revolutionary, dangerous threats to their ability to control the work force. If discipline has been somewhat lax and holding people accountable for what they do has been more the exception than the rule, these bosses may believe they can get away with openly resisting change. As their senior boss therefore, you must at least have embarked on squaring away your support systems and <u>demonstrated you have the grit to continue</u> before middle management can be considered ready. Once you have demonstrated a strong but fair hand on the helm, these lower level bosses might voice skepticism of "talk back to the boss" and "self-control" through values, but they won't dare sabotage your efforts.

If you pay strict attention to the details of your leadership, the response by your troops will amaze you. They will demonstrate indebtedness and appreciation for being released to their own motivations. They've been wishing for the day they could try out their own ideas, rather than just be a robot or another number. They will seize this opportunity in a serious and grateful manner and will try hard to be worthy of your trust in them.

IN CONCLUSION

There are very few original ideas in this book. The book's contribution lies in fitting together many pieces into a coherent, compatible, comprehensive whole and in providing the glue of compelling whys to hold the pieces together.

The book's only startling revelation is that 5Star non-followers can be a majority rather than just a small minority, and that every person has the potential to be 5Star. While working to high standards through following the boss's lead is a big step forward, being freed from the bondage of following to our natural 5Star, strong and independent, non-follower self is real glory. For the boss, the power of 5Star people is truly awesome because of a myriad of reasons; 300 percent productivity gains, reduced costs of turnover and sickness and absenteeism etc, worries about change/diversity/conflict disappear, anxiety and stress almost disappear, morale is high, and creativity and innovation become abundant.

The boss' role is that of a gardener who, *in harmony* with Mother Nature, brings forth a great bounty. *Harmony* is the key. <u>The boss must act in</u> <u>*harmony*</u> with the concept of 5Star and the three human characteristics shared by subordinates; identical good and bad values from which stem important traits, most of us being followers, and an innate ability to choose. The road to *harmony* is paved with high quality leadership through supporting, listening, GOTYP and group meetings. Paying attention to every detail of your leadership is your road to excellence. In accordance with the natural law, *"you will reap what you sow"*.

Please read the Appendices since you will need the hows and whys of their principles in order to march down the 5Star road with flags waving!

THUMBS UP TO MANAGING PEOPLE,
AN EXTREMELY SATISFYING ENDEAVOR!!!!!

APPENDIX A

WORKPLACE CONDITIONS

The chapters of this book have provided whys and hows for conditions that are a part of any workplace, such as discipline, training, peace of mind, coaching, conflicts and leading/following. There are thirteen more recurring conditions for which bosses require whys and hows. They are; bosses, peers, change, bureaucracy, unions, customers, priorities, competition, relief of the boss, communication, committees, discrimination and life's problems. As we enter the workplace, we have little knowledge of how to effectively manage these conditions, even though they have a considerable potential for disruption of ourselves and our bosses. On the job trial and error or learning from peers are often ineffective and frustrating.

But easy to understand and effective solutions do exist. If our boss helps us with these when we are experiencing problems, we are very appreciative, even indebted. For the boss, finding a need and coaching to provide the knowledge necessary for excellence are the mechanisms to prevent the frustration, disharmony and lost productivity that otherwise result. It should not be surprising that the solutions comply totally with 8-10 value standards and the six Rationales. I will start with a discussion of bosses and a prevalent misconception that can cause frustration in subordinates.

BOSSES - Can the Boss be a Friend?

Everyone has an opinion on this issue. My experience indicates an overwhelming majority believe the answer is yes. Whatever your opinion is, the correct answer should be discernible through analysis.

Friends accept each other warts and all, enjoy each other no matter what, share many things and above all, act out to each other that a friend in need is a friend indeed.

By comparison, juniors do not have to like bosses, but must carry out their orders. Subordinates are valued by their bosses in proportion to their success in execution. The smart ones go to their boss for help.

Conversely, bosses treat juniors to orders, instruction, correction, reprimands, discipline, praise, promotion and demotion. In addition, they are obligated to lead, support and develop the junior.

Do the above three descriptions appear in any way to be equivalent or even similar? The answer is a resounding No! In fact, the friend/friend and boss/junior relationships would appear to be at opposite ends of a spectrum.

The only apparent connection I can find is when the junior is in need, the boss should support and help the junior wherever possible. This could extend to just a shoulder to cry on or some advice or time off to handle a personal problem, possibly a leave of absence, or whatever. But in no case should the boss go to the junior for similar succor when the boss has a bad day in the barrel. In addition, juniors do not have power over their boss' pay check or over permission to leave work early. So this apparent similarity turns out to be the opposite as well.

Bosses who attempt to be a friend as well as a boss are quick to extol the virtues of this path. Of course, they don't suffer much from it. Only the junior does that. The junior who has such a boss is never quite sure when he/she will act as a boss or as a friend. These situations are always confusing and lead to many uncertainties for the junior. The other possibility is the boss fails to reprimand when reasonably required because of friendship loyalties. This is also of negative value to everyone involved, including the company that pays the salaries of both. Clearly, this is a case of misplaced loyalties that cannot validly be justified by the excuse of friendship.

So bosses and juniors cannot be friends! They can, however, share the joys of success and that is called comradeship. In view of this, the obvious remaining question is whether peers can be friends. Once again, let's turn to analysis.

Peers as Friends

Peers are people who know each other because in some way they interact in the course of business. One of the two needs the other's support in order to meet the requirements of the job, or both need each other or some mixture. High standards of performance by both is never a problem, but how about low standards?

Let's assume the first shift foreman always leaves a mess for the second shift to clean up. Assume the two foremen have discussed this issue several times, but the situation does not improve. An obvious next step would be for the second shift foreman to take the problem to the boss in the hope the boss will make the first shift clean up their own messes. But if the two foremen are friends, this rarely occurs.

In the above case, the second shift foreman owed loyalty four ways; to his/her boss, juniors, self and friend. Are these loyalties compatible? Loyalty to juniors would be to get it fixed quickly so the juniors don't have to clean up after someone else and suffer bad morale -- "why must we do it if they don't have to?" Loyalty to the boss would cause similar action since the boss would certainly want cleanliness and neatness as well as fairness and morale. Besides, the boss' boss may have been watching and wondering why the problem has not been fixed. Loyalty to self and to family indicate that making the troops feel good brings good feelings for self and keeping the boss out of hot water would be good as well. Therefore, these three loyalties are fully compatible.

On the other hand, the fourth loyalty to the friend would mean protection of the friend, accepting all the warts and thus no report. This incompatibility, between the peer as friend relationship and the normal job related loyalties to bosses, juniors and self, is a fact of life and will always occur. Compatibility of loyalties to bosses, juniors and self is also always a fact! For this reason, a friendship with peers in the workplace is difficult to successfully manage, so much so that I strongly recommend against it.

There are other hazards. If we permit friendships, we will reap expectations of favoritism as a minimum. And how about those who are not our friends? Will they then be enemies? And what of teamwork and cooperation with all? How will we do that? And what happens if we are promoted over the friend or vice versa. The message is - <u>do not develop friendships</u> with a peer, boss or junior unless you want to be disloyal to your juniors, your bosses, yourself and your family.

COMRADESHIP

In place of friendship I recommend comradeship, the good feeling we all get toward each other when together we have done a difficult job well. The more blood, sweat and tears put out in the course of the job and the tougher the job, the tighter the bond of comradeship. The tighter the bond, the more these groups want to celebrate their perseverance and success. Parties, picnics and the like turn out to be uplifting, very enjoyable events with plenty of warm handshakes, tight hugs and friendly kidding/cajoling. Group gatherings without these accomplishments, these bonds, are rather stiff, false affairs where courtesy attempts unsuccessfully to substitute for comradeship.

Comradeship is not friendship! Do yourself and your subordinates a favor! Forget friendship and go after 5Star accomplishments and comradeship between Associates. It's much more fun and the payoff to the bottom line is great.

Now that we understand the hazards of friendship and are prepared to coach subordinates who show signs of suffering from a lack of understanding, let's look at the hazards of peer relationships.

DEALING WITH PEERS

Bosses must know how to deal with their own peers and how to help juniors do likewise. So far, we know we cannot be their true friend unless we want to be disloyal to ourselves, our juniors and our bosses. What else do we need in order to help a frustrated subordinate?

Peers must help each other in time of business need. Peers do not work for each other and so cannot do what juniors do to bosses or what bosses do to juniors. Therefore, no criticisms or orders, reprimands, instructions, demotion, promotion, etc., etc. What can they do? The expectation of your peer is that you should be a friend! So if you treat a peer in a <u>friendly fashion</u>, "you get more with honey than you do with salt", the relationship will be a more productive one.

In fact, if you attempt to criticize, reprimand or in any way talk down to a peer, you invite disaster. One of these days, the peer will slip a knife in your back. You will be greatly surprised, but no less stabbed. This is just a fact of life. So don't ever use salt, or at least any salt that can be traced to you unless you want some bad effects.

In fact, don't judge peers against your value standards. If they fail, you will not like them. And if you don't like them, you will have difficulty cooperating or harmonizing with them or treating them in a friendly way. Judging tends to become emotional and while it is one of the worst possible things you can do to another person, you are the one most damaged. You are the one saddled with negative thoughts and emotions that decrease your energy available for constructive action. There is no gain to judging peers, only adverse effects. So the relationship must be a friendly one. Always use sugar.

Now assume your subordinate, Alice, is upset and frustrated with a peer named Joe because Joe will not provide what Alice needs. Alice reports that the friendly persuasion of "Gee Joe, I really wish you could help me out on this one" didn't work, even though it's Joe's job to provide what was asked and no other way exists to get it. What counsel should you give to your soon to be frustrated subordinate?

Assuming you believe your group must have what Joe didn't provide, advise Alice to use the "blame it on the boss" tactic. Alice raises the pressure on Joe by bringing her boss into the equation. For instance, say "Gee Joe, I really wish you could do it for me. My boss threw me out of the office yesterday and told me if I was so ineffective that I couldn't get such a little thing done, maybe I'd have to be replaced. I was ordered to report back today and there's no telling what he might do. Well, I'm sure you've got your marching orders too. Boy, we really get caught in the middle sometimes." Note that Alice did not say she would report this to the boss. That would be a threat of consequences that Alice had initiated. Alice can avert being knifed in the back by Joe by blaming the whole distasteful event on a demanding boss.

The above approaches are nice ways to warn Joe that he should stand by for a call from Alice's boss to Joe's boss. The key is that it must be obvious it is the boss and not Alice who is being so demanding, that she would never do this to good old Joe and that the outcome is beyond her control. Besides being true, this protects the junior from retribution and <u>keeps the peer relationship functioning</u>.

As boss, you must use the same guidelines for conduct with your peers. At high levels, the "blame it on the boss tactic" may not be appropriate and may be a negative action. This is a judgment call. Maintaining good working relationships with peers and reporting problems up the chain are the only hard and fast requirements. If your group has a valid need, this process provides the best chance that someone will realize it and give orders down the other chain to fill that need. This may have a positive effect on Joe the next time your junior calls. In this way, a large organization can come to the <u>correct decision as to the proper assignment of resources</u>. Peers will never know if the requester's need meets this resource test, so occasional refusals are undoubtedly best for the overall efficiency of the company.

Part of the wisdom of this approach is not to waste your time thinking bad thoughts about your peers or criticizing other people. <u>Assume they are good.</u> They work for bosses too and their priorities may not be, and correctly so, the same as yours. That is why there is a common boss up there and he/she will have to be presented the problem before any decision can be made. This is a strength of a chain of command organization, not a weakness.

In addition to increasing the overall effectiveness of juniors, these guidelines significantly <u>reduce their stress and frustration</u>. If you choose to judge your peers and decide they are bad, dealing with them creates stress and nothing becomes easier or better. Since they do not work for you and you cannot effectively change them, you must, in accordance with the Serenity

Prayer of Rationale #5, have the courage to accept them as is or suffer considerable frustration.

If a boss actively coaches subordinates with these techniques, juniors will come to understand their value. They result in a considerable increase in cooperation and group effectiveness and a good feeling (peace of mind) that interdepartmental difficulties can be resolved to the common good. Leaving your people to the various other tactics that I see in use damns them to unnecessary failure, failure that often adversely affects quite a few people. Courtesy, cooperation and humility toward others are truly the rule for all of us.

DEALING WITH BOSSES

While a peer expects friendship, a boss expects respect for authority, the boss' authority. While violation of these expectations will get you enmity and a knife, getting it from your boss is far more serious and therefore deserves our total attention.

The authority issue comes down to carrying out the boss' <u>orders or desires in a manner acceptable to the boss</u>. Juniors must not only be timely and accurate in executing orders, but must make the boss aware of possible outcomes and at the same time gain the boss' comments on their acceptability. The boss may be open and candid, or may not be particularly clear in transmitting orders and desires.

In short, a junior's boss may be authoritarian or egalitarian or somewhere in between. In order to be effective, a junior has no choice but to be assertive in gaining sufficient guidance at appropriate times. Continuous effort is a necessity to learning what the boss really wanted as compared to what he/she appeared to want. This struggle by the junior is what respect for authority is all about and juniors who view it as a primary responsibility will never be far from the mark. Juniors who view this as the boss' problem or fault may convince themselves they are justified in not making it all come out right. This, however, is a recipe for failure through the excuse box. As a boss, you must make subordinates who are having trouble dealing with one or more bosses aware of this aspect of their job, this manner of being 5Star.

Who Owns The Relationship?

Before further discussion, we should address an issue that is the key to understanding any relationship. Who owns the quality of the relationship between a boss and junior? The answer is either can own it, <u>but from the viewpoint of the junior it is imperative that the junior take control</u>. While bosses are generally content if their orders and desires are being reasonably executed, this standard will not be adequate to the junior's purposes.

The junior may want the boss to provide better pay, promotion, new opportunities, support, or just continued employment when the need for downsizing eventually occurs. Support may include a multitude of different actions and approvals; resources to procure the tools of new technology, freedom to expand into new markets, promotion or reward of the junior's subordinates, aid in getting other corporate organizations to better support the junior's group or just backing of the junior's efforts to correct his/her people and policy problems. An outstandingly good relationship will make most of the above possible and it is therefore <u>in the junior's best interest to take charge of every aspect of the relationship to make it as good as possible</u>.

Beyond a significant effort to meet or exceed the expectations of the boss's orders and desires, making a good relationship means the junior must <u>gain the boss' trust</u>. The extent of this trust will play a big part in determining the boss' response to any requests made by the junior. The boss will have complete trust in the junior if; the junior's statements are always a true and complete representation of the facts, the junior's commitments are always met and the junior never fails to keep the boss informed of errors or other noteworthy events (no short-fusing or blindsiding).

Telling the boss every problem within a time interval that is appropriate to its consequence and providing timely solutions are a part of gaining the boss' trust. Juniors must expect unknown persons to inform their boss of problems in the junior's area of responsibility. Nothing is more satisfying to a boss than finding that these reports from others are far less complete and/or timely than those directly from the junior. This reduces the boss' anxiety about unknowns and develops trust.

Being open, candid and forthright with your boss about problems pays big dividends. If you make certain not to saddle your boss with the job of solving the problems, the only difficulty is that your boss may decide your group has too many problems if no other group-head reports problems. <u>Carefully accentuating the positive</u>, so as to counterbalance the negative image of problems, and <u>focusing on the improvements</u> that problem resolution always gains, effectively prevents any bad effects. Don't stop reporting problems. Reporting makes you a hero to your troops, shows high standards for several important values, including admission of error and sacrifice, and is something of which you can be truly proud. Your troops sorely need good leadership and your boss will become impressed by your loyalty to the company. Your relationship with your boss will improve through these reports.

Problem reporting can also be viewed from the perspective of the boss' responsibility. Bosses cannot fix anything they do not know about and juniors who deny them knowledge only cause the boss to be irresponsible. <u>Bosses who do not learn of problems tend to get hit by trains</u> and we do them no favors by keeping them in the dark. As a boss, I tended to view non-reporters as <u>first class enemies who should be changed or removed from their positions as fast as possible</u>. Non-reporters tend to view themselves as survival experts who are protecting themselves from the boss' irrational response to reports of problems. In my own experience, bosses eventually learn of a few of these unreported problems and as this list grows they become more and more frustrated with the non-reporter. Juniors can choose their strategy, but must <u>live with the consequences</u>.

An outstandingly positive attitude on the part of the junior is also an overriding answer to the above. Bosses love enthusiasm in juniors and respond positively to it. Juniors who permit their bosses to affect their attitude, to deflect it from being extremely positive, are making a big mistake, both for themselves and their subordinates, and should study this book. As with everyone, the junior's attitude is his/her most important weapon. Volunteering to work for a boss includes acceptance of the boss' criticism and warts. "Sticks and stones will break my bones, but words will never harm me" is as true today as ever. Even verbal abuse is not a big deal. Get your attitude up to an extremely positive level and you will discover solutions to problems with your boss, or in accepting criticism without negative reaction.

Because your boss is authoritarian or stressed out is not an excuse for you to be negative. Bosses are people too. They make errors. Are their errors problematical to subordinates? Mostly not so. Subordinates can choose how to adjust and can usually eliminate any real damage. Problems in the workplace are many and a few more from the boss are seldom of real consequence if the junior makes the correct choices. The boss' errors are problems for the boss' boss since he/she is in a position to make necessary changes. So while loyalty to the boss requires that the junior try to get the boss to correct the error, the serenity prayer of Rationale #5 allows the junior to accept a boss' errors. In this way, the junior accepts the boss as unchangeable and thus prevents any frustration or damage to an otherwise positive attitude.

The bottom line to the above two paragraphs is that <u>juniors must never, never judge their bosses</u>, or lose control of themselves. Judging leads to the conclusion that your boss is somehow inadequate or, in the extreme, immoral. This makes the junior's job of working for a boss almost impossible, far more difficult than most juniors can handle. Choose to stop such thoughts and <u>focus</u>

on respecting his/her authority, building trust and maintaining your own very positive attitude. These are the real secrets to success with bosses. Use your value standards as rules for your own behavior, not as criteria by which to judge your boss. I have never seen anyone enjoy more success with the latter, only more problems.

Short-fusing is another relationship pitfall. Juniors often look for a quick decision from their boss to a problem that they have been evaluating over a period of time. The junior has gathered more facts, has had plenty of time to get thoughts in order and additional time to disclose more facts. Both the junior and the boss tend to get upset when the junior expects a quick decision without the boss having had time to come up to speed.

The solution is for the junior to tell the boss about problems as they occur. The boss will never be far behind in the need for decisions and may even volunteer a few before the junior is convinced of the need. After all, have you ever seen Mother Nature produce a flower without first planting a seed and allowing time for it to grow. Bosses are no different. Reporting as they occur is a far better tactic than short-fusing and is just another reason why the problem reporting rule is necessary.

As with all workplace situations, acting in accordance with the Six Rationales and all high value standards is the perfect solution, best for everyone. In dealing with our bosses, issues often get so emotional as to obscure this truth. Do not allow yourself to get off the right road by any such mechanism. Follow the Golden Rule, Rationale #4, do unto others as you would -----.

BUREAUCRACY

Note: This discussion is meant to augment, not replace, the information presented in Chapter 6 under Authority.

Bureaucracy is a place where lots of people can say no and you almost cannot find a person who can say yes. The ones who can only say no are willing to talk about it, send memos about it and have endless meetings about it since they all have plenty of time. Normally they have no line responsibilities, only staff.

It is also a place where getting a decision to move forward takes a long time by anyone's measure, but that can develop a plausible justification for each month of delay, month after month. "We were getting this or analyzing that or getting them on board." "You can't be hasty you know." "Well, we have this procedure that ----." It is a living, breathing, voracious beast that consumes time, money and people.

People? Did I mention people again? Bureaucracy is a beast that demotivates, frustrates, demoralizes and otherwise turns off all involved. If the people had any entrepreneurial spirit or any creativity when they started, it may disappear. The beast is a shared responsibility scheme so diverse that no one can get control over it and no one can be held accountable for its interminable delays or its failure to make a decision. "I don't know where it is, doesn't Barbara have it?" "Well if Barbara doesn't have it, ask John when he comes back from vacation." Somehow it's OK if the bureaucratic process grinds to a halt for vacations, weekends or sickness, but don't even mention such a possibility for a line job of producing products or serving customers.

The attempts made at getting around this system are time-consuming, costly and heroic. The costs in terms of human frustration and in disrespect for bosses, both inside and outside the bureaucracy, are likewise very high. This is to say nothing of the costs associated with the long delays and with employing so many non-producers.

Bureaucracy replaces excellence through value standards with mediocrity through politics. It becomes important who you know, not what you know. Name dropping and power politics become survival skills.

Those unhappy internal customers who object are labeled by the bureaucrats as trouble-makers, uncooperative wave-makers who are certainly not team players. In order to escape these labels, everyone turns to consensus management techniques. While these are important to making major corporate decisions, they are totally inappropriate for use between organizations. But in a bureaucratic environment, they become the method of choice for many decisions, large and small, through committees and task forces that in the end only serve to perpetuate mediocrity through compromise and negotiation.

Consensus management serves to justify the bureaucracy since who else has the time to conduct the many lengthy meetings needed in order to keep the ball rolling, even if ever so slowly. <u>Line management decides to cooperate since without the ability to object or to act as a real customer, there is simply no other way to improve anything.</u>

Thus bureaucracy violates many of the value standards we all hold dear; creativity, caring, decisiveness, risk-taking, positive attitude, fairness, humility, strong and independent, excellence and the like. If a boss wants to send strong negative Leadership to subordinates, have bureaucracy. Subordinates will no doubt follow and start using those value standards (low good or bad) in their everyday performance as well. Fight the beast and you get points for grit and heroism, as well as for caring, creativity, et al.

Bureaucracy is an opportunity. Detection consists of going down to the little people and asking what stops them or frustrates them. Perhaps it is better to begin by asking who helps them, who is of value to them, as this is less offensive. From these responses, produce a list. Support and staff groups not on this list are a perfect place to start. As bosses, we fail to seize these opportunities at our own peril.

Bureaucracy Prevention

The first rule to prevent bureaucracies from forming, or to stop one already formed, is that <u>staff cannot be allowed to exercise authority over line management</u>. Staff may be used to support the line, but <u>the line must be given full customer rights</u> over that support, <u>including the right to replace it with an alternative</u>. Being successful at line management requires the fitting together of a myriad of skills and capabilities in just the right way to produce a superior product. To the extent that control and "customer rights" over these elements are absent, excellence in production degrades.

All bosses tend to allow their staffs to exercise the boss' authority over the line, in the name of getting more "things" done "right". This is often extended to authority over procedures, purchasing, training, engineering, computers, hiring and firing. This is a choice for bureaucracy since more bureaucracy always results. The boss' only alternative, the rule above, is a choice for excellence since more excellence always results. I presented this choice in Chapter 6 as <u>matching responsibility with authority</u>. Whole books could be written on this subject alone, but the secret to success will always be found by meeting high standards for all good values. Your own experiences should be sufficient to bear out my counsel.

The second rule is for the boss to decide exactly what purpose each element of a staff will fulfill. If they serve a support function, who are their customers and what are their products? Since these people report to the boss, he/she must know how to judge their performance. <u>Listening to external customers is how to judge the line and listening to internal customers is the only way to judge a staff.</u> If a staff function cannot satisfy its internal customers, it is unnecessary baggage.

The third rule is not to use staff to critique their own internal customers. Listening to them as they critique their customers is hazardous since this degrades their ability to serve and tends toward bureaucracy, toward allowing the staff to use the boss' authority directly or through name dropping to gain power over line management. Get out of your office and find out "what is" in the workplace and perhaps have an inspection group whose sole purpose it is to inspect performance. But <u>do not use staff who support the line to critique the line</u>.

With these three rules, staff will no longer need to have long meetings over how to design "one size fits all" rules for how they will serve their customers. Line will no longer need to attend meetings with staff in order to ensure that their ox is not gored too badly by rules. Besides, staff will be too busy serving the needs of their customers to waste time in long meetings. Customers will dictate to suppliers rather than vice versa. Committees and task forces will be much fewer. For those you must have, observe the rules provided later in this Appendix, under Committees, in order to escape their form of mediocrity.

All of the above actions reflect leadership of high standards, whereas bureaucracy is leadership of low or bad standards. The effects of each are remarkable in their extent.

CHANGE

"May you live in a time of change" is an old Chinese curse. Compared to the western "go to hell", it may sound tame, but is it? The curse implies that change can be particularly disruptive and difficult for humans. What it does not say is if managed properly, change can be particularly rewarding and challenging for humans.

Change is essentially an unknown and most of us strongly dislike and shy away from unknowns. Unknowns can be dangerous. They are compared to darkness and forces so associated. Unknowns, when borne by our friends and family, are called surprises. We love them because we expect something good from good people and we were never given a bad surprise. These surprises do not require change on our part.

So change is perceived by most of us to be bad. Most children hate to move because they don't want to leave the apparent security of their friends and neighborhood, the known. My children had to move many times and learned to look forward to new faces and new places, only because my wife discussed the good things with them for several months before each change. So change, attended by time for enlightenment, can become acceptable to us.

Therefore, if change is presented as an event, "this is a change so just do it", we cannot expect it to receive anything but rejection. This results from not carefully explaining the reasons for the change, not allowing time to digest these reasons and not allowing time to develop commitment to a particular form of change. Without firm commitment by those involved, change will fail, so why even bother to attempt it?

Change must be a process for everyone involved and it must include all the elements natural to change. We start with a necessity, something that "ain't so good" judged against some value standards. Then we start to look at alternatives, possible solutions. Then we closely study each solution and compare them against value standards including cost-benefit criteria. Only when convinced of a sizable gain do we decide to change.

Every human being who can share in this process, with time to understand each and every step, is able to accept the validity of the end result. And each of them will be able to work with high spirits to make the change successful -- unless it will result in the demise of their own job, and often even then if the gain is significant enough.

Bosses become aware that a change is appropriate before they know of an acceptable alternative and well before it can be implemented. The time to bring subordinates into the process is when the need for change becomes apparent. Don't wait! As alternative changes are examined, all affected people can be brought along in the process. The group meetings of Chapter 9 are great forums to get the troops to bring up the necessities on their own and to supply alternatives that they know, while the boss fills in knowledge gaps with what he/she knows. Most of this method's aspects were given in the Chapters for listening (commitment from two cents) and GOTYP (procedure to address corrective action). Most important is the boss' role as a brake rather than as an accelerator so as to gain compliance with all high value standards, including those that respect people and their need for commitment.

The way humans willingly accept change is just another law. If you choose to violate it, you get burned. If you choose to take advantage of it, you reap great benefits from the commitment that results. It is always the boss' choice. So take the time to allow your people to become convinced of the problem, its possible solutions, the chosen solution and its benefits. This is called loving your neighbor. Without these elements, marching up to your people with a change is disruptive and could be called hating your neighbor or "the hell with you".

Loving humility by a boss is not invoking a change if those affected cannot willingly accept and enjoy it. A change will not succeed, no matter how good the boss' intentions are, if it is not accepted by the troops. Many bosses use the arrogance of "my right is more right than your right" in order to absolve themselves of the responsibility to gain wide acceptance before action. This is the error of hubris and always fails through high negative costs, both human and financial. I certainly made a batch of these errors before getting it right. Most of us do.

Change is therefore a real chance for the boss to show respect for subordinates. Managing people rather than managing "things" always has great paybacks and a time of change makes the need for this axiom very clear.

UNIONS

Management's union problems can be viewed as originating from granting power to the union, indirectly and directly. Those who represent the union use this power to control union members and to increase the union's influence at the bargaining table. <u>It is management that creates this power.</u> Let me explain.

Recalling the excuse principle, management can choose to provide low quality support that violates the value standards of subordinates. This choice causes disrespect, distrust and other negative reactions to bosses while providing juniors with reasons to excuse any incorrect/bad performance on their part. This managerial choice grants "indirect" power to union leaders since they can now gain membership support by criticizing management and by calling for solidarity in facing down these "bad" management people and their practices.

"Direct" power is gained when management turns over partial or complete control of managerial functions to the union. This power could be over such events as job or overtime assignments, special requests, training, vacations, or promotions. These fall into the realm of "If I (the union member) don't do what my union stewards want, I won't get what I want from them when I want it." This is a very real fear and one that union bosses learn to use effectively since they have no power of their own.

The above choice to grant "indirect and or direct" power to union leaders always causes severe problems for both management <u>and</u> union members. The union members effectively <u>lose their status as customers who can demand performance from elected union leaders</u> and become controlled by those same leaders through the mechanism of fear.

If on the other hand, management chooses to grant little or no "indirect or direct" power to the union, management will be greatly respected by union members and a true team spirit will ensue. Union leaders, in order to keep their elected positions, will become team players out of a need to satisfy constituents. As politicians without power to grant constituents special favors, these leaders will only be able to be "against" what their members are "against" and "for" what their members are "for". If the union members are trusting of management, union leaders will be also.

AND BEYOND THE ISSUE OF POWER

Juniors need to know that success in any business environment requires three distinct groups be satisfied; customers, employees and owners/stockholders. If any of these groups become dissatisfied enough to pull out, the business will fail. If owners and employees act as a team to satisfy customers, sharing in the good and the bad times, they may be able to please enough customers to keep the business healthy. As the degree of their cooperation, dedication and professionalism degrades from 8-10, pleasing their customers becomes more difficult and money available for distribution to employees and owners will decrease. In stiff competition, less proficient teams do not survive.

A union is a choice by individuals to band together and hire others to represent them to senior management. The hope is to gain a "fair shake", to share fairly in the proceeds of the business enterprise. Union officials are hired by and paid by the group to serve this purpose. It is just like hiring a doctor or a lawyer to help to solve your problems.

Employees must be assisted in understanding this difference between an employer who pays and directs them (deserves a decent day's work, don't bite the hand that feeds you) and a union that the employees pay and should direct. Your budding 5Star people need to know that whoever is paying the bills should have the right to decide what is done. They will start to control their own union rather than have it control them. <u>This change takes no longer than management takes to create 5Star people.</u>

Management must never be for or against union representatives, must never lobby employees to take sides against their union and must treat their union officials with the courtesy and respect due any peer. To do otherwise violates federal law and several value standards. At the same time, management must not allow the union to stand between itself and its employees. To achieve success in the business environment, team members must have uninhibited access to each other over all issues. How else can we be forthright, show integrity, be cooperative or show that it is everyone's company?

The existence of a union in the workplace is only a hazardous condition if management decides to use it as an excuse to violate high standards for values. <u>In this excuse mode, management leads its work force in the wrong direction and then blames bad results on the union.</u> Abdication of the management role by executives, for whatever excuse, is never a solution. The solution to lead through high value standards in support applies to union relations as well as to those with customers and subordinates.

As with any relationship with others, nothing takes the place of excellence in the human values. Honesty, integrity, forthrightness and humility get you the best quality relationship, while movement in the opposite direction measurably reduces your chance of success. <u>Problems in union relations are the result of management's decisions and as such can only be resolved by management, not by the union.</u> The mechanisms of forthrightness and integrity are a boss' most important assets in this process. Open and candid discussion of all aspects of the business (the 52 Card principle), rather than playing the cards close to the vest, is the answer. Managements who keep their employees ignorant of company matters make employees susceptible to union propaganda. <u>The closer the majority of employees is to 5Star, the fewer the union problems.</u>

CUSTOMERS

In the business environment there are two types of customers, internal and external. The rules for both are identical. Bureaucracy and bosses who believe in managing "things" but not people cause the greatest violations of rules for handling customers. Violations of internal customers always result in similar treatment of external customers because of the natural law. The rules for success with customers are simple.

Rule 1- THE CUSTOMER IS ALWAYS RIGHT.

Rule 2- WHEN IN DOUBT, REFER TO RULE NUMBER 1.

Always give customers what they need in a way that meets high standards for all values. Make a concerted effort to understand the customers' needs and if these are different from what you have, get them what they need or send them to a place that can meet those needs.

If customers are unhappy, do whatever is necessary to make them happy. If the customers are incorrect, respectfully show them what is correct and help them to understand how this would affect their needs. Afterwards, give them what they want whether it has changed or not.

If what they want is definitely not what they need, use the guidance above to sort that out. If they do not change and if what they want will be a waste of their money, it is time to politely but firmly take the position that you cannot supply what they want because they will hate you later. The customer is left to do what they will.

The only other choice is to stop serving particular customers since what they want is not what you are willing to provide. As a boss to a junior, this is transfer to another job or termination. For other internal and all external customers, this is sending them to other suppliers.

PRIORITIES

People prioritize their work for the purpose of deciding what to do next. The most frequent result is that there are many parts of their job that are never done. These are left undone because they never get high enough on the priority list to become the next thing to do in the work time remaining. The fact that we are responsible for these, and can be considered irresponsible if we take no action, is just one more unhappy thing to accept about the workplace.

I suggest taking a different approach to our responsibilities. Prioritize nothing. Decide when each task must be done on the basis of its characteristics. Each task has an associated time that if met would satisfy everyone, a time that would dissatisfy everyone and a time that would be in between or questionable. Armed with this knowledge we can now decide when the task should be completed. Removing less worthwhile requirements, delegation to juniors or working late are the three methods available for meeting dates. Carrying out these methods and not allowing any slippage will effectively resolve the prioritization issue and provide a positive sense of accomplishment. It also stops bosses from believing that their deadlines are not being given sufficient attention.

COMPETITION INSIDE YOUR COMPANY

Against other people is the normal competitive mode and it always creates more problems than it solves. Inside your company, competition goes against the caring values of charity, compassion, humility, loving your neighbor and doing unto others as you would have them do unto you. People or groups in competition have trouble with cooperation, sharing and harmony while selflessness, sacrifice and comradeship cannot even be discussed. Healthy competition among people is, in fact, only one more oxymoron, inappropriate to any purpose.

Competition against high standards of human values is the solution. This policy puts everyone in your company on the same team and resolves all of the apparent inconsistencies and incompatibilities between different values. This makes values into a universal decision set applicable to all workplace endeavors to the exclusion of all other possible criteria. In order to get stiffer competition, we merely raise the standards higher. With this policy, there's no limit on progress and no telling how high you can go.

Unlike those vanquished human competitors, value standards never go away in the short or long term. Therefore, this solution permits us to stop competing against other people and to start "doing unto others as we would have them do unto us" -- rather than "doing unto others before they do it to us".

RELIEF OF A BOSS

Assume a new boss is taking the reins and the post is other than a CEO position. Should there be a turnover period between old and new? Should the new boss undergo some indoctrination before taking the reins? The answer may be easy after some analysis.

Let's start by looking at the job itself. What knowledge of technical issues is needed? What rules, regulations, procedures and policies govern the work done by the subordinates? Are there any corporate procedures and policies that apply? How many and what types of equipment, tools and other support will the new boss control and in what condition are they? Who are the customers and how do they feel about us? How many subordinates of what type skills are there? What is the current status of group culture and of 5Star? What technical and personnel problems exist? What are the group's goals and what has been the progress over the past few years? What is the financial condition of the group? What planning mechanisms are in place? What computer applications are in place? What are the prospective boss' responsibilities to subordinates on a daily, monthly, or annual basis? What are all the problems?

These are just a few of the many questions that could be asked. The answers would provide some feel for the degree of difficulty a newcomer would have in gaining control over the group. But there are more questions of particular concern to a newcomer's boss and/or CEO. Do we want the newcomer to flounder for many months or more before securely grabbing the reins? Or do we want a decisive, confident person at the reins? Do we want his/her juniors to flounder for the same time frame attempting to educate the boss while forsaking their own jobs in the process? Was the group mostly on course before this change and will going off course while the new boss gets acclimated be of any concern?

Often, the new boss is only given one day to relieve the outgoing one. Unless the relief is thoroughly familiar with all aspects of the organization and its functions (almost impossible), this quick process has some very bad side effects. Juniors are greatly disrupted. The relief will go through a period of very low confidence and possibly low esteem in trying to gain knowledge of and control over the group, while playing catch up as to knowledge.

In addition, many problem solutions previously discovered will be lost. Subordinates may take advantage of the confusion to drop things that were displeasing and to start things that had once been thrown out for good reason. The new boss will be completely unprepared to protect those things that the old boss did protect or even to miss those things that subordinates have normally performed. Thus, anarchy will prevail for some period of time and recovery will be one to two years away.

There are two alternatives. The first is to keep the old boss around for the 30 days it will take for the newcomer to learn everything about the group; policies, procedures, problems and such. The old boss will continue to be the boss and will help to pass "what is" and what was planned to the newcomer. If the old boss must depart quickly, the second alternative is to appoint an acting boss for the same duration. This would probably be the same person who took charge when the old boss went on vacation.

The intent of these two alternatives is to allow the newcomer to come up to speed on all aspects of the organization before being required to take charge. The new boss gains a working relationship with all direct reports by learning from them about their areas of responsibility and existing problems. A similar approach would be used with other levels as appropriate. All policies/procedures as well as equipment and personnel issues would be reviewed. He/she would inspect records and the physical plant facilities to grasp most existing problems and begin to formulate how to go about correcting them.

This process gives a significant boost to the relief's confidence, totally removes any disruption to juniors, permits the organization to retain its learning from past errors and allows it to move forward without having to wait for the new boss to come up to speed. It also provides to this person's boss a golden opportunity to comment on what the relief believes are problems and the intended solutions to them. Creating this sort of contract is important to the future relationship between these two.

The above procedure also sends some strong messages of high value standards. Taking the time to do it right presents a high standard of quality to all subordinates. Most importantly, it shows the new boss we must always take the time to do it right. In addition, it allows the new boss time to be with the people and to begin the process of gaining their respect and of showing them that he/she cares. Direct reports will be particularly appreciative since most problems will have already been discussed and thus will not be surprises when the boss does take the reins. In fact, this process fosters real honesty, integrity and forthrightness.

The issue in picking a relief procedure is whether or not we want the new boss to manage by whim or by purpose. Comprehensive indoctrinations support control by purpose, building on old gains in order to get new ones and learning from old errors to avert their reoccurrence. Quick reliefs force bosses to manage any way they can, a sort of dog-eat-dog mentality of survival. They are not carrying on or building on what went before because they don't know what it was. What they do know is their boss didn't care to take the time to prepare them. Also, these new bosses get the distinct impression that whatever exists must be of questionable value, so why not do what they want, their whim. This may be the major flaw of the quick relief, but the sum of all the flaws spells a myriad of new problems that no one needs.

The gain of using the recommended procedure to a company in monetary terms is significant. If the group's culture was in good shape to start, this process will best maintain it. If the culture was in need of change, this process will greatly assist the new boss in understanding it and proceeding to the fix stage in an expeditious manner.

COMMUNICATION

Damaging rumors and bum dope are the normal by-products of any attempts at communication. As previously indicated, chains of command are generally capable of distorting any information or policies being passed down and of filtering partially or completely any data being passed up the chain. Distortion and filtering create considerable havoc among subordinates and bosses, and are the cause of all sorts of problems. Unfortunately for the bosses, there is no real way to train or legislate away all of these errors of communication and their resulting problems.

In addition to distortion on the way down, communication can also suffer from being incomplete. Most managers do not feel any responsibility to keep their subordinates well informed and many believe subordinates should not be told what's really going on or why. This can stem from a basic distrust or a belief that juniors have no need for such information. Playing management cards close to our vest can also be a sort of self-preservation tactic. Add to this those managers who shy away from communication because they are uncomfortable or inept and we have a significant number of subordinates who are poorly informed. Although managers can be trained and communications can be dramatically improved over time to better conform to the 52 Card principle, serious problems will still exist. Is there no superior solution?

There is one! If we accept that miscommunications will occur, the appropriate response would be to listen for it and to take appropriate corrective action when a case is found. Since this alternative also causes an increase in human interaction between boss and subordinates, the overall effect is extremely positive. This approach is used in GOTYP of Chapter 8 and Group Meetings of Chapter 9. While group meetings serve to accomplish other more important goals, they are also an opportunity to correct all of the existing miscommunications. This is a powerful solution that is immediately effective. Use of it influences subordinate bosses to be more accurate and complete the first time since their errors will now be so obvious.

COMMITTEES

It is said that a committee once tried to design a horse, but the end result was a camel. Most committees achieve very little of value and most bosses know this. Members are accountable to different bosses and collectively can only agree on the "lowest common denominator". This is called consensus management wherein opinions and status are all important, while facts and standards take a back seat. The emphasis is mostly on getting agreement to proceed, rather than on quality and cost in order to best the competition. The result is a compromise of standards that gives competitors an advantage.

There is a way out. The committee members must report to a single boss who has sufficient authority to approve/disapprove and direct whatever the committee decides. This boss must personally provide the committee's charter, direction to use only facts and high value standards and not politics, and continuous oversight. The boss must also direct that all decisions be unanimous and that cases wherein one or more dissenting votes exist be referred to the boss for resolution. Members are directed to dissent whenever they believe high standards are not being met. Oversight consists of meeting separately with each member to assess achievement of that person's goals and meeting periodically with the entire group to discuss progress. The boss should have the authority to unilaterally replace any member believed to be of low value to the committee.

With the above solution, the normal power struggle disappears for two reasons: one person has all the power and is not on the committee, and the members are all granted equal power. Notice that I purposely did not mention a chairperson (they will need one for the meetings) because the boss never meets with that person as chairperson. Discussing committee progress is done with everyone present and with each member separately, with no special power or influence being granted to the chairperson. I have watched this solution in action for years and never cease to be amazed at how simple and executable it is. It also consistently produces superior results respected by all and never produces the value standard compromises and monuments to mediocrity for which committees have gained renown. A business environment should not promote power politics over reason and value standards. Once again, this is the boss' choice.

I must admit, in an authoritarian/bureaucratic setting, making committees effective will be a very difficult task. So removing bureaucratic controls through adopting the rules for customers may be a necessary prerequisite.

DISCRIMINATION

In chapter 4 while discussing Group II "caring" values, I stated there are many opportunities in today's world for disharmony and discrimination between people. I also stated that the resulting ill feelings and bad habits are brought into the workplace. Before proceeding with analysis and solutions, what about the world from which this problem emanates?

My conclusion is that the outside world is a bad influence. The observations that drew me to that conclusion are:

1.   violence is rising
2.   more people are in court suing other people and organizations for all sorts of new reasons.
3.   families are weaker and less reliable havens.
4.   the concept of "the right to do your own thing" seems to have replaced that of personal obligation and human values.

5.   government makes more of our decisions, making us more dependent on it and less responsible for our own lives.

6.   communication is faster and we learn of bad events more quickly than ever before.

7.   and much more.

All of the above creates more uncertainty and less stability for each of us. And these translate into less ability to interact with other people. Only if we know who we are, feel comfortable with ourselves, act responsibly and use high value standards, can we establish smooth and effective relationships with others. In short, I believe disharmony and discrimination to be a natural result of today's world. For a boss, the wisdom is in understanding the influences behind this unproductive behavior are pervasive and powerful and any effort to counter them must be more powerful and more pervasive.

Not to worry for we have already covered all of the solutions. Once any boss has changed to being "caring" (that's about a month after you start really listening and responding to the troops), he/she is in the position to attack discrimination. The boss brings it up in the course of a group meeting and uses values/Rationales to show how wrong it is to our success as a team and how none of us wants it. Be sure to get the answers out of the troops and not to be caught preaching. But ensure respect, humility, trust, fairness, compassion, admission of error and the first four Rationales (Ch 6) are used to analyze the issue.

This effort must be ongoing and must be a part of the normal indoctrination of new associates. The only other action, beyond the boss' routine actions to move toward 5Star, is to provide harsh discipline to people who violate discrimination codes. Include apologies to the injured party by yourself and the violator. In addition, the offender should be assigned to read books and/or attend special training outside of normal working hours.

My own experience indicates that harmony between sexes, races and ages can be achieved with common sense and value based solutions. I am certain the current tendency toward diversity training is well meaning, but it will fail in the long run if you don't establish the value based culture of this book. Caring bosses and 5Star associates are the lasting solutions to discrimination because they have the power required to effectively combat the outside world's negative forces.

LIFE'S PROBLEMS

All of life's problems are not necessarily in the workplace, but their effects certainly are. Fate throws a variety of boulders at us. While we each get a different set, the available alternative reactions to these boulders are basically the same, regardless of the boulder's characteristics. And each reaction results in about the same effect for each of us, regardless of our current status.

The boulders are deficiencies from our childhood and problems from educational, health, financial, marital, mental, familial, interpersonal, physical and other circumstances. These, as well as fear of nuclear war, cancer or impotence, can be all consuming issues or pebbles brushed aside. We have very little control over which boulders are presented to us and the frequency of their arrival is fairly constant over a lifetime. In any group of 100 people, there are a few fairly large ones each year and a larger number of small ones.

But we can control our response to them. We can choose to consider each as just one more opportunity to show the strength of our character. This choice is to work as hard as is necessary to resolve and overcome the problem while burdening other people as little as possible. A second choice is to show the weakness of our character by assuming a very negative "Oh, poor me" attitude that adversely affects others as well as ourselves. And in between these two extremes lie mixtures of these two basic reactions. Incorrect reactions always have negative impacts on the workplace, only varying in extents.

This presents a choice to the boss; to ignore the whole thing or to attempt to compassionately be a sounding board and provide values and the Six Rationales of chapter 6, so the person can make an informed choice. I would contend that the <u>business reasons</u> for doing the latter are quite compelling on their own, without recourse to any standard for kind, merciful, compassionate and humane treatment of subordinates. I would also contend this fits perfectly with the goal of becoming 5Star and being strong and independent. The more practice in becoming 5Star that the boss can generate, the more progress will be made toward utopia. And every little bit counts.

CONCLUSION

This completes discussion of workplace conditions for which all associates need the whys and hows of success. Those presented, plus all of those discussed within the book's main body, are necessary knowledge so a "caring" boss can truly act the part. Likewise, the whys and hows of Appendix B for personal behaviors, such as negative attitudes, stress or ego, are also necessary.

APPENDIX B

UNDERSTANDING PERSONAL BEHAVIORS
AND HOW TO CHANGE THEM

Appendix A covered the whys and hows of successfully dealing with workplace conditions not covered in the book's main body. Every workplace condition is a potential cause of frustration and de-motivation if we don't handle it properly.

But what of the effects from these causes, the frustration itself or other personal behaviors such as stress or bad morale from which so many of us suffer? If frustration or stress has become a habit, is there no way to turn it around and avert further damage to self and family (#1, 2 and 3)?

In this Appendix we will examine the whys and hows of eight personal behaviors that limit us in ways none of us need. They are our personality, likes and dislikes, ego and prestige, assumptions, bad morale, bad attitudes, stress and emotionalism. All of these are hazards that interfere with our quality of life and degrade our professional and personal performance. These hazards are often considered as "only being human", but they cause violations of value standards and seriously get in the way of excellence. While bosses are more susceptible to them than are working-level people, each of the eight can be removed.

First, we need a sound understanding of behavior in general before we can discuss the eight specific ones. What exactly is behavior? How do we go about creating it? And most importantly, how can we change it? For reasons that will become obvious, I call this the "3x5 Card" principle.

The Human Brain

The brain! What a fantastic device. Many books have been written about it and this is no attempt to summarize what others have said. Rather, my goal is to impart a simple, easy to understand model of the brain that explains your own human behavior. Using this model, you can then proceed to develop and change your own behavior as a boss. Using this model, you can also help others to change their behavior.

Understanding human nature is, in my opinion, very dependent upon the direction from which one approaches. In my own search for human understanding, studying digital computers proved invaluable. In the beginning, I was struck with the realization that the computer could only add two numbers or compare them to determine if they are the same. I then learned how these two functions are manipulated to produce multiplication (adding many times), subtraction (negative addition), file searches and the like. And then I was amazed to find that these simple actions can be arranged by writers of computer programs to produce chess playing computers that lose only to the best players.

Computers are also very fast. Individual actions take place at the rate of at least many millions each second. The computer can thus appear to be doing many things simultaneously. This is only an appearance, because our reference point is the speed of our conscious brain, which is very slow by comparison. Could the speed of a computer compare to that of the sub-conscious brain?

I also learned computers never make mistakes. That is, the computer always carries out the exact instructions (program) provided to it and always uses the exact data provided to it. If the program is flawed, the result is garbage. Likewise, if the data is in error, garbage-in produces garbage-out. But the program itself is always executed flawlessly, without error, on the data provided.

I began to realize that the human brain, in order to carry out a multitude of required body and mind functions, must be similarly constructed and therefore the sub-conscious brain is most likely methodical, predictable and repeatable, even flawless --just like computers. I recommend some study of computers in order to develop your own understanding. The terms compute, program, algorithm, decision tree, memory, data base, re-program, faulty programming and garbage-in garbage-out directly parallel the behavior of our human brain. Humans often have a lot of bum dope to feed their computer-brain and the programming/decision tree may be flawed as well. So they also have lots of opportunities for flawed decisions or garbage out.

Programs for Racing

The simple example of a racecar driver best illustrates what the sub-conscious brain does for us. The driver I have in mind wins races with cars that travel at 200 miles per hour. At those speeds, the driver has little time for conscious thought in order to direct actions that must take place in the next half second. The speed of conscious thought is far too slow for such a purpose, so we use the term "fast reactions" or "reflex actions" to describe how the car is quickly maneuvered to avoid an accident or to take advantage of a momentary opportunity to pass the driver ahead. What's really going on?

When first learning to drive a car we have to literally tell our limbs with a conscious order when to push the brake, when to engage the clutch, when to pull the steering wheel to the right, when to shift, etc. We can all remember these thoughts as we first learned how to drive, but we rarely remember when we ceased having to think about it. Timing the clutch and the gearshift lever were particularly critical and an error ground gears and produced very jerky starts and stops. But soon, after many repetitions, this became of no concern -- it became properly executed through an effective program.

As we learn how to drive through repetition, we pass action control from the conscious to our sub-conscious brain. The normal experienced driver thinks in the conscious about going to the store and where it is while the sub-conscious gets him/her in the car, puts the seat belt on, starts the car, backs out and gets the car moving on the road. Very little conscious thought is expended on the actual driving once we have learned how to do it, once we've programmed our sub-conscious. What the eyes see is sent to the sub-conscious that evaluates the scene (the data) for action based on criteria (more data) previously provided, such as where the store is and how fast to drive. If after using the program and data a decision for action is generated, the sub-conscious (through programs) orders muscle actions, hundreds of them, in order to carry out the action.

When the action is in response to external conditions, such as stoplights and other cars coming close, we call this "automatic"! In truth, the program was constructed to use sensors (eyes and ears) to provide data at regular intervals. The program then evaluates this data against programmed standards such as too close for cars or red/green for lights in order to decide on action. The program then sends a routine set of instructions to our hands and legs in order to carry out the chosen action. If done without conscious thought, we call it "automatic".

For another example, think of a high jumper who has tried to "program" the sub-conscious to produce that perfect sequence of muscle actions that will result in jumping over, not touching, the bar. Think of the sheer number of different muscle actions that must be directed by the sub-conscious almost simultaneously. Think of learning from the coach over a period of years all the little things that must happen to be successful. Think of the fact that the jump itself is over in a couple of seconds and that conscious brain speed is far too slow to direct the thousands of required actions in the correct sequence. But the sub-conscious can do it all if the conscious brain takes the time to program and practice action, build muscle strength, program the sub-conscious and practice, again and again and again!

Let's return to the racecar driver. After learning to drive a normal car, the driver quickly finds that some of the things that were learned for normal driving aren't helpful for racing. The sub-conscious was programmed to slow the car down considerably before entering a sharp corner, an automatic response. Since the racecar has cornering capabilities far beyond those of the normal passenger car, this response will lose a lot of races if not changed. So the driver begins to force him/herself to take the corners faster, i.e. reprogram the sub-conscious. This means the sub-conscious has no stored knowledge (data) of what that looks like and thus can make no comparisons to decide the correct speed. Therefore, conscious has to take over a normal sub-conscious function in order to re-program. Once reprogrammed to go faster and faster into sharp corners, the sub-conscious has gained a new history or new database of visual comparisons. We can say it has been reprogrammed to recognize the new "too fast" or "too slow" rules based on a racecar versus a passenger car.

Actually, the sub-conscious must be taught many new conditions and circumstances that did not appear to exist in normal driving. Once learned, technology changes occur that also require new responses. Sub-conscious must be taught new techniques for handling these so it can continue to successfully manage a 200 mph problem. If conscious does a great job of programming and testing, sub-conscious can handle most 200 mph problems without crashing. Quite a motivator! What if the person had decided "I can't!"? The racing challenge is to be able to re-program and provide data to the sub-conscious as the situation dictates. What are the operating characteristics of the other cars and drivers and at what point on the track can they best be passed? How are track conditions changing? Conscious brain spends time on these in order to prepare sub-conscious (by checking programs and data) since there will be no time for such during the fractions of a second available to sub-conscious for analysis, decision-making and action at 200 mph. If sub-conscious can't detect through the eyeballs an oil slick (data), determine correct action and execute it perfectly (a superior program), the result may well be a crash. If conscious brain talks too much or worries too much, it may distract the sub-conscious (loss of concentration) and result in a crash.

Conclusion

The significant conclusion is, in order to meet the needs of speed in execution, the conscious brain creates a program, a specific set of instructions in the sub-conscious. And only considerable repetition allows the program to become more and more complete and to eventually include an automatic initiator feature. Automatics are a prerequisite to achieving excellence in racecar driving where time is a real problem.

However, <u>automatics and speed are unnecessary and, in fact, totally inappropriate for business interactions between humans</u>. Because we didn't understand this, we programmed our sub-conscious to conduct some of our routines in life. This is a source of dysfunctional behavior, our problems in dealing with other people and events.

Do not fail to appreciate that the conscious brain has no real habits or programs. It can easily be taught new things and it can change instantly, on demand so to speak. It is not capable of the great speeds of the sub-conscious brain, but it is infinitely more flexible. The conscious brain's capacity for reasoning and creating action from this reasoning is what differentiates us from other living species. And only the conscious brain can program and/or reprogram the sub-conscious where all the programs reside.

The point is, <u>when interacting with people or routine events, such as work or traffic jams, the conscious brain should always be used</u>, not the sub-conscious. But we need a few more details before arriving at the fix.

Growing Up

Programming is mostly done unconsciously (without a clear decision to do so) when we are young. Programs exist only in the sub-conscious and only to create action. The action could be internal such as increased heartbeat, worry, anxiety, strong emotion or a boiling Gut. It could be external such as facial expression, eye movement, twitching, hand or leg motion and the like. Internal means not necessarily detectable by others. Internal and external actions could be simultaneous and could range from being consistent to inconsistent (appearing to be cool on the outside while boiling on the inside). These actions or reactions were not with us at birth and must be learned and developed.

This process of developing behavior or habits was described in the Chapter 2 section "Behavior Without Value Standards". All of us were forced to do some copying just to develop some behavior since we started with none, followers and non-followers alike. We see examples and we copy them.

Beyond copying what we see and hear, our behavior is strongly influenced by the demands of our parents and other authoritarians bent on making us follow. These often cause negative reactions and therefore the resulting programs are dysfunctional. The theory and the result were adequately explained for subordinates in Chapter 6, Support Through Direction, and are as applicable to the parent-child as to the boss-junior relationship.

Of course, we not only create programs for external behavior, what we do and say, but also for internal responses such as emotions or adrenaline flow or stress. Signals from the good-bad compass of our Gut are often used to trigger a sub-conscious program creating what we call an "emotional response".

Reactions that result in an emotional response have been learned/programmed. These can be reactions to failure, criticism, the other sex, other races, responsibility, bosses, finances, weather, road traffic, security, etc., etc. The rule is that emotions that go beyond being signals from the Gut of good or bad are generally dysfunctional and require reprogramming of the sub-conscious.

Reprogramming using the 3x5 Card Principle

The first and most important point to the above is that we are <u>not</u> programmed by others. Only we can do this programming of our sub-conscious. It is presently physically impossible for someone else to do it for us. And therefore, our right to <u>make a choice</u> permits us to decide whether to do it or not. This is what 5Star people do whether they know it or not.

The second is that we can re-program at any time. It matters not what the dysfunction is. We could have been born into:

1. a wealthy family wherein we learned to disrespect and arrogantly look down on the financially less fortunate.
2. a family on the dole wherein the world appears as a place of no hope and we resort to violence or drugs since life has no value.
3. an environment that practices dislike for people of a different race and we ---------.
4. a family wherein a violent father mistreats the members and we ----.
5. an authoritative family wherein we are told what we should do and we are closely controlled with the result that we --------.

There are a myriad of dysfunctions that can be brought into the workplace, from lack of confidence to hating management or unions, from being too kind to being too critical. While we all make the same errors, we each turn only a few of these errors into programmed habits. The secret is not to confuse these programs with our birthrights, but to mark them for destruction. Minor changes we make all of the time and getting rid of the entire program is just as straightforward, the 3x5 card.

An Example Of 3x5 Card

My own experience may help here. By the time I got to my third naval ship assignment I knew that correcting and reprimanding people was a real emotional negative. I disliked it. It turned me off even to think about doing it. I knew it had to be done and forced myself to do it, but it made my stomach boil and I didn't want to continue boiling.

Although no one knew or could tell from my actions that I had such strong emotions, because of them I decided the Navy might not be for me. While contemplating a return to civilian life, I realized I would want to be in a managerial position as a civilian and would still have to correct and reprimand subordinates. I soon recognized I could only escape this responsibility by becoming a laborer responsible for no one else or living on a deserted island. I didn't have the money for the island and, as concerns being a laborer, I wanted to be the one giving the orders rather than the recipient of them.

So I decided to analyze whether my negative emotions were proper. I made one list of all the reasons that supported my liking correction and reprimand and a second list of reasons that supported disliking it. I tried to look at it from every possible approach -- Navy, man, family, shipmate, country, God, taxpayer, as well as law, religious, ethical, Gut and, of course, value standards. I forget exactly how the first cut effort stacked up, but it was about 60% supporting like and 40% dislike. After considerable review and objective analysis, however, all the reasons ended out supporting like, none supporting dislike. I realized that if I disliked doing it, I would not do it as well as could be done and everyone would suffer, including myself and the person in need.

Armed with such overwhelming evidence, I carried the list with me on a 3x5 card and reviewed it every time the bad feelings emerged. I told myself repeatedly what a dummy I was for boiling, how I had emotions that made no sense and must be changed, and how I almost left the Navy over such an error. I also thought about each and every reason on the card. I never damaged my morale or self-esteem, but talked firmly to my sub-conscious.

The more I talked to my sub-conscious, the less my stomach boiled. Little by little the boiling disappeared, most of it in six months. About 2 1/2 years later I reprimanded a very senior person. Afterwards I realized I had felt very good about the whole thing; the planning, the doing and the aftermath. In essence, I had thrown out the prior program and reprogrammed to be able to enjoy the considerable satisfaction of another job well done. I had changed what I first perceived to be me, granite rock, my birth right, but which only turned out to be the hard packed earth and gravel mixture of a sub-conscious directed response, a program I had built and could therefore change.

How had I learned such a dysfunctional emotion/response? The truth is, attempts to find a cause or someone to blame will not solve the problem. Once we are adults it is our job to find our faults objectively and give a good go at correcting them before they do too much damage to others and ourselves. We should expect to be judged by our correction of error and not by the error itself. "To err is human, to forgive divine."

Notice in the above case, I never mentioned any feelings about not being able to change my own dysfunctional behavior. I owe this to my father. He taught me a very simple concept; our Creator made a beautiful world in which there is a "good" solution for everything and each person was given the wherewithal to find it. So if the chosen solution is not good for everyone and everything involved, it is only because of our lack of understanding of what the Creator did. So we should try again to find the "good" solution that surely exists. Whether the required action is to learn more and/or to change ourselves, it is always within our power to accomplish, something we may choose to do. We all need to believe this wisdom.

So this was my rationale for not wasting time on "I can't". There are a multitude of excuses for "I can't", many of which have been discussed in this book. Any leader must appreciate how limiting "I can't" really is. Once an emotional response has been made into a habit, people have a large tendency to believe it is then their birthright, made of pure rock. The bottom line is, if it is dysfunctional to us or to others, unhappy in any way, it is not locked in cement and there is great value in changing it. The more we keep of these negatives, the more we hurt others and ourselves. Take Care of #1 and #2 and #3!!

Another Method

In the above, I slowly but surely changed an internal response. For external responses, while the procedure is the same through making the two lists, the next step is always to stop the behavior. Dysfunctional actions (gestures, facial expressions, words) occur in association with some event and if one concentrates sufficiently, these actions can be interrupted before they begin. The conscious brain thus reasserts control over the body actions dictated by the sub-conscious brain's program.

Once control has been proven several times, it becomes possible for the conscious brain to direct actions that would be correct for the given event. And after the proper behavior has been sufficiently practiced, it will become your new norm. This solution is the same as was given under Listening, chapter 7.

Another Example Of 3x5 Card

At the time, I was in charge of about 300 people. I learned one of our experienced operators was terribly upset. His superiors were concerned he would not be able to continue to function as an operator.

In talking to this man, he disclosed the cause of his distress. He had been beating his two children, ages 4 and 2. He would get mad at them, give them a beating and feel good about it for two days. By the third day, he would realize what a bad thing he had done and be upset and feel terrible for a few days. These feelings would eventually wear off and he would repeat the process again. But after each event he became more upset than before and it began to adversely affect his work.

I learned that from the age of 9 he had been regularly left by his parents to take care of a two and four year old brother and sister. And if everything wasn't in good order when his parents returned, his father would beat him.

I offered to help, but he didn't accept. Knowing he could be a hazard to safety as an operator, I ordered him to immediately report to me if he beat his children again.

About a month later he was in my office. He had beaten his children three days before and was in tears, quite unfit for work. We discussed the event and what led up to it in detail. He could remember starting to get upset at his children, but had little further recollection until he was almost through beating them. He had gone from a feeling into an automatic program execution by the sub-conscious brain. It was then I knew we could fix his problem.

We made a detailed plan. He committed to listen to his feelings. Whenever he realized he was starting to become upset with his children, he would immediately get up, leave the house and start walking a pre-determined course armed only with a 3x5 card of reasons why he should not beat his children. His wife would know of this plan and would say nothing to him if she saw him suddenly leave the house. He would walk the pre-determined course while reviewing each item on his card, again and again until he no longer felt upset at the children. He would then turn around and retrace his steps at the same pace while still reviewing his list. This plan would ensure his negative feelings had subsided by the time he arrived home.

In the beginning, I spoke with him once or twice a week to assure he stuck with the plan. In fact, he was very proud of himself for getting out of the house and was talking a lot to his sub-conscious brain about how wrong it was to get upset rather than just feel love for his children.

And I vividly remember the day, six months after we started, he came into my office and broke down in tears. When he returned home from work the previous evening, his two children had run out to meet him and hugged his legs, rather than shy away as they had done in the past. I cried with him.

The Procedure For Changing Behavior

1. Keep in mind you are a good person. You are your value standards and they are all good.

2. Your behavior is not you, rather something you do. It stands a good chance of being incorrect because of how it was developed from the hodgepodge of behaviors you attempted to use as models.

3. Behavior includes all emotions. There are internal as well as external reactions to perceived events. While both varieties are capable of producing significant damage, the internal reactions may be the most harmful.

4. You need to stand back and evaluate each and every one of your behaviors against your own value standards. <u>Those that flunk should be marked for change.</u>

5. Automatic dysfunctional behaviors are always triggered by specific events. Traffic, mother, boss, George, finances and criticism are just a few of the triggers. Think these out ahead of time, make your lists and when the event occurs concentrate on stopping any and all actions emanating from the sub-conscious. Zip your lip or whatever. If it will be a physical reaction, leave the area rapidly. Concentrate solely on <u>interfering with the expected behavior</u> and thereby gaining control over it. Often, there are internalized mental reactions that bother us, distract us and cause stress as in my case. A large number of our dysfunctional behaviors fall into this category. The secret is to <u>talk to your sub-conscious with your 3x5 card in hand</u> and do what's necessary to regain control with the conscious brain. <u>Proving we can stop the sub-conscious is a real proud, momentous day!</u>

6.   For external behavior, once in control, you can take the time to develop the correct behavioral response to the trigger and then return to that person and give this correct response. Apologize for not having the presence of mind to bring it up before and then give it. This gives you new correct practice. Design a small response, such as "thanks very much" or "I'll think about it and get back to you", which you can give at the time of the trigger and before you leave, in order to get out of there more gracefully. After several events of being in control and returning later with the "perfect" response in accordance with your value standards, you may begin to try a somewhat longer response at the time of the original trigger. Slowly but surely work toward doing it perfectly without leaving and returning.

7.   Making lists and carrying them with you on a 3x5 card, as I did in the example, are not only valuable but also <u>mandatory</u>. Convincing arguments help us to sustain the effort. Review of these important motivations every time the dysfunctional reaction is experienced is the key to correction. <u>Talking to your sub-conscious</u> in a respectful, but firm manner with solid reasons <u>is a must for reprogramming to occur</u>.

8.   All of this will be a great boon to your confidence. There will be many good feelings inside as you gain on the problem. Pure heaven!

YOUR OWN WORST ENEMY

It is often said we are our own worst enemy. The reason is while non-5Star followers complain and blame others for their circumstance, 5Star people are out doing things to make their circumstance better. 5Star people know that everything is within their power and is only waiting for them to do something about it. 5Star people have no limits while non-5Star are creating limits through use of excuses, reasons why they can't do something. These are <u>self-imposed limits</u>.

Self-imposed limits are far more restrictive than any external ones can ever be. The big payoffs come from working to improve ourselves, not from blaming the actions of others for what is happening to us. Get out of the blame game and into a self-improvement game.

CONCLUSION ABOUT FIXING OUR BEHAVIORS

Our behavior is not us. We are our value standards and they are good. Our behavior may be dysfunctional, for work or family or whatever functions. We can recognize it because it causes unhappiness either in ourselves or in others or in both. We can change it when we choose. Why be our own worst enemy when we can be our own best friend? Use the 3x5 card principle! It works!!

EIGHT PERSONAL BEHAVIORS WORTHY OF CHANGE

Now let's get on with the whys and hows of the eight personal behaviors. And when you are thinking about the fixes, don't forget the Six Rationales of chapter 6.

PERSONALITY

This is a well-used excuse for not being able to successfully interact with other people. Rather than learning to do what the people circumstance requires and honing that skill through "practice makes perfect" to a high standard, we excuse ourselves on the basis of our own personality from even trying, or excuse a half-hearted attempt. To make matters worse, we expect others to accept this excuse and the damage that results.

In sharp contrast, no one uses personality as an excuse for poor performance with machines. With them we tend to be objective and make the necessary behavioral changes to achieve competitive results, or seek a different field where such actions are not required.

Meekness, laid back, introvert, extrovert, bull in a china shop and other personality traits all have their strengths and weaknesses. All reflect actions that we learned to do in our youth. They are not us. They are our behavior. We are our value standards that are good. We are not our personality that may or may not be dysfunctional through whatever vehicle, be it meekness or abrasiveness.

While the technical manuals tell us about care and operation of machines and how to detect problems, our biggest guideline for people is "Do unto others as you would have them do unto you". For example, take the case of Sally who is one of your finest workers, one who creates great output and quality, very dependable. Today Sally made an error and is personally crushed. Her own sense of pride is hurting and she needs some tender love and care, some uplifting. Can you as her boss with a naturally cold personality meet Sally's needs? Have you learned to provide encouraging warmth in spite of yourself? If not, Sally is going to suffer and so will everyone else watching. Down goes productivity! And can you with your warm, loving personality hand out a large dose of salt, even termination, to handle Bob who is a very low achiever and a hazard to the group?

The solution is to ignore your personality and make plans to perform those actions that are dictated by an objective review of the person and applicable value standards. Conduct a careful analysis of what needs to be done and how to do it, and then get plenty of practice and self-coaching. Discuss the results, experiment, study alternative techniques and experiment some more. Diligence, perseverance and tenacity are also solutions to handling people problems. Throw your personality into the river and let it drift away with the tide or leave it at the door when you come to work. <u>Do not believe consultants who advise you to pick a management style to fit your personality.</u> There is no such thing! There is only a right way and then many more incorrect ways from which to choose. Invoking personality as a limit is one of the incorrect ways. <u>Use your 3x5 card!</u>

Personality Clashes

Personality clashes can be public or relatively private events between two peers. One person may claim "I can't work with John. He's an xx xx xx person. Keep him away from me!" They can be between a junior and a boss or between a supplier and an internal or external customer. Whatever the case, they are used as excuses for sub-standard behavior. Not so surprisingly, they are often accepted by others, including bosses, as part of life with people. They appear to be like the fifteen "conflicts" of chapter 3, things that we "can't" escape, only accept.

These clashes always produce disharmony coupled with a sizable reduction in cooperation. The damage does not stop there, however. The onlookers who are always present quickly divide into three groups. There are those who support A, those who support B and those who cannot decide who to support or want to be neutral. A's supporters grow to dislike the B group who likewise dislike A's supporters. Both groups dislike the neutral group for not backing their person and the neutral group reciprocates with various real or imagined epithets. These three groups will never become a happy family of high producers, never be a high performance team. Any boss who accepts this condition deserves the reduced performance that ensues.

Personality clashes between a boss and a junior are simply insubordination at its best. It is not necessary that the two like each other. It is necessary that they <u>treat each other with respect and common courtesy</u>.

The boss wants only to have orders carried out effectively and the junior only needs to receive them, make whatever reports are requested and receive whatever guidance ensues. Personality has nothing to do with this process. If the junior elects to get mad at the boss and be in "conflict", the boss should coach, provide consequence through discipline if necessary, and eventually terminate the relationship if correction cannot be achieved. If the junior goes public, the boss must order this guerrilla action to stop immediately, publicly apologize to onlookers and terminate sooner if the publicity continues. Do not allow insubordination to wreak havoc.

Personality conflicts between peers can be just as damaging. These are likewise insubordinations since harmony and cooperation must be considered conditions of employment. The boss must not take sides without first hand knowledge of their relationship, knowledge that is normally not available. The best solution is to discuss with each participant the possible damage and the formation of the three groups who are reaching for each other's throats. Once again, peers are not hired to like each other, only to treat each other with respect and to cooperate harmoniously.

The boss' next step is to order each person separately to cease and desist or be treated as an enemy of the organization. Getting them to go out to lunch together, to agree to disagree and to report those disagreements up the chain for resolution is a necessary step. Whatever you do, do not put them in the same room with you, each trying to justify their positions. No excuses are acceptable so discussion is inappropriate. Remember, any clash requires two people, so each is wrong for the same reason.

LIKES AND DISLIKES

Along the way to puberty, adulthood and middle age, we acquire a set of baggage termed things we like and things we dislike. All of these have been learned and some of them directly affect our performance in the workplace. Paper, discipline, working with the union, opening up to other people, coaching, reading, speaking to a group, computers, handling older subordinates, reprimanding and admission of error all seem to crop up regularly as being disliked. There are many more.

There are also a multitude of likes, a list not much different in length, but most often devoid of people issues, unless it is handing out rewards. You will not find many bosses who take satisfaction from tackling a personality conflict amongst juniors or terminating a subordinate whose performance warrants it. Bosses must learn to get satisfaction from each since doing these tasks well is so beneficial to all concerned.

We have all witnessed people who like being a first line foreman so much that as third line managers they continue to act the role of a first line foreman. We have all seen "operations" managers who, when promoted to being responsible for both maintenance and operations, continue to spend most of their time with operations. Everyone has experienced bosses who cannot bring themselves to terminate anyone with the result there is plenty of deadwood hanging around the office. We have all seen the lack of care that stems from dislike and the overkill of the meddler who likes a certain aspect of the job. Unfortunately for subordinates, a disproportionate share of the boss' dislikes apply to people functions.

Likes and dislikes are managerial land mines similar to personality, often accorded the same status. Doing what you like to do is always an error! It causes you to meddle in things that probably don't need you while other aspects of the business flounder from lack of attention. By way of a fix, bosses must be able to objectively determine what needs to be done in every facet of the business and, in some priority order, work to address these. The list must be re-ordered/re-worked at least monthly.

Recognize that disliking some facet of your responsibilities always dooms you to being a sub-par performer compared to others who were not dumb enough to get their emotions involved in their work. A bad choice for #1 (you)! The old axiom, "if it's worth doing, it's worth doing well", is a real truth. So you need to evaluate all workplace likes/dislikes and, after examination, modify your behavior until you can be proud of your performance in all aspects. Use your 3x5 card!

Likes and dislikes of individuals are also damaging and produce favoritism and cliques. Objectivity and merit are replaced by politics and access. Remember, your non-5Star will be following your lead and so everyone will be neglecting whatever the boss neglects.

Throw away your likes as well as your dislikes. Likes only serve as excuses for engaging in something that doesn't need you. Without likes or dislikes, you are left with performance over which to be proud or not proud. Work to improve all aspects of your performance to meet high value standards and do not neglect any aspect of your job through likes or dislikes. They are a snare and a delusion, an Excuse for poor performance by yourself or others. Throw them in the river and let them drift away on the tide.

EGO AND PRESTIGE

Bosses are particularly susceptible to these. "I was the one promoted. I must be OK!" "What I believe to be right is certainly more right than anyone else's right, so do as I say!" Bosses are paid more, have been promoted and are flattered by the attentions of subordinates and others. They are also awed by the power and influence that they appear to have. The hazard is they fall prey to this game. Rather than recognizing they are getting farther and farther away from the battle and that the pay, power and flattery are only seductions, they become impressed with their own self-importance.

Prestige is dangerously seductive. It can quickly draw us away from the use of our Gut level good value standards, away from selflessness toward selfishness, self-importance and ego. With a large ego you are in real trouble in the workplace. Humility, charity, fairness and forgiveness standards go out the window and you are left in the hollow shell of arrogance. Meeting the whims of your dictates, rather than the high standards of good values, becomes the requirement. "How dare the employee--------!" Weighed down by responsibility, the boss decides that only he/she cares or can protect the jewels of the kingdom. In this mode the boss listens less to subordinates and starts down the road toward reports, more reports and bureaucracy, all of which stifle people.

While we must have confidence in our ability to achieve, ego is a negative that projects arrogance rather than humility. Believe in yourself, but get rid of projecting "I'm the best ----" or "Look at me! I ------!" or other demonstrations of ego. Think about how people respond to these protestations of ego as compared with their response to the humility of "You are superior to me" or "You are more important than I". No one can meet high standards of good values with an ego because it stops us from "doing unto others as you would have them do unto you" or achieving the "caring" values (forgiveness, fairness, compassion, courtesy and forthrightness). With ego we shoot messengers and no one dares tell us a serious problem. <u>Ego only tolerates yes-men</u> and no one wants to deal with an ego. Vanity destroys our sensitivity to the feelings of others and makes us incapable of true listening. Ego is a menace to outstanding decision making. Leave your ego at the door or throw it in the river and let it drift away on the tide.

To the extent you suffer the ills of prestige and take on an ego, to that extent do your employees follow in this wrong direction. The farther the boss gets away from meeting 8-10 in the values (arrogance is in the negative direction), the worse the performance of subordinates since they follow the boss wherever he/she leads them. Damage to productivity, quality, efficiency, safety and other workplace values can become significant.

Ego and prestige are clearly workplace enemies and should be treated as such. <u>Recognizing the boss is a supplier to subordinates, and remembering that the answers are always at the worker's level, are the keys to maintaining humility</u> and defeating the enemies of ego and prestige. <u>Use your 3x5 card!</u>

ASSUMPTIONS

I was often surprised by the actions of others and found myself muttering "I had assumed they would --" and "If I had known they were going to---, I would have ----". In addition, I would take action after seeing a person do something I "assumed" was incorrect. In retrospect, my assumptions caused me to react in a certain way, but had I used a different set of assumptions, the person's actions would have made sense. After reviewing past assumptions, I came to realize I had never made a totally correct assumption in my entire life.

After taking the time to listen, rather than just to criticize, I learned every person has good reasons for doing what they do. I also learned that quick judgments on my part prevented me from showing love and compassion for my neighbor or caring for my subordinates, and they were an extremely negative and arrogant, "you are wrong" response on my part. As you might expect, these responses elicited negative reactions from every witness as well as from those directly involved.

Why did I make these assumptions? Was I lazy or was it that I just didn't Care about people? Judging myself also got me nowhere. During my upbringing, I may have copied this behavior from my surroundings, but for the life of me I know not from whom or where. But knowing how it happened is of no value. <u>Let's just fix it.</u>

These flaws also extended to my assumptions about "things" like machines and the future. Many of us are taken with strategic planning, an art that mostly attempts to predict the future. You might just as well use a crystal ball because these are nothing but assumptions and they too are worthless. The only viable strategy is to sketch out your pictures or visions of excellence, visualize achieving them and head for them. Make the future by using real facts and basing actions on them. Some examples of real facts to use are:

1. The competition will always catch up so better to obsolete your own products than wait for the competition to do it for you.
2. Change is a part of life.

3.   There are no quick fixes, but hard work and turned-on brains will always find them.

4.   A culture of 5Star people will surmount all difficulties and meet every challenge.

So, all of my assumptions have led to bad surprises, negative reactions and excuses for all. When I acted upon them in dealing with people, they also led to negative reactions. It was as though I was blaming them for something. Blaming others for your own incorrect assumptions is arrogance. No one needs to learn arrogance from the boss.

Needless to say, I have attempted to stop making assumptions other than that people are good and will do what they think is right. I have thrown away my crystal ball since it was never more than 20% correct. <u>I now decide my own actions by weighing the consequences of failure and the abilities of the people assigned.</u> For minor consequences, I leave them to their own devices and infrequently inspect results. As consequences rise, I pay more attention to abilities and proper preparation, plans and audits, as well as execution. When there are major consequences, I might be on scene to provide direct support if not to participate.

After making these decisions, whatever goes wrong I accept as my choice as well as theirs, and do not waste time with assumptions. I trust they and I were trying hard, unless otherwise proven. When problems strike, I can then attend to determining what we can each do better in order to improve, rather than blaming them. Rid yourself of assumptions and develop expertise in judging the consequences of failure, your people's abilities and real facts in order to determine your own actions. <u>Use your 3x5 card!</u>

BAD MORALE

This is our own mental condition with respect to courage, confidence and self-discipline. High morale is being willing and able to meet the demands of any challenge or the trials of any problem as opportunities to excel. It is also actively seeking out these challenges and problems.

Courage is an ability to be brave and undaunted in the face of hazards and danger. Confidence is a belief that whatever we undertake will turn out to be successful no matter the difficulty. Self-discipline is an ability to conduct ourselves in an orderly manner with sufficient self-control to accomplish obedient execution of a plan. These three are our morale.

As our inventory level of courage, confidence and self-discipline decline, our morale decreases. We first lose our desire to actively seek out challenges and problems. Next, we begin to see problems as problems and hazards to be avoided rather than opportunities to excel. As our morale drops further, problems become tangible fears and challenges become problems. Low morale is making mountains out of molehills, the "oh, poor me" syndrome of a real victim.

The message for the boss is, people without high morale will function at well less than 50 percent of capacity, often at 10-20 percent. They also pull down the morale of others. Unfortunately, they may constitute a majority of the boss' subordinates, workers and managers alike. How did they get to have less than high morale?

Morale and the Follower

From birth we are taught to do what is "expected" of us or what we "should" do as defined by "they", whoever "they" are. We are taught and required to please others, particularly parents. Since most parents believe "children don't know any better", children are told when to get up, when to go to bed, what to eat, when to do their homework, what to wear, who to have as friends, how to act and a myriad of other requirements. Some parents even tell their children when to feel good or bad. Unfortunately, many teachers do almost the same thing to us in school and the influences of our peers, television and other media, etc. etc. are similar. Though the effect of all of this training in doing what's expected varies between us, it strongly tends toward making us into a follower who copies behavior from others, a person who is directed by and dependent on external messages in order to function.

Because of this process, non-5Star followers have little practice in producing actions or feelings through the careful analysis of necessity and available criteria such as value standards, Rationales and principles. The extreme is a person who does not initiate, does not take charge of self, but reacts to external stimuli. As followers they haven't learned how to handle naturally occurring events of life, only how to react to them. What they perceive to be bad events tend to turn them off, while perceived good events tend to turn them on. Unfortunately, most of us are too close to this extreme for comfort, our own comfort.

In this increasingly complex and small world, there are a multitude of events that followers can seize upon to make themselves unhappy; traffic jams instead of a clear road, rain instead of sunshine as well as authoritarian parents, teachers, bosses, neighbors, politicians and others. And since many other people seem to react to these stimuli in a similar fashion, their own unhappiness is validated over and over again by other people. This is the "I'm only human" excuse.

<u>Unhappiness as a steady diet degrades morale</u> through a feeling of powerlessness. The follower brings this about through the reactionary process of <u>listening to external rather than internal messages</u>. These create unhappinesses that saddle the person with lowered morale and result in a lowered productivity level.

Low morale can also originate from low self-esteem, a characteristic that I have termed confidence. Parents and others often hand out a rather steady diet of criticism and negative barbs to children that can be interpreted by the child as meaning "I'm no good." or "I'm stupid". Follower adults are susceptible to exactly the same fate from bosses and peers, and from it they experience the same low morale. These people have a strong tendency to subject others to exactly the same overly critical, demeaning treatment as they received. As bosses, they can do great damage to morale in general.

The Fix

Bosses cannot buy morale. It doesn't exist as a separate entity, only as a condition within a person. An observer can determine causes, but control can only be exercised by the person themself. The fix is to help the person to gain control over their own morale. There are three pieces to the fix available to the boss; success, praise and 5Star.

First, success. The person who has succeeded at nothing has nothing to be proud of until he/she succeeds at something, even at a very little thing. Bosses can easily create success at small things by their team members and this can be nurtured into success at big things. The positive feelings of satisfaction and self-worth brought on by a small success are so different from low morale the person will start looking for other things at which to succeed. The road to high morale always starts with small successes and can be started by the boss. Continuation down the success road will eventually be done independently of the boss.

Second, praise. Bosses should run around finding things being done right and handing out praise. Praise is the most effective action any boss can take because of its positive effect on morale and the positive effect on corporate performance that increased morale causes.

Third, 5Star, Make the person strong and independent (5Star) and place them in control of their own morale. Take the time to convince people their morale is the fire in their boiler and without it they accomplish very little. People must learn that they own their morale and can control it. Lowered morale is bad for #1, #2 and #3. Bosses should articulate a persuasive argument based on the Six Rationales of chapter 6 and values. Handing over their morale to the whims of Mother Nature, to the availability of spare parts or to the perceived unfairness of their bosses means forever being disappointed. Using excuses for lowered morale harms us and others and is never the correct choice in view of the Six Rationales. High morale is a personal choice, everyone's right.

Thus the third fix is a move toward the self-direction and independence of 5Star and away from the external direction and dependence most of us were required to accept in our youth. Bosses can return us to our original, as born 5Star status of being independent of external direction. How the boss should accomplish this third fix for morale was the main thrust of chapters 8 and 9 on GOTYP and group meetings, especially the latter.

Morale is so important that the boss cannot leave it to the whims of life or of other people. The corporation can sink or swim on its courage, confidence and self-discipline. Bosses who can tune in to people's unhappiness can provide them with solutions through success, praise, self-defense by way of independence, and improved support and direction. All avenues must be utilized and all unhappiness confronted. Recall that every person wants to be a superstar, 5Star for the good of #1, #2 and #3. They need you to help them. Get them to use their 3x5 card!.

BAD/NEGATIVE ATTITUDES

Negative attitudes are different from bad morale. "This place makes me mad". "Who do you think you are telling me what to do?" "Why don't you ask someone else to do that?" Eyes turned down, head down. Surliness. Lack of cooperation. The world owes me a living. Refusal to learn new things. Anti-management or labor. Prejudice. Sexism. Things were always better in the past.

These negative attitudes result in degradation of performance, most often by a large amount. These all adversely effect anyone in contact. No one wants to work with these people and no boss wants them as employees. These attitudes are carried into the person's personal life and thus are very detrimental to #2 and #3.

These people are very expensive to keep around because they actively destroy others. They are real enemies of the workplace and take a devastating toll on attitude and thus indirectly on productivity and quality. Taking away one of these people probably has the same effect as hiring 3 employees who want to work.

A few of these people are strong and independent! These can really be superstars, just as effective in the positive direction as in the negative. But only if you can persevere to give them the right facts and the right consequences to cause them to change. Theirs is a problem of bum dope or ignorance of what's really true. Turning one of them around has the equivalent effect of hiring six good people since they not only turn around, but become very active in the positive direction. These people are easy to recognize so take advantage of this payback.

The remainder of the people with negative attitudes, those who are not strong and independent, represent serious problems. But most will turn around when faced with enough consequence and respectful education. Those who don't in the course of your placing into effect the guidance of this book, are either too close to retirement, medically unfit, or ready for termination through your disciplinary procedures.

STRESS

In response to a perception, a mental state develops that disrupts the person involved. The severity of the disruption can vary from slight to severe. This disruptive condition is variously described as being stress, pressure, mental tension, frustration, strain, worry, anxiety and unhappiness. These words are generally related to perceived causes, but the disruption is always the same. Stress is a behavior and exists in humans only as a self-creation by the person. Two people experiencing identical events can totally differ as concerns stress; one can suffer considerable stress and the other can feel no stress. While the difference can be one of habit or one of using contrasting beliefs about stress or life in general, stress is a choice we each can make.

Stress in a person can be likened to an automobile pushing against a brick wall spinning its tires. Engine power is normally used to move the car and good tires normally last 40,000 miles or more. If the engine is used to spin the driving tires, the engine power is expended in heating these tires and causes destruction of them in thirty seconds or so. Stress likewise results in the dissipation of body energy inside the body, an event that always creates damage to body parts. While fingernail biting, ulcers, heart disease, grinding down teeth at night, high blood pressure and other outcomes are possible, the ultimate effect of severe stress is a catatonic state in which the person's brain ceases to perform other than internal body functions. There is nothing good about stress and anyone who chooses to play with this fire will be burned.

Events in our lives have a higher tendency to cause stress as their importance to us increases. Since for most of us gaining an adequate livelihood is so important, the workplace has a very high potential for stress. The peer, junior, boss and work related stress possibilities are numerous; embarrassment, intimidation, disrespect, humiliation, confusion, corruption, politics, failure, frustration, competition, criticism, peer pressure, responsibility, accountability, skill inadequacies, job loss and the like. People who experience stress from these or any other work related events believe themselves to be normal and thus accept the stress as a necessary evil of life. So what's new?

Frustration is probably the most common workplace stress malady. We are frustrated by bureaucracies that hold us back, by bosses who will not support us or make timely decisions or let us know what's really transpiring, by juniors who will not take orders or do what's expected or be reliable, and by a host of other people and events. And all of this is considered normal! In fact, it is so normal as to be accepted practice, something we can discuss and pass around to others without fear of rejection. In short, it has become normal for us to demoralize ourselves and others, believing we are doing the right thing for all. Should it be so?

Frustration cannot exist in people who follow the Golden Rule. It also cannot exist in people who properly act out the "serenity prayer" about changing or accepting what cannot be changed (Rationale #5). Neither can frustration exist in anyone who will use their right to choose in order to pick a different alternative since anything is better than frustration. In fact, use of the Six Rationales, value standards and a reasonable knowledge of the workplace are all that is needed in order to understand that frustration is not a friend to be embraced, but an enemy to be cast out. And the same analysis can be performed for every other cause of stress, with the identical result.

Therefore, the fix is relatively straight forward. Stress is an automatic sub-conscious directed response to a perceived external condition. More simply, it is one among many behaviors that we have learned. The unlearning process is to analyze our values and Rationales and then to make a choice. That choice must be to convince ourselves how wrong it is to create stress. Perseverance in "self-talk" every time stress is experienced leads to success. Coaching by bosses is a great aid to stress victims. Get them to use their 3x5 card!

EMOTIONALISM

Emotionalism must be removed from the objective process of deciding how to do something. Emotionalism will only cloud the facts and get in the way of determining the best alternatives of "how to". It is as equally ineffective as using your personality or likes and dislikes. If emotions are present, get them to subside before beginning to analyze "how to" or your analysis will be badly flawed.

One of the sources of emotionalism is criticism, whether it be from the boss or from others, whether in jest or not. Emotionalism is an automatic behavior in defense of our own self-esteem, a defensive response to a perceived threat. It floods our brain with unconstructive thoughts, prevents us from hearing more than a small fraction of the communication and stresses our bodies. It makes establishing a trusting relationship with our bosses very difficult, if not impossible.

Severe negative emotions are Gut level responses that have been magnified far beyond their original purpose as signposts or the fire in our boiler. These responses are caused by <u>flagrant violations of our <i>value</i> standards</u>. The greater the violation and the higher its repetition rate, the greater the response, possibly becoming a severe emotional reaction. Bad bosses create bitterness and desires for revenge.

These negatives eat away our insides. Because of them we self-create stress, low self-esteem and health problems. Negative emotions are a self-destruct button. Fortunately for bosses, <u>they are easy to detect and correct</u>.

The bottom line is that there is nothing good about emotionalism. We should be thankful for constructive criticism because errors are our best friends and knowing another one is a chance for you to do better. Also, we should be flattered by gibes or apparent verbal attacks. We must have really "arrived" to warrant such attention. Try to say "thanks very much for the attention, I can surely use some today". That should serve to squelch your emotions as well as future gibes.

The corrective action for the problem of emotionalism is the same as for stress or any ingrained behavior. <u>Use your 3x5 card!</u>

RECAP

We all experience the eight hazards explained above to a greater or lesser extent. Most of us accept their bad results by using the "I'm only human" excuse. But we can alternatively choose not to accept the bad results and to change them. People can be helped to realize they have been duped by society and the truth lies elsewhere.

These hazards should be discussed when they occur and treated objectively as the normal routine human problems that they are. With discussion, practical example, boss encouragement, boss admission to his/her frailties and provision of the means to correct, they can be effectively combated. Remember, these hazards are more prevalent in management than in working levels.

The less open and the more secretive a boss is, the more people will use the excuse box and behavior from the sub-conscious rather than the objective conscious brain. Open frank discussion always produces many more solutions and is particularly effective at group meetings. These problems are so pervasive that the potential productivity gain from addressing them is significant.

Use your 3x5 card. It is a practical, easy to use solution that really works, again and again.

Printed in the United States
100446LV00002B/13/A